GOAT

GOAT

MEAT ∗ MILK ∗ CHEESE

BRUCE WEINSTEIN & MARK SCARBROUGH

PHOTOGRAPHS BY MARCUS NILSSON

STEWART, TABORI & CHANG

NEW YORK

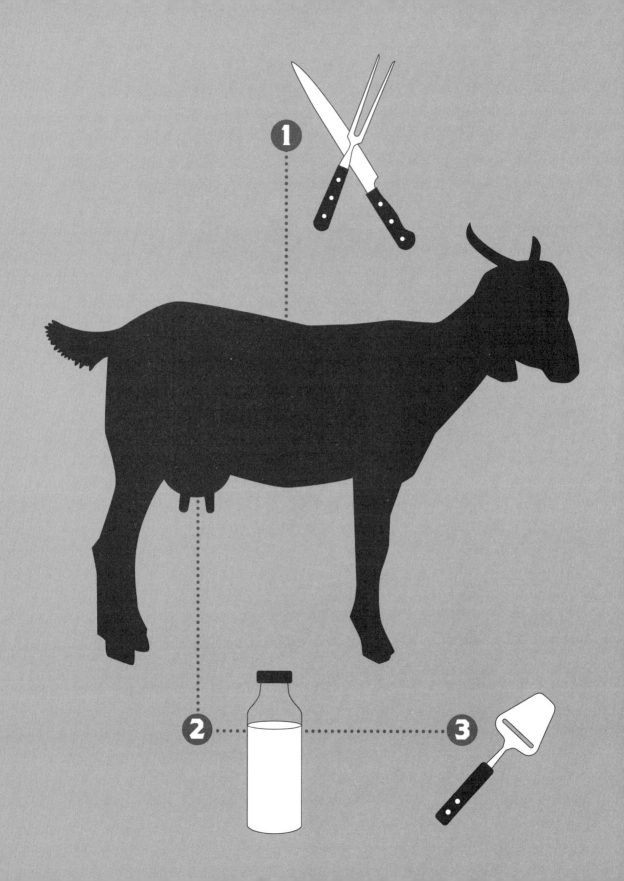

CONTENTS

IN WHICH A LIE BECOMES A COOKBOOK..........6

1: MEAT

GET YOUR GOAT 15

HUNKS 16

CHUNKS 50

CURRIES 70

MOLE 82

GROUND 90

IF YOU'VE GOT NOTHING BUT
TIME—AND GOAT—ON YOUR HANDS 104

2: MILK & YOGURT

THE SMELL OF GOAT IN THE MORNING........122

SAVORIES 132

SWEETS 146

3: CHEESE

BITS & BITES 174

A MATCH MADE IN NORWAY 190

COMFORT FOOD 196

LITTLE NOTHINGS 220

BIGGER SOMETHINGS 228

IN WHICH A WORLD-CLASS POET
SURPRISES ME WITH A GOAT TALE............244

ACKNOWLEDGMENTS 247

INDEX 248

IN WHICH
A LIE
BECOMES
A COOKBOOK

I LIED AND I WAS WEARING MAKEUP.

Not a lot. Just concealer and foundation. No lipstick, for heaven's sake.

First off, it's a bit ironic—or funny or tragic or something—that I, a gay guy who tried to play it straight for years, ended up in a career where I'm expected to wear makeup whenever the cameras are rolling and the lights, blaring.

Truth be told, I've never really gotten comfortable with the spackle. I don't do drag. Don't go to drag shows. Don't even like them. Maybe it was all those years I spent in the closet. I don't need to pretend I'm something I'm not. I already did that. With a wife and six-course-dinner parties. To great success.

These days, I do my best. Picture this: me, behind the scenes of some national TV show, sitting in front of some makeup artist with blemish pencils and greasepaint trowels wedged between her lips, getting pasty gunk dabbed on my face, all the while jumpy as hell that whatever is in the skillet out on the set is going to burst into flames any minute.

Around me in the dressing room, serried in front of klieg light mirrors, are the show's celebrities. I swear to God, they're usually reading about themselves in the tabloids. Did they forget where they had dinner last night? I once saw one highlighting passages with a yellow marker.

Bruce usually tells me to settle down, but this much I know: no amount of makeup can cover up words. An age spot? Oh, sure. Claiming to be sixty when you're really a hundred and thirty-seven? You bet. But a lie gets caught by the mikes.

Mine did. Here's how it happened. About five years ago, Bruce and I sold a TV show. Sold it, I might add, without ever shooting a pilot. Sold it with nothing but a pitch on a piece of paper: a show all about the process of what it takes to write a cookbook, the successes and failures.

Sounds great, no? But here's the problem: When you sell something with just words, you eventually have to produce said thing in the flesh. You know, like with online dating. Somebody eventually has to show up at the door. And they'd better be good, what with all that buildup. More like, they'd better have been accurate.

As I had to be that morning. I found myself makeupped and standing under the lights, desperate to vindicate the words we'd used. Despite the pressure, our executive producer was a kind man, a Borscht Belt comic with a clipboard—and not what I'd imagined producers were like. I'd been trained on *I Love Lucy*, on Dore Schary.

"You sure you're OK with this?" he said with a chuckle.

The lie, that is. Because it was. And we all knew it. But it was a little late to back out, what with all the directors, editors, assistants, sound guys, and cameramen.

I glanced at Bruce for support.

"Hey, it's reality TV," he said.

Oh, right. Still created and crafted, just not by a formal script. They rely on run-of-the-mill liars.

Of which I am not one. I grew up under the heel of Southern Protestants. As I had been told repeatedly, the worst thing would be to be caught with a lie in your mouth at the moment of the rapture. One minute you're telling someone you just love that pink chenille sweater and then in midsentence you're telling it to Jesus.

I'm not an actor. (Well, except for those thirty-five years where I pretended to be straight.) But we had to build a story for the cameras about writing a cookbook. So we came up with this doozy: Bruce and I had already finished *The Ultimate Cook Book*—nine hundred brand-new recipes—but we'd somehow "forgotten" to put a brownie recipe in it.

Mind you, those were those heady days before Facebook, Twitter, and the rest. Back then, cookbooks were trying to compete with the Internet by *being* the Internet: a zillion recipes packed tight on the pages. If you could get everything in there, people wouldn't go online. Shoot, we had to have put a brownie recipe in there just to get them out of the chat rooms.

What's more, Bruce and I had already written a brownie book. Why would we forget such a recipe when it came to writing our so-called ultimate book?

And then there was this niggling detail: There *were* brownie recipes in the book.

With all that in mind, here was the scenario:

Bruce was being the happy homemaker, throwing together a quick lunch of poached salmon in a dill-cucumber-yogurt sauce for our ever-so-fabulous life, and I was writing away at the kitchen table. Suddenly, I stood up, horrified. I fluttered the page proofs at him, pointed to my laptop, and declaimed, "Bruce, I just realized we forgot to include a brownie recipe in the book!"

I said it. And said it again. And said it again. Because it sounded like a lie. To me, to Bruce, to everyone. We watched it over and over on playback. It was wrong. And it was already midmorning.

I sidled up to the producer. "You know what? There *are* brownie recipes in the book."

"So I've heard." He smiled. "Again and again."

"I know, I know. But listen: There's no goat in the book."

He said nothing.

I laughed.

He still said nothing.

Because there'd already been way too many discussions about it.

First, between Bruce and me. When we started to write that big book, we pitched back and forth about including goat. How could it be the ultimate cookbook if there was no goat? We'd written a recipe for seared foie gras, for Pete's sake. But no goat meat. Or goat milk.

Second, there'd been discussions with this very producer. The day I'd pitched goat to him for the first episode, he reared back and looked at me over his glasses. "We're not airing this in Egypt."

"But . . ."

"Mark, people love brownies."

"People love goat."

"Where?"

"Across the world. The Caribbean. South America. Asia. More and more, right here at home." I thought I'd risk it. "Hell, I love goat."

He eyed me, then laughed. "Oh, you goyim with your ideas. No goat. Brownies."

"But . . ."

"Brow . . . nies."

Even if he was turning into Mr. Mooney, I could have continued to argue my point. Certainly, the last decade had watched goat cheese come into

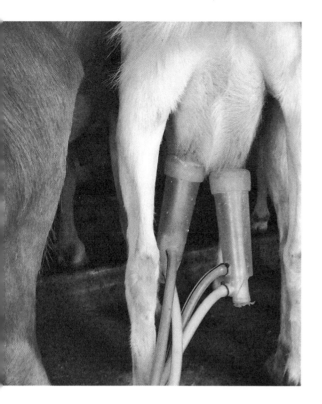

its own. It was no longer just a fancy, Frenchified product, adored by culinary snobs.

And goat milk? It was in almost every supermarket, thanks mostly to the tireless efforts of a handful of producers.

Even the meat was coming into its own, served high and low in restaurants and some home kitchens across the United States.

But not that day on the set. We did the brownies. And I could feel the lie rankle the back of my neck, like wool in August. There was a truth behind the lie: We'd forgotten goat. *It* was what was missing.

Thus began this pursuit. We walked off the set and started working on a book proposal. We played with it for two years: visiting farms, ordering up whole goats, testing some recipes. Then we started talking about it. At first to more unfavorable responses like our producer's. Then to silence (which in this business is sometimes a sign of hope). And finally to acceptance.

What happened after that is between these covers: touring many more farms, taking classes in cheese making, simmering endless pots of stew, ripening our own goat cheese, and discovering what may well be some of the best artisanal agri-entrepreneurs in North America. All because of a lie.

If there's anything I've learned in life, it's this: The important things that go missing rarely are really missing. They come back. Because they have to.

Oh, that TV show? It never saw the light of day. By the time my lie was edited into a segment, the channel had changed management, programming direction had morphed, and the deal had fallen apart.

Because *that's* the other, maddening truth: The things that really do go missing were never truly real in the first place. They were all mirrors and hopes. Makeup, in other words.

What's left is the unvarnished truth. For us, that's a whole book devoted to goat. What's important comes back.

So here we go.

CHAPTER 1

MEAT

Goat is the world's primary meat. Upwards of 70 percent of the *red* meat eaten globally is goat. Not cow, not pig, not dog (for you fans of gross-out food shows on basic cable). Goat.

By all measures, these bearded head-butters outdo white meat, too—like chicken. And they can even take on all sorts of fish—except shrimp. But that may well be changing, what with the sustainability problems associated with catching or farming those squirmy critters.

Surprised? Think globally: India, Thailand, China, Bali, Nigeria, Kenya, Jordan, Saudi Arabia, Israel, Mexico, Costa Rica, Barbados, and Brazil. Goat can be kosher. Halal, too. In other words, it suffers from few cultural no-nos.

Except in the United States, where coy cartoon animals gaze out from every screen or monitor. Here, we like our animals with five-inch eyelashes; our meat pretty tasteless—if not cellophane-wrapped.

On a radio show the other day, Bruce was going on and on about spice rubs for chicken breasts.

"Well, they sure need it," the host finally said, "since they don't taste like much."

They don't? Has she ever had a pasture-raised, grub-worm-fed chicken? It has a slightly gamy, even smoky flavor. It tastes like, well, chicken.

Only in North America do we identify a neutral taste as *chicken*. Mostly because the chicken we eat doesn't taste like chicken.

In the end, we've constructed a hall of mirrors: Everything is like everything else—which is really like a fat lot of nothing. Which all got that way because it was penned in enormous lots, was fed its own kin ground up into a tasteless meal, lived an unspeakable life of utter privation—and then, in a final indignity, has to be tarted up on the plate to attract any attention.

Not goat. This world-class meat flies under our radar, so it has managed to escape these horrors. Although there are enormous feedlots for pigs in South America, there are no similar nightmares for goats—this on a continent that consumes a hefty bit of the world's production. In the United States, there are no hormones approved for goat production—and few antibiotics, to boot.

Put another way, goat may be eaten across the globe, but it's still a cottage industry: in Argentina, on the Caribbean island of Dominica, and in the United States. Goat is small scale. Always has been, still is. Want to reduce your carbon footprint? Eat goat.

Which is all sort of strange, since these animals have been raised for meat for millennia, domesticated for almost as long as humans have made dinner together. Archeological remnants of goat farming go back at least eleven thousand years among the ancestors of the Kurdish people, in some of the oldest established settlement patterns known. In fact, studies carried out under the aegis of the U.S. National Academy of Sciences have discovered that almost every domesticated goat in the world can be traced genetically back to herds still abundant in the Zagros Mountains along the Iran-Iraq border.

Nobody has morphed the DNA of goats so that they have breasts so big they can't walk (hello, chickens) or hooves so weak they are prone to rot (hello, cows). Over thousands of years, goats have been gleefully consumed by millions, if not billions—and yet have escaped the modern food chain.

However, the meat has been at the crossroads of some pretty important moments. Like that time Rebekah got her husband, Isaac, to bless the wrong son, to bless Jacob, who became the father of the twelve tribes of Israel, mostly through a trick played with a goat stew.

You see, the old patriarch, blind and dottering, had called in his eldest son, Esau, to ask him to go hunt up some game for supper. "Prepare for me savory food, such as I like, and bring it to me to eat, so that I may bless you before I die."

Esau deserved the blessing based on birth order. But Rebekah concocted a scheme for her favored son, Jacob: "Go to the flock and get me two choice goats, so that I may prepare from them savory food for your father, such as he likes, and you shall take it to your father to eat, so that he may bless you before he dies."

Theologians can argue the meaning. For Bruce and me, it's this: Goat is so tasty it can change history and secure an eternal blessing.

No wonder we're addicted to the stuff. But then again, I've always been impatient with boneless, skinless chicken breasts. I'll admit I had a strange childhood—sometime I'll tell you about having to ride around in the backseat of a Galaxy 500 under a paisley umbrella—but I grew up thinking almost all barnyard animals were for eating, even the bits and parts, snouts and tails. I thought hearts, livers, and the like were the tasty bits, saved as a prize for the only grandchild. True, my forebearers were stern prairie Methodists. They wasted not, nor wanted for anything. (Those two might be connected, you know?) But those ethics had nothing to do with giving me the inner bits. They thought they were spoiling me.

If this book has a constant refrain, it's this: Get thee behind me, blandness. There's a lot of research out there on how we in the developed world overeat dramatically and constantly because our food is so darn flavorless. We eat stuff that tastes like *chicken* (which, in fact, doesn't taste like chicken), miss the cues to satiety, and so eat more—and more and more. Goat in all its forms is a remedy.

Still, for some it's a hard sell. When we first signed on to write this book, I posted a big "Hurrah!" on Facebook, only to be met with a high school connection who wrote "Yucky goat" on my wall. I defriended her.

Nonetheless, her response fits in with goat's history. What once could secure an eternal blessing soon became the stuff of nightmares. Israelite priests would lay hands on a goat and drive it into the wilderness, the sins of everyone vanishing into the sand's maw. Jesus would tell his followers that the damned were goats, rather than the saved who were sheep. Soon, even the devil would be showing up tricked out in goat togs.

As Bruce and I were working on this chapter, we encountered that prejudice time and again among friends, only to have it evaporate in the face of an actual goat stew.

Because goat *is* savory: delectable, scrumptious, and lip smacking. It's definitely not sweet like pork, beef, or shrimp. It's got an earthiness that stands up well in deep braises and sophisticated stews—and even on the grill.

Because it has remained a cottage, clean-food industry and, I suspect, because we're all a little tired of boneless, skinless chicken breasts, goat is fast gaining acceptance in the United States. In 1989, the USDA inspected 230,297 goats for butchering; in 1999, 463,249; and in 2009, it was estimated the USDA took on over 830,000 animals. Growth like that is unprecedented, especially in the midst of an economic downturn.

Part of the reason for its rise in popularity may have to do with the fact that goat is a nutritional wonder. Check out this comparison for hefty, 6-ounce (170-g) servings of various meats.

PER 6-OUNCE (170-G) SERVING	GOAT	CHICKEN	BEEF	PORK	LAMB
CALORIES	244	324	358	360	350
FAT (IN GRAMS)	5.2	12.6	15.8	16.4	16.2
SATURATED FAT (IN GRAMS)	1.58	3.4	6.0	5.8	5.8
CHOLESTEROL (IN MILLIGRAMS)	127.6	152	146.2	146.2	156.4

What's more, it's easier to get your goat these days. You can now find it at high-end grocery stores. You can also often buy it at kosher or halal markets—or at East Indian, Pakistani, Turkish, Caribbean, and Latin American grocery stores. Or check your local farmers' market.

Then there's the Internet. State department of agriculture directories will often list goat producers near you. Or check out sites for small family farms. They'll ship the meat overnight to you—and the attendant mailing cost is barely noticeable, given the inexpensive but high-quality meat they're selling.

Just know what you're looking for. Goat may have gotten a bad reputation because some cultures prefer smelly old bucks for celebratory meals. For some Caribbean festivals, the stinkier, the better.

Um, no. Bruce and I are all for big tastes, but there's no reason to go over the edge. Besides, we have a feeling the odiferous cuts are desired because they're rubbed with habanero chiles and other incendiary devices. You need something pretty potent to stand up to that kind of burn.

In general, look for goat slaughtered between six and nine months of age. Much older, and the meat will start to go island on you. Call it the troll's revenge. Remember the fairy tale *The Three Billy Goats Gruff* with the troll under the bridge? He let the two smaller, younger goats go in hopes of getting their bigger brother coming along behind. The bigger brother, of course, head-butted the old guy into the ravine—but the troll should have held his ground early on and took one of the younger goats, particularly the smallest one. So don't be a greedy troll. Go for the young goat.

You also want to make sure you've got some marbling in the meat. There won't be a lot because goat is so darn lean. Leaner than chicken breasts. But some marbling is preferable to none.

We'll start off with the hunks, the recognizable bits.

Recognizable, that is, if you're a real carnivore, someone who doesn't just eat boneless, skinless bits of tastelessness. The hunks all look like ones from other animals: chops, tenderloins, legs, and shanks. Easy enough, right?

Actually, no. Goat is the Wild West of meat. Sometimes, it's hacked up by people who don't know any better. Or think it's "just like lamb." Most animals long enjoyed in European culinary traditions are processed according to standardized butchering practices. Not goat.

We know a small-time farmer up in our part of New England who raises goats to sell to us locals. Boy, have we gotten some strange cuts from him! Mostly because he goes at the carcasses with a hacksaw in his barn. We once bought a gangly hunk that included some rib chops (tender quick-cookers if there ever were any) still attached to the breast (a long-stewer for sure).

Our bad cut was indicative of a bigger issue. Most goat meat is the long-stewing stuff. The only exceptions are the chops (and only some of them), the tenderloin (seldom seen by consumers), and the legs (if you prepare them in one certain way—more on that in a bit). The rest is for braising or roasting. Goat is the original slow food.

So talk to your supplier. Where does the goat come from? Is it local? How was it raised? What is this cut best for? How should it be prepared? Do I need to do anything special to it? Because these questions make you a better eater. Ignorance is not bliss. It's just ignorance.

GET YOUR GOAT

Beery Farms
Mason, Michigan
www.localharvest.org/farms/M28202
(517) 676-4686 (local pickup only)

Brookside Farm
Portland, Oregon
www.brooksidefarm.org
(503) 449-3679

Chaffin Family Orchards
Oroville, California
www.chaffinfamilyorchards.com
(530) 533-1676 (local pickup only)

D&W Meat
Newton, Alabama
www.dandwmeatproducts.com
(334) 692-9977

Ferndale Farms
Ferndale, California
www.ferndalefarms.com
(707) 986-4322

Full of Life Farm
St. Paul, Oregon
www.fulloflifefarm.com
(925) 876-6720

Goat Peak Ranch
Red Wing, Minnesota
www.goatpeakranch.com
(651) 248-7443

Grande Premium Meats
Del Norte, Colorado
www.elkusa.com
(888) 338-4581

Heritage Foods USA
Brooklyn, New York
www.heritagefoodsusa.com
(718) 389-0985

Koether Ranch
McGregor, Iowa
www.eatwild.com/products/iowa.html
(563) 873-3385 (local pickup only)

Laurel Creek Farm
Maryville, Tennessee
www.laurelcreekmeat.com
(865) 873-3385

Little Brush Creek Farm
Buffalo, Kentucky
www.localharvest.org/farms/M19449
(270) 932-5388 (local pickup only)

Moon in the Pond
Sheffield, Massachusetts
www.mooninthepond.com
(413) 229-3092

Nicky USA
Portland, Oregon
www.nickyusa.com
(800) 469-4162

North Hollow Farms
Rochester, Vermont
www.vermontgrassfedbeef.com
(877) 304-2333

Preferred Meats
Oakland, California
www.preferredmeats.com
(800) 397-6328

Riverslea Farm
Epping, New Hampshire
www.riversleafarm.com
(603) 679-2629 (local pickup only)

Shepherd Song Farm
Downing, Wisconsin
www.shepherdsongfarm.com
(715) 265-7637

Slanker's Grass-fed Meats
Powderly, Texas
www.texasgrassfedbeef.com
(866) 752-6537

Thyme for Goat
Dresden, Maine
www.thymeforgoat.com
(207) 737-8737

CANADIAN GOAT MEAT SUPPLIERS

Boucherie Nile Eng
Montreal, Québec
(514) 271-9130

Canadian Meat Goat Association
Annaheim, Saskatchewan
(306) 598-4322

Frazierview Meat Shop
Vancouver, British Columbia
(604) 327-1724

Dave and Pat Griffith
Vanderhoof, British Columbia
(250) 567-2860

Koenig Farm
Clyde, Alberta
(780) 348-5872

La Chèvrerie du Biquet
Warwick, Québec
(819) 358-2594

Les Élevages du Sud
St-Denis, Québec
(418) 498-2167

Single Oak Farm
Upper Rawdon, Nova Scotia
(902) 632-2827

UNITED KINGDOM GOAT MEAT SUPPLIERS

Cockerham Boers
Lancaster
www.goat-meat.co.uk
0796 2812528

Abraham Natural Produce
Devon
www.organic-halal-meat.com
0791 2040267

Alternative Meats
Shropshire
www.alternativemeats.co.uk
0844 5456070

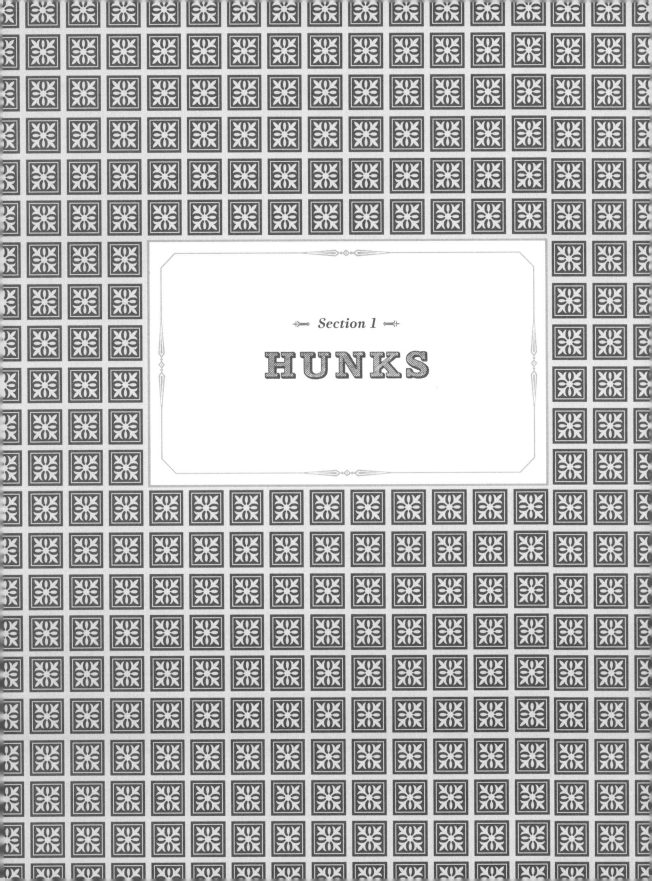

Section 1

HUNKS

A GOAT IS A BONY CRITTER, much like all the other four-legged, long-backboned types. Imagine feeling along the underside of a dog. (Or not, if you're squeamish. But our collie willingly stands in for anatomy lessons during cooking classes. He poses, we point to the cuts, and he gets a cookie. He's never complained.)

The spine supports a set of arching bones from just below the neck all the way to the abdomen. On a goat, these can all be cut into various chops. Most are long-stewers, but some are tender, juicy quick-cookers—the loin chops and the rib chops.

Another quick-cooker lies toward the back of that stretch of ribs: the tenderloin. In goats, it's not as tender as in cows; but it's nonetheless delectable, if frightfully exotic, and also terribly small, no more than a few ounces. A lot of goat butchers never even fool with the thing. What's more, it's too far back in the animal to be kosher without a lot of fancy knife work along the sciatic nerve. So it's often just ground—or chopped into stew meat. If you can lay your hands on a whole one, you've got a rarity indeed.

OK, those are the quick-cookers: the loin chops, the rib chops, and the tenderloin. Now for the long-stewers, the real treats in my opinion. Let's start again at the front of the animal.

First off, there are the neck slices. These are quite esoteric, just that long, goaty neck sliced into rounds, ½ inch thick (1.2 cm) or so. They're tasty, but I'd be negligent if I didn't add this: They're a bit dodgy in the United States. It's illegal to sell much of the tissue of the central nervous system—and those neck slices indeed have the spinal cord running through them. We've gotten goat-neck slices from plenty of U.S. suppliers; we've eaten them in some Indian and Southeast Asian restaurants, particularly in Queens, New York, and around the Bay Area. They're some of our favorite bits. And I've never thought of us as lawbreakers. But there you have it.

At the base of the neck, running between the front legs and a bit under the animal, we'll find the so-called breast. It is not a breast, except in the way that military generals pin medals to their "breasts." In other words, it's the chest. With the exception of some of the back rib chops, this is the fattiest cut, a piece of rich luxury when long-braised.

Near it lie the shoulders. Yes, it's odd to talk about *shoulders* on a four-legged creature. I mean, we're really talking about hips. But in culinary parlance, the shoulders are the meat at the top of the two front legs (although—and please don't ask me why—this meat on a pig is called the *butt*. Sheesh!). The shoulders can be cut into their own sorts of bony chops, all long-stewers, like lamb shoulder chops. The shoulders can also be left whole as long-cooking or long-braising roasts—or even cubed into stew meat.

All that said, remember this: We're talking about the Wild West of butchering. Bruce and I have seen back haunches cut up and called *shoulders*. Ask questions. And don't accept a shrug as an answer.

There are also sets of back rib chops that are long-cookers—as well as dribs and drabs throughout the animal that are cut off the bones as stew meat.

Finally, there are the four legs, front and back. Although the front legs are sometimes sold as *leg of goat*, they're more often boned out and chopped up as stew meat. The back legs are usually the ones labeled *leg of goat*—that is, the big haunch on which the goat can rear up when head-butting, more muscled than a pig's back leg, from which the fat-ass ham is taken.

And below those four legs? The shanks. The shins, as it were. These are long-stewers, for sure—stocked up with collagen and connective tissue.

So those are the hunks we'll work with. But there are others. A goat heart ground into an Italian meat *ragù* is a thing of beauty. (Stick with me here.) A goat tongue ground into a pâté? Equally gorgeous. But if this is your first go at goat, perhaps we should leave the esoteric morsels for another day.

That said, never forget the point: If you're going to take an animal's life to eat it, then eat it—and as much of it as you can. Waste not, as my prairie Methodist forebearers would have counseled. A life is precious and sacrosanct. To toss out this and that bit for no other reason than squeamishness is mere profligacy—if not much, much worse.

PAN-ROASTED CHOPS WITH BLACKBERRIES AND SAGE

THIS WILL MAKE TWO PLATES. DOUBLE THE RECIPE AT WILL.

Bruce calls this technique sear-and-shove: *Sear the chops in a hot skillet, then shove the skillet into a hot oven. Make sure your skillet is oven safe, preferably cast iron or heavy stainless steel. And with no wooden or plastic handles. I once left a dish towel wrapped around a skillet's handle after I'd shoved the thing into the oven. You know, firemen are the nicest people.*

MORE TO KNOW

Almost all the bad pests that lurk in goat meat are killed off at about 137°F (58°C). The good people at the USDA are all about safety, so they want to make sure you get the meat well past that temperature. However, because goat chops have so little fat, they can dry out pretty quickly. Thus, Bruce opts for a slightly lower but still safe temperature in a bid for more juice. It's your call. Just know what you're doing.

MORE GOATY
GOODNESS

Can you make this dish with plain ol' cow cream? Of course. But you're making a goat dish. Don't you want to go all out? The goat milk will not give you a tongue-coating sauce the way cow cream will, nor will it offer as heavy a punch of fat—yet it will offer more flavor, a little zip to match the berries.

---

1 tablespoon goat butter (or unsalted cow butter, if you must)

1 pound (455 g) goat loin chops or rib chops, each about ½ inch (1.2 cm) thick

½ teaspoon salt, plus more as needed

½ teaspoon freshly ground black pepper

1 small shallot, minced

1 teaspoon minced fresh sage leaves

⅛ teaspoon ground cinnamon

2 tablespoons dry white wine or dry vermouth

¼ cup (60 ml) whole goat milk

¼ cup (55 g) fat, sweet fresh blackberries

A crunchy baguette

1. Set the rack in the center of the oven. Fire up the oven to 400°F (205°C).

2. Melt the butter in a medium-sized, oven-safe skillet over medium heat. Season the chops with the salt and pepper, then slip them into the skillet. Brown for 2 minutes, shaking the skillet to loosen them up.

3. Turn the chops and shove the skillet into the oven. Roast until an instant-read meat thermometer inserted into the center of one of the chops registers 140°F (60°C) (Bruce's recommendation) or 145°F (63°C) (the USDA's), 4 to 5 minutes.

4. Remembering that the skillet is ridiculously hot, remove it from the oven, set it over medium heat again, and transfer the chops to a serving platter or individual serving plates.

5. Stir the minced shallot into the skillet and cook just until soft, probably less than 1 minute. Add the sage and cinnamon; stir until aromatic, about 15 seconds. Now pour in the wine or vermouth. As it boils, scrape up any browned bits in the skillet. The amount of liquid is tiny; it will boil instantly. Work fast.

6. Pour in the milk and drop in the blackberries. Bring to a full boil and cook for 1 minute, or just until somewhat reduced. Check for salt, then ladle this sauce over the chops. Tear the baguette into pieces so that some can accidentally fall into the sauce as you eat the chops.

GRILLED HERBY CHOPS

YOU'LL FEED FOUR IF YOU'VE ALSO GOT SALADS AND SUCH.

Know the chops you're getting. Despite little standardization, there are essentially four kinds: loin, rib, shoulder, and then the rarity of back rib chops, cut by some butchers, deboned as stew meat by a few, but ground by most. We'll get to the latter two kinds of chops in a bit, both long-stewers. This recipe calls for either of the first two types, loin chops (sometimes called T-bones*) or rib chops (sometimes called* rib steaks *or even* bone-in rib eyes*). That should tell you everything: They look like either T-bones or veal rib chops—but way smaller. You want a plentiful platter. Double or triple the recipe at will.*

MORE TO KNOW

Almost all the goat meat you'll ever cook will be done in a technique Bruce calls *low and slow*—that is, low heat, a little simmer, and a lot of time. Not so with loin or rib chops. These babies have little marbling, so they cook fast. That said, there's often a lip of fat that runs around the outer rim of each chop. Leave this in place to protect the edges of the chops as they cook over the hot coals or in the smoking pan. Listen, a little fat won't kill you.

LESS TO DO

You don't have to go whole hog (or goat?) with all those herbs. Bruce likes lots—and develops recipes as such. But you can pick two from the list: say, 2 tablespoons of thyme plus 2 tablespoons of one of the others.

1½ pounds (680 g) goat loin chops or rib chops, each about ¾ inch (2 cm) thick

2 tablespoons olive oil

3 medium garlic cloves, minced

1 tablespoon minced fresh marjoram leaves

1 tablespoon minced fresh rosemary leaves

1 tablespoon minced fresh dill fronds

1 tablespoon fresh thyme leaves

1 teaspoon finely grated lemon zest

½ teaspoon salt

½ teaspoon freshly ground black pepper

---

1. Mix everything together in a big bowl, cover it, and refrigerate for at least 2 hours, swapping things around in the bowl from time to time. Since there's almost no acid in the marinade, you can let the chops go for a long time for more flavor (up to 24 hours). Like sex, more is better—within reason.

2. Fire up the grill. Either heat a gas grill to high heat (around 550°F [288°C]) or prepare a high-heat, high-coal bed in a charcoal grill, eventually raking the coals into a searingly hot layer. While either is heating up, take the bowl of chops out of the fridge and let the chops sit in their marinade at room temperature, so you're not trying to grill cold meat. If you do, the inside of the chops will take too long to cook, the outside blackening before the rest is done.

Don't want to mess with the grill? You can do this whole operation in a well-seasoned, cast-iron grill pan. Heat it up to smoking over medium-high heat on the top of the stove. Turn on the vent or open a window. Or do both. And still plan on setting your smoke detectors off.

3. Stir the chops in the marinade one last time and set them on the grate directly over the heat or in the super-hot grill pan. Grill for 3 minutes—for heaven's sake, leave them alone: no prodding, poking, or futzing—then turn with a wide spatula and continue grilling until an instant-read meat thermometer inserted into the center of one of the chops registers 140°F (60°C) for a pink, hot center (our recommendation) or 145°F (63°C) for safety's sake (the USDA's rec), 2 to 3 more minutes. Remember: Meat is never done based on a stopwatch. There are a variety of factors at work: marbling, the animal's diet, its stress levels, your inability to quit prodding. The only reliable guide is internal heat. (Feel free to use this as dating advice, too.) Transfer the chops to a platter and dig in.

MORE GOATY
GOODNESS

Use this technique to prepare goat tenderloins, usually between 3 and 6 ounces (85 and 170 g) each. They will take about the same amount of time, maybe a minute or two longer. Figure on one tenderloin per person, particularly if you've got teenagers. Then again, if your teenagers are eating goat, either you're a culinary Dr. Spock or you just married someone with kids and are still new on the job.

MUSTARD-AND-HERB-RUBBED RACK

IT'LL FEED FOUR—ALTHOUGH IT CAN BE HALVED OR DOUBLED AT WILL.

When those tender rib chops—that is, the ones we've been working with, the small ones with a round eye of meat on only one side—remain joined together, the whole thing is called a rack. *Think of it like a rack of lamb: a lineup of bones, an eye of meat at the bottom of each, an elegant meal, great dinner-party fare.*

MORE TO KNOW

A rack is often *frenched*. All the meat and cartilage is removed from between and among the little bones so they arc out of the meat in a clean, ribby chorus line, the little eyes of meat the only bits left at their ends. This classic technique is aesthetically pleasing, but it doesn't really work for goat. First off, the meat is not that fatty. So there's no reason to remove those bits of heat protection. And second, the meat is not that plentiful. Better to leave every scrap for gnawing.

Two 12-ounce (two 340-g) racks of goat (8 bones each—do not trim)

¼ cup (60 ml) Dijon mustard

⅔ cup (150 g) fresh bread crumbs (see page 96)

⅔ cup (150 g) ground walnuts

1 teaspoon minced fresh sage leaves

½ teaspoon salt

½ teaspoon freshly ground black pepper

1. Preheat the oven to 375°F (190°C).

2. Check out that rack. (I promise that's the only time in my whole life I'll ever write that sentence.) One side has the eye of meat lying on top of it; the other is mostly the curve of the unadorned bones. Work only with the side with the fleshy bumps. (No jokes, please.) Rub the mustard on that side, getting it up the bones as well.

3. Mix the bread crumbs, walnuts, sage, salt, and pepper in a medium bowl, then press this mixture onto the mustard coating. You can spread the coating on a cutting board and roll the racks in it, but you might pick up too much on the first rack, giving the second short shrift. Better to get your hands messy patting it into place.

4. Set the racks, coating side up, in a heavy, solid roasting pan. Don't have one of these IRA-emptiers? Use a heavy, stainless steel, oven-safe skillet. Roast until an instant-read meat thermometer inserted into the thickest part of one of the racks without its touching bone registers 140°F (60°C) (Bruce's recommendation) or 145°F (63°C) (the USDA's), about 20 minutes, maybe a little less, a little longer, depending on the amount of interstitial fat. Start checking after about 15 minutes to know how close the racks are to being done.

5. Remove the hot pan or skillet from the oven; transfer the racks to a cutting board. Leave them alone for 5 minutes. Here's why: As meat roasts, internal juices are squeezed out by toughening and flattening muscle fibers; when it sits for a while, the fibers relax and the juices slip back between the fibers, giving you a more flavorful dinner. To serve, use a large, heavy knife to slice between the bones, separating the chops from one another.

GOAT CACCIATORE

CONSIDER IT DINNER FOR FOUR.

Now let's turn to the other kinds of chops: here, primarily shoulder chops, taken from up the rib cage, closer to the neck. These are full of cartilage, collagen, and other interstitial goodness. In other words, they're long-cookers—and so the basis for the first of our low-and-slow recipes. Bruce's recipe loosens up all that gorgeous stuff, turning it into tender goodness, slowly melting it all into this old-fashioned, tomato-based, mushroom-laced, Italian stew—which requires everyone at the table to slurp the meat off the bones. Some polenta in the bowls would also be a great treat. One more thing: Why no goat bacon here? Well, um, no one's making it. Interested entrepreneurs, take note.

LESS TO DO

The amount of mushrooms Bruce has used is a tad over the top. Believe me, it is delicious; but if you want to simplify things, keep the dried porcini and feel free to substitute 1½ pounds (680 g) sliced cremini mushrooms for the others.

MORE GOATY GOODNESS

You can also use neck slices (see page 17). These are stocked with even more connective tissue than shoulder chops—and therefore when done are almost sticky, sort of like oxtail, one of my all-time favorite cuts off a cow. If you use neck slices for this recipe, the stew will need to go longer, probably up to 3 hours.

---

1 ounce (30 g) **dried porcini mushrooms**

2 cups (480 ml) **boiling water**

4 ounces (115 g) **bacon, chopped**

1 cup (125 g) **all-purpose flour**

2 teaspoons **salt, plus more as needed**

1 teaspoon **freshly ground black pepper**

2½ pounds (1.2 kg) **bone-in goat shoulder chops**

1 large **yellow onion, chopped**

1 large **green bell pepper, stemmed, seeded, and chopped**

3 large **garlic cloves, minced**

8 ounces (225 g) **brown (or cremini) mushrooms**

6 ounces (170 g) **portobello mushroom caps, thinly sliced**

4 ounces (115 g) **shiitake mushroom caps, thinly sliced**

1 tablespoon **minced fresh oregano leaves or 2 teaspoons dried oregano**

1 tablespoon **minced fresh rosemary leaves or 2 teaspoons dried rosemary, crumbled**

½ teaspoon **freshly grated nutmeg**

⅔ cup (165 ml) **dry sherry, dry vermouth, or dry white wine**

3½ cups (800 g) **canned reduced-sodium diced tomatoes, with juice**

¼ cup (55 g) **pitted black olives**

1. Souse the dried porcini with the boiling water in a small bowl. Set aside for 30 minutes; then drain in a colander set over a bowl, reserving the mushroom-soaking liquid separately. Chop the porcini into small chunks.

   But before you go on, check that soaking liquid. If it's sandy, you'll have to run it through cheesecloth to clean it up—or through a paper coffee filter, if you don't have fancy chef paraphernalia lying around.

2. Fire up a large Dutch or French oven over medium heat. Drop in the bacon and cook, stirring occasionally, until crisp, about 4 minutes. Use a slotted spoon to transfer the bacon to a bowl, leaving its luxurious rendered fat behind.

3. Use a fork to mix the flour, salt, and pepper on a large plate. It's more than you'll need, but better safe than sorry. Dredge a couple goat chops in the flour, coating them in a thin layer, then put them in the pot and brown them on both sides, maybe about 4 minutes in all. Transfer them to the bowl with the bacon and continue browning more chops, first coating them lightly with flour before they hit the heat. The pot is going to get good and crusty, lots of browned bits, even blackened ones, all speckled and shellacked across it. All the better. Don't be afraid. You've come this far.

4. Once all the chops have been browned and are out of the pot, dump in the onion and bell pepper. Cook, stirring occasionally, until the onion turns translucent, about 4 minutes. Add the garlic and stir over the heat a few seconds.

5. Toss in all the mushrooms: the cremini, the portobello slices, the shiitake, and the chopped porcini. Stir over the heat several times; then cook, stirring occasionally, until they release their liquid and the mixture reduces to a glaze.

What does that mean? When you drag a wooden spoon through the sauce in the bottom of the pot, the line you make should not instantly flow back in place but keep discrete margins for a few seconds.

6. Stir in the oregano, rosemary, and nutmeg; cook until fragrant, just a few seconds; then pour in the sherry or one of its substitutes as well as the reserved (and possibly strained) mushroom soaking liquid. Bring the sauce to a simmer, scraping up any browned bits on the pot's bottom. Continue simmering until the liquid in the pot has reduced by about half, probably several minutes.

7. Pour in the tomatoes; add the olives, all the browned shoulder chops, the bacon, and any juices in their bowl. Bring the whole kit and caboodle to a full simmer.

8. Cover the pot and drop the heat to low. After that, there's not much to do: Read a good book while the stew simmers slowly until the meat is meltingly tender, about 2 hours, stirring it every once in a while. By the end, the shoulder meat should sag and wiggle off the bones. You know, like your favorite starlet below the neckline. And one last thing: Check the stew for salt before serving. Maybe a little more?

BRAISED BREAST OF GOAT

ONE BATCH WILL MAKE DINNER FOR FOUR TO SIX.

This cut is from the front of the animal, at the base of the neck, like a breast of veal. Goat breasts are naturally smaller than those off calves, so you'll need two to get the requisite servings. One note: You might be shocked at the amount of fat, but don't start trimming. A breast is not a cut for fat-phobes.

MORE TO KNOW

If you spend enough time doing cooking classes, you soon learn people are afraid to brown meat. Don't get me wrong—you don't want to blacken a filet mignon, turning a diamond back into carbon. But whenever you're braising or stewing and the recipe asks you to brown the meat, do so—with abandon. Brown is flavor, even on the bones. Because of complex evolutionary changes, we taste short-chain proteins and caramelized sugars far better than long-chain or raw ones. And the only way to get those? By searing long-cooking cuts like breasts and shanks over high heat.

1 tablespoon olive oil

Two 1½-pound (two 680-g) **goat breasts**

2 small yellow onions, chopped

2 large carrots, peeled and cut into 1-inch (2.5-cm) pieces

2 large parsnips, peeled and cut into 1-inch (2.5-cm) pieces

1 cup (240 ml) dry white wine or dry vermouth

3 medium tomatoes, chopped

2 teaspoons ground sumac (see page 97)

1 teaspoon dried thyme

1 teaspoon salt

½ teaspoon ground allspice

½ teaspoon freshly ground black pepper

2 cups (480 ml) reduced-sodium chicken broth

1. Heat a large, heavy Dutch or French oven over medium heat. Swirl in the oil, add one of the goat breasts. Brown it well on both sides. Transfer it to a plate and add the other one to the pot, doing the same operation. It should take 4 to 5 minutes a side—and with two sides to each breast, up to 20 minutes in all.

2. When both the breasts are on the plate, add the onions, carrots, and parsnips to the pot. Stir until the onions soften, about 5 minutes.

3. Crank the heat to high and pour in the wine or vermouth, scraping up any browned bits on the bottom of the pot as the liquid boils. Let it bubble madly, stirring once in a while, until reduced to a glaze.

4. Dump in the tomatoes, sumac, thyme, salt, allspice, and pepper. Stir over the heat until the tomatoes begin to break down, maybe a few minutes.

5. Pour in the broth before setting the breasts back into the pot, stacking them on each other as necessary, but trying to get them as flat as possible. Pour any juices left on their plate over them in the pot.

6. When everything in the pot is at a full simmer, cover, reduce the heat to low, and simmer slowly until the meat is incredibly tender when poked with a fork, about 2½ hours. One note: In an oval oven, the two breasts will overlap; in a round one, they may be on top of each other. Flip them once or twice as they cook, if one is more immersed than the other.

To serve, cut between the bones, sort of like the fattiest spareribs you ever had, only goat.

SHOULDER ROAST

IT'S A MEAL FOR FOUR TO SIX, DEPENDING ON THE SIDES.

Goat shoulders—that is, the meat over the front legs—are sometimes cut into chops (see page 17); but they can also be left whole and roasted or braised, each a long-cooking method to get all that connective tissue melty and irresistible. Bruce kept it simple here, using a French-inspired technique to create a great Sunday dinner.

1 tablespoon goat butter (or unsalted cow butter, if you must)

1 tablespoon olive oil

One 3- to 4-pound (1.4-kg to 1.8-kg) bone-in goat shoulder

2 small yellow onions, sliced into paper-thin rings

2 medium carrots, peeled and cut into 1-inch (2.5-cm) pieces

1 small fennel head, fronds removed, the bulb roughly chopped

6 medium garlic cloves, halved

3 fresh thyme sprigs

3 fresh oregano sprigs

2 bay leaves

1½ cups (360 ml) reduced-sodium beef or chicken broth, plus more as needed

1 cup (240 ml) red wine

1 tablespoon reduced-sodium tomato paste

2 teaspoons red wine vinegar

½ teaspoon salt, plus more as needed

½ teaspoon freshly ground black pepper

MORE TO KNOW

Here's the real deal with all the internal-temperature folderol: There are only three temperatures that matter for goat—140°F (60°C), 150°F (66°C), and 160°F (71°C). At 140°F (60°C), any interstitial fat has melted, bathing the meat in its goodness. In fact, it's about all melted at that point. By 150°F (66°C), it's gone, evaporated, dried up; the meat has become fit for shoes. Which means you have to push the temperature a bit, to around 160°F (71°C) (or even a little above for some cuts), where you get collagen melt—which then returns "juice" to the meat, making it again moist and luscious. Collagen is not fat; it's the main protein found in connective tissue. Watch the temperature to make sure you hit the right spot—collagen can get squeezed out, too, if the temperature goes too high. Here's the visual cue: Once the bones get waggly in the meat, you can be assured that the collagen is melting and everything is turning gorgeous. But that said, always go by temperature. After all, some connective tissue might have been thin or not in the best shape. Think of your knees after a game of tennis.

1. Set the rack in the center of the oven, then get the oven heated up to 325°F (165°C). Use a fork to mash the butter and oil in a small bowl until you have a loose paste. Massage this all over the roast.

2. Put all the veggies and herbs in a big roasting pan: the onions, carrots, fennel, garlic cloves, thyme, oregano, and bay leaves. Stir everything up, then set the fat-slathered goat roast on top.

3. Pour the broth and wine into the pan (but not over the meat) and shove the whole thing into the oven. Roast until an instant-read meat thermometer inserted into the roast without touching bone registers 160°F (71°C), 2½ to 3 hours, turning the roast twice during the time it's in the oven and basting it fairly frequently, maybe every 20 minutes or so.

4. Transfer the roast to a cutting board. Strain the sauce from the (hot!) pan through a colander set over a bowl in the sink. Discard all the solids in the colander. Pour the liquid into a small saucepan. You'll need about 1½ cups (360 ml). Add a little broth if you need to compensate.

5. Bring the pan juices to a simmer over medium-high heat, then whisk in the tomato paste, vinegar, salt, and pepper. Reduce the heat to low and simmer slowly for 5 minutes, whisking occasionally. To serve, carve the goat shoulder into slices (although it will also fall apart into chunks—do the best you can, since there's little rhyme or reason here). Serve these with the pan sauce on the side—all of which may need more salt.

PULLED SHOULDER

CALL IT A MEAL FOR EIGHT WITH ENOUGH SIDES—
LIKE SLAW AND POTATO SALAD.

No, not like you get after raking the yard. Instead, Texas-style. If the breast of a four-legged animal is part of Bruce's culinary tradition, pulled meat is part of mine: long-simmered cuts that get slathered in a fragrant chile-doped sauce. Goat is a lot less fatty than pork shoulder, so feel free to add extra mayo to the potato salad on the side. Pulled goat also needs the right accoutrements: hamburger buns, pickle relish, sliced tomatoes, shredded lettuce, and lots of napkins.

4 dried New Mexico red chiles, stemmed and seeded (see page 59)

4 ancho chiles, stemmed and seeded (see page 59)

Boiling water

2 tablespoons olive oil

4 pounds (1.8 kg) boneless goat shoulder roast (probably 2 boneless shoulder roasts—each tied around with butchers' twine so it holds its shape while cooked)

1 large yellow onion, chopped

⅓ cup (76 g) raisins

4 medium garlic cloves, minced

2 tablespoons packed dark brown sugar

2 tablespoons Worcestershire sauce

2 tablespoons mild smoked paprika (see More to Know)

1 tablespoon dried oregano

2 teaspoons ground cumin

3½ cups (800 g) canned reduced-sodium diced tomatoes, with juice

¾ cup (180 ml) reduced-sodium beef broth

⅓ cup (76 g) sliced pitted green olives

2 tablespoons cider vinegar

1. Swamp the dried chiles with boiling water in a large bowl. Set aside for 1 hour. Drain them in a colander set over a big bowl in the sink, reserving ½ cup (120 ml) of their soaking liquid.

2. Plop the softened chiles in a food processor fitted with the chopping blade, then add ¼ cup (60 ml) of their soaking liquid. Grind them to a fine paste, adding more liquid in 1-tablespoon increments as necessary and occasionally scraping down the inside of the canister with a rubber spatula to make sure every bit takes a death spiral onto the blades.

3. Heat a large Dutch or French oven over medium heat. Swirl in the oil, then add the shoulders, probably one at a time, browning them well on both sides, about 7 minutes per shoulder. Don't crowd the pot. As they're done, transfer them to a cutting board.

4. Add the onion and cook, stirring often, until softened, about 4 minutes. Then add the raisins and garlic. Cook, stirring constantly, for 1 minute. Hungry yet? Just wait.

5. Scrape your homemade chile paste into the pot; then add the brown sugar, Worcestershire sauce, smoked paprika, oregano, and cumin. Stir

over the heat until ridiculously aromatic, probably less than a minute; then dump in the tomatoes, broth, and olives.

6. Nestle the shoulders back into the pot and bring the whole thing to a full simmer. Cover, reduce the heat to low, and simmer slowly until the shoulder meat is falling-apart tender, 3 to 4 hours. You're going to have to poke and prod a bit to see how tender the meat is. In the end, a fork should be sufficient to rend the meat without effort.

7. Transfer the shoulders to your cutting board. This is way easier than it sounds, since they'll tend to fall apart, even when tied. Plan on drips and spills. Put the dog outside. Remove and discard the butchers' twine. Shred the meat with two forks, then stir it and the vinegar into the still-hot sauce in the pot to serve.

MORE GOATY GOODNESS

Goat shoulder can be difficult to obtain because the meat is often cut into chops or stew meat. So you can use 6½ to 7 pounds (3 to 3.2 kg) of bone-in goat shoulder chops for this recipe. Or go all out and use 7 to 8 (3.2 to 3.6 kg) pounds goat back ribs, the really fatty ones from way down the animal, toward the back legs. In either case, you'll spend a good 20 minutes picking the bones out of the sauce before you can serve the dish. But that's not the worst thing: standing over a pot, sucking the sauce off bones.

THE SEVEN-HOUR LEG

IT'S A MEAL FOR SIX WITH SOME SIDES LIKE ROASTED
SWEET POTATOES AND BRAISED SPINACH.

This is the first of Bruce's four ways to prepare a goat leg: a French technique called gigot de sept heures, *pronounced something like* zjee-GOAH-duh-set-UHR—*that is, "leg of seven hours." I used to struggle with French while sitting in small cafés, sipping espresso and pretending to master irregular verbs. I thought it was a good strategy to meet someone classy. Instead, it was a good strategy for meeting someone easily impressed, usually in sassy prints. Fortunately, Bruce came along in earth tones when I wasn't otherwise conjugating. Anyway, I did a lot of calling around among our French friends to find out if a* gigot *was anything other than a lamb leg. Could it be goat, despite always referring to lamb but not really being anything but a fancy word for leg? A gigot de chèvre, as it were? No one had an answer. But, boy, did I get in the middle of some long discussions! After all, language is the national sport in that country. Which really tells you another reason why learning French is not a smooth road to romance. Endless talk of vocabulary, grammar, and syntax rather spoils the mood.*

MORE TO KNOW

La chèvre is a goat; *le chèvre* is the cheese from said goat. Ah, French. Were you invented just so nuns could torture children?

3 tablespoons olive oil

One 4-pound (1.8-kg) leg of goat

2 whole garlic heads, the cloves not peeled but broken up from the bulb and the core/stem discarded

1 tablespoon minced fresh rosemary leaves

1 tablespoon minced fresh sage leaves

1 tablespoon fresh thyme leaves

4 bay leaves

2 cups (480 ml) dry white wine or dry vermouth

2 cups (480 ml) reduced-sodium chicken broth

1 tablespoon goat butter, optional

1. Get the rack set in the center of the oven and warm the oven up to 300°F (150°C).

2. Set a large, serious, flame-safe, no-holds-barred roasting pan over medium-high heat on top of the stove. Let that pan get good and hot, then swirl in the oil. Add the leg and brown it all over, holding it up so that even its narrow, thin sides sear against the hot pan. One warning: You'll splatter everything. Plan ahead and have children to clean up the mess. (Thus, you may need to start the recipe years earlier. Call it the *fourteen-year leg.*)

3. Transfer the leg to a carving board, drop the heat under the pan to medium, and toss in the garlic and all the herbs. Stir them around for a few seconds, then pour in the wine and broth. Whoosh! Scrape up any browned bits in the roasting pan as the liquid boils.

4. Set the leg back in the pan. A goat leg is not rounded; instead, it has two meaty sides. You'll want to roast it with the meatier side facing up. Cover the pan tightly with aluminum foil. Place it in the oven and bake for 3½ hours, basting occasionally. This is a tricky bit: uncovering, basting, re-covering. It's probably why this dish is such a classic: Only French grandmothers have this much time on their hands. Of course, they do because of their 35-hour work weeks and universal health care and state-backed pensions and . . . Sorry. Just make sure the foil is sealed tight after each basting.

5. Uncover the roasting pan and drop the oven's temperature to 275°F (135°C). Continue roasting for 3½ more hours, basting occasionally, making sure that the leg stays moist. Baste more now than you did before, because the thing is uncovered. At the end of it all, that leg will almost be confit: tender, meltingly sweet, crazy-delicious, and perfect. Transfer the leg back to the carving board. The task of carving this thing isn't that big a deal, since it will basically fall apart into chunks and pieces. You can slice these down into more manageable bits.

6. Finally, if you like, swirl the butter into the very small amount of pan juices left in the hot pan, to make a simple sauce. Bruce thinks this excessive. (Cooking a goat leg for 7 hours, isn't?) I think of butter as a beverage. In any event, remove the bay leaves before serving the sauce.

MORE GOATY GOODNESS

As I've already said, when we call for a goat leg in culinary parlance, we're talking about one of the two back legs. But there's little standard-ization. Sometimes, you'll end up with a front leg—which may not be as large, the meat lying in less defined planes, but which will work just fine in any of these recipes for the gams.

SCHWARMA

YOU'LL GET A MAIN COURSE FOR SIX TO EIGHT—OR STUFFED
PITA POCKET SANDWICHES FOR MANY MORE.

When I was in graduate school and still a weekend foodie, there were several places along State Street in Madison, Wisconsin, that offered schwarma: hunks of processed and extruded meat, heavily spiced, gray but somehow livid, turning slowly on big silver sabers. The guys at the counter hacked off pieces and put them in sandwiches. Or I think they did. I never tried the stuff. I don't eat street food. I don't care how many food writers promise it's the only way to know a culture. I don't eat it. Plus, I wasn't sure I needed to know any more about Madison culture, besides the patchouli and Birkenstocks. The long and the short of all this? I moved to New York, found Bruce, who is the master of long roasts with delicately sweet rubs, and now understand the pleasure of schwarma. At home.

6 medium garlic cloves, peeled, then mashed with the side of a heavy knife or put through a garlic press

2 tablespoons olive oil

2 teaspoons salt

1½ teaspoons ground mace

1½ teaspoons ground cardamom

1½ teaspoons mild paprika

1 teaspoon ground cinnamon

1 teaspoon ground cumin

½ teaspoon cayenne pepper

One 4-pound (1.8-kg) leg of goat

1. Mix the garlic, olive oil, salt, mace, cardamom, paprika, cinnamon, cumin, and cayenne in a small bowl. Smear it all over the goat leg and set the leg in a big, heavy roasting pan.

2. Set the rack in the oven's middle and crank the oven up to 350°F (175°C). It'll take about 15 minutes. Leave the goat leg in the pan on the counter the whole time so that the flavors of the spice mixture will begin to infuse the meat at room temperature.

3. Roast the leg in its pan until an instant-read meat thermometer inserted into the thickest part of the meat without touching bone registers 160°F (71°C), about 2 hours. Transfer the leg to a carving board and leave it alone for 10 minutes.

4. Now you'll need to carve it. And doing so with a goat leg can be tricky. With The Seven-Hour Leg (page 30), it's no problem, since the thing goes well beyond a rational point and simply falls off the bone. But in the case of this recipe, you'll want to carve the leg without hacking it to pieces. Position the leg on your carving board with the meatier side up. Starting at the fatter end of the leg, slice the meat against the grain. If you take a thin slice off the top, you'll see which way the meat's fibers are running, sort of like the grain in wood. Now, position the leg so that you're slicing at a 90-degree angle from the way the "grain" is running. But here's the tricky part: There are several muscle groups in a leg. Once

you get through one, the grain will change and go a different direction in another part. You'll have to keep turning the leg to slice thin strips against the grain. There's a little bit of trial and error here, but don't worry: No one's going to know the difference if a couple of slices are going with the grain. If someone makes a comment, seek new friends. Or a marriage counselor.

GO ALL OUT! GO ALL OUT! GO ALL OUT! GO ALL OUT! GO ALL OUT!

Once you slice the meat into bits, you'll want a flavorful sauce—either to ladle over it on the plate or to drizzle on it in pita pockets before you add some chopped tomato and shredded lettuce. An easy lemon tahini sauce is best: Mix 1 cup (240 ml) strained goat yogurt (see page 154) or Greek-style yogurt, ¼ cup (60 ml) tahini, ¼ cup (60 ml) lemon juice, ¼ cup (60 ml) minced cilantro leaves, 1 crushed large garlic clove, 1 teaspoon salt, ½ teaspoon ground cumin, and ½ teaspoon freshly ground black pepper in a bowl until smooth. You can make the sauce up to 3 days in advance; store it, covered, in the refrigerator, but let it sit out on the counter for 10 minutes or so before serving so that it's not ice-cold.

My First Time

It was in 1977. I was seventeen. I had skipped out of high school and gone right to college. Where I'd told no one I was seventeen. Or gay. Waco, Southern Baptists, Baylor. You do the math.

Still, I was game when my roommates cooked up a plan to go to Cancún for Christmas.

"Think of the girls," they said.

I smiled. Thinly.

You should know something about Cancún in 1977. It wasn't Cancún. There was a dusty airport with a couple of gates. There was a small town populated by Aussies, Germans, and their detritus, mostly prostitutes. And there were a few hotels on the beach. The El Presidente was the classy one.

We didn't stay there. We couldn't afford it. We stayed in a flop joint. But on the beach. As I said, it wasn't Cancún.

I'd brought a hundred bucks or so with me. (More math problems.) It didn't cover much more than my bar bill and some meals in the hotel's faded restaurant where the cracks in the walls were covered with load-bearing Christmas lights.

Since I could afford only simple things, I ordered in like manner. Or tried to. I didn't speak Spanish. A Texas boy studies French. Because that will do him a lot of good.

After I had stammered over the menu for a while, the waiter finally said, "*Señor? Tacos? Sí?*"

"*Sí*," I said.

Apparently, my linguistic skills were picking up.

I eventually got those tacos. They looked plenty good, stuffed with shredded meat, laced with fiery chiles.

Still, meat, Mexico, 1977. I asked what was in said tacos, using that finger-flailing technique common to Texas boys who study French, are gay, go to college early, and end up in Cancún trying to pretend they're looking for girls in a flop joint. You know the gesture I mean.

"*Cabrito*," he said.

I had no idea what he meant.

"*Sí*," I said. And took a bite.

It was searingly hot. Blindingly so. I coughed. Sat up. Tried to act tough. No tears, I thought. No tears.

I guzzled my drink. A Tom Collins. Oh, go ahead and laugh. My friends still didn't know. I had that poster of Farrah Fawcett on my dorm room wall. A load-bearing poster.

Despite the fire in my mouth, that meat was sweet, a little musky, and crazy-good.

"What is this?" I spluttered.

"Goat," one of my friends said. He was the worldly one. He drove a Trans-Am.

I couldn't spit it out. Because my friends were looking at me. Showing any sign of weakness wasn't worth the hassle. They might finally notice that I wasn't picking up any girls. Or so I thought in my constant attempt to square the circle.

I took a second bite.

It was my madeleine. Something pinged in my head. Yes, the chiles. But that intense, earthy flavor. Something beyond the bland stuff that passed for meat in the Mexican restaurants I'd known. Something elemental. A celebration of all things carnivore.

I'd like to tell you my career as a food writer began right there. It didn't. There's a lot between: street-preaching at Texas state fairs, getting married, going to graduate school, learning medieval Italian, getting a divorce, moving to New York, writing screenplays for persnickety celebrities, meeting the love of my life, getting married again. You know: the usual stuff. But at the back of it somewhere was goat. It led me out of myself and into a much bigger world.

JERK LEG

YOU'LL END UP WITH ABOUT SIX SERVINGS.

Jerk is a sweet, spicy, herbaceous Jamaican spice rub—but in the United States, all too often just a frat-boy excuse for "as hot as anyone can stand it." Listen, jerk needs to be hot, no doubt. But it also should be aromatic, as Bruce's blend here, stocked full with garlic, leeks, dried spices, and even vinegar. All these things are needed to manage the habanero, a fiery ball but also astoundingly fruity, once you get the heat balanced.

MORE TO KNOW

If you've ever worked with hot chiles, you know the problem: the hot chemical fandango still on your hands when you go to touch your lips, ears, eyes, or even more sensitive bits. Sheesh! Bruce has the most ingenious way of dealing with this problem. Capsaicin, the hot stuff, is not water soluble; it's fat soluble. That's why iced tea won't calm the burn in your mouth, but whole milk or a buttered tortilla will. So after you've worked with a fiery chile, rub your hands well with vegetable or olive oil, getting it along the sides of your fingers and under your nails. Now clean your hands with soap under warm running water for about 20 seconds, about as long as it takes to sing a full chorus of "Jingle Bells." Or forget this song-and-dance and simply wear rubber gloves when working with chiles—then throw the gloves out afterward.

LESS TO DO

Substitute a bottled jerk seasoning marinade for the one given in the recipe. However, look for a brand that's not (1) a ridiculously hot prank or (2) simply a corn syrup vehicle, sweet without aromatic overtones.

1 medium leek (white and pale green parts only), halved lengthwise, washed carefully for any grit in the inner chambers, then thinly sliced

4 medium garlic cloves, quartered

1 habanero chile, stemmed for sure, seeded or not, depending on how much of a masochist you are

2 tablespoons soy sauce

2 tablespoons red wine vinegar

2 tablespoons dried thyme

1 tablespoon smoked paprika (see page 28)

1 tablespoon ground allspice

1½ teaspoons salt

1 teaspoon freshly grated nutmeg

1 teaspoon ground cinnamon

1 teaspoon chipotle chile powder (see page 49)

1 teaspoon freshly ground black pepper

One 3- to 4-pound (1.4- to 1.8-kg) leg of goat

1. Combine the leeks, garlic, habanero chile, soy sauce, vinegar, thyme, paprika, allspice, salt, nutmeg, cinnamon, chipotle chile powder, and pepper in a mini food processor and whir it up into a coarse paste, about like wet sand.

Don't have a mini food processor? Then do the operation in a mortar with a pestle, grinding everything into a coarse paste.

2. Rub the chile mixture over the leg of lamb and set it meatier side up and uncovered in a heavy roasting pan in the refrigerator for 6 to 8 hours.

3. Position the rack in the middle of the oven and preheat the oven to 350°F (175°C). Set the leg in its roasting pan out on the counter while the oven preheats, about 15 minutes.

4. Roast, basting occasionally with the pan juices after the first hour, either (1) until an instant-read meat thermometer inserted into the leg without touching bone registers 160°F (71°C), about 2 hours, or (2) until the meat is falling off the bone, coming apart in shreds—somewhere above 160°F (71°C), but with no real temperature indication, just an overall feel.

What's the difference? At 160°F (71°C), you'll be able to make thin slices of meat, more as you did with *Schwarma* (page 32). At the higher temperature, the meat will be more tender (the cartilage and collagen will have begun to melt), so the meat will be more like "pulled goat" (see page 28), not really sliceable but quite luscious, coming apart in shreds and hunks without much prodding, not as far as The Seven-Hour Leg (page 30), but somewhere in between that and the more sliceable *Schwarma*.

The call is yours. Are you serving it at a dinner party with roasted roots and some sautéed collard greens? Then go for the lower, sliceable temperature. Are you serving it family style with a pot of rice and some fresh tortillas, with sour cream and grated cheese on the side? Then go for the higher temperature to make hunks and bits.

In either case, take the leg out of the roasting pan, set it on a cutting board, and wait about 5 minutes before carving or shredding it up.

MORE GOATY
GOODNESS

You can also use Bruce's jerk rub to flavor goat chops. Simply substitute it for the herb mixture in Grilled Herby Chops (page 20), marinating the meat for no more than 3 hours because of the added vinegar. Then grill or broil the chops as directed in that recipe.

SPANISH-INSPIRED LEG ᴼᶠ GOAT ON A BED OF CHICKPEAS, TOMATOES, AND SAFFRON

CALL IT DINNER FOR SIX WITH A STARCHY SIDE DISH AT THE READY.

Bruce's technique here is something of a fusion: Call it a braise/roast. There's not really enough liquid for it to be a true braise, but there's too much for a roast. In the end, the leg roasts until the meat falls off the bone in chunks, the melting collagen only further enriching the aromatic sauce. The whole thing cries out for rice, polenta, or even Goat Cheese Mashed Potatoes (page 185).

MORE TO KNOW

Saffron is the stigmas of *Crocus savitus*, which grows in southern Eurasia; the plant flowers in mid-autumn and is harvested by hand, backbreaking work to remove Lilliputian bits from low flowers. Although ground saffron is cheaper than the dried threads, it's best to go with the more expensive stuff because the ground is often of inferior quality and sometimes mixed with turmeric and other fillers. By the way, the stamens of the crocuses in your garden will not do—and can sicken you terribly. The dried stamens from the proper plants will infuse any dish with a musky, earthy flavor and a red/yellow color.

3 medium garlic cloves, peeled

2 tablespoons packed fresh oregano leaves

2 tablespoons olive oil

1 teaspoon salt

1 teaspoon freshly ground black pepper, halved and used in two places in the recipe

One 4-pound (1.8-kg) leg of goat

3½ cups (800 g) canned reduced-sodium diced tomatoes, drained

3 cups (680 g) canned chickpeas, drained and rinsed

2 cups (480 ml) dry sherry

1 medium yellow onion, chopped

½ cup (115 g) chopped fresh parsley leaves

1 teaspoon smoked paprika (see page 28)

1 teaspoon ground cloves

½ teaspoon ground cinnamon

½ teaspoon saffron threads, set in a small bowl with 1 tablespoon hot tap water for 10 minutes (see More to Know)

2 bay leaves

½ teaspoon freshly ground black pepper

1. Mash the garlic, oregano, olive oil, salt, and pepper together into a paste. You can do this in one of several ways:

   ☞ with the side of a large chef's knife on a cutting board,

   ☞ in a mortar with a pestle,

   ☞ or in a mini food processor.

2. Spread this mixture all over the goat leg and set the leg aside at room temperature while the oven preheats to 350°F (175°C), about 10 minutes.

3. Mix everything else in a large roasting pan (including the saffron in its soaking water and the remaining ½ teaspoon black pepper). Put the pan in the oven and set the prepared goat leg on top of the vegetables.

4. Roast until the meat is pulling away from the bone and quite tender, between 3 and 4 hours. Don't go by temperature on this one—just notice how tender the meat is and how it is pulling away from the bone, particularly at the joint. In fact, there's no real worry about its internal temperature; just let the leg go until it's ridiculously tender.

But don't just leave it alone. After the first hour, baste it with the pan sauce repeatedly, about every 15 minutes. Look, you don't have anything better to do; you're roasting a goat leg.

To serve, transfer the leg to a carving board (the bones and meat will fall apart, so be careful and keep kids from underfoot), then slice the meat into chunks and bits, worrying less about making neat slices and more about getting cheeky chunks of it ready for the platter. Remove and discard the bay leaves. Serve the chunks in bowls with the pan sauce lapped over the top.

MORE GOATY GOODNESS

You can also roast a bone-in shoulder roast with this technique. Give it about 2 hours, maybe up to 3, basting quite frequently to keep it from drying out.

Bruce's First Time

It happened at his kosher grandmother's.

By this point in her life, she lived with her home health aid, a Jamaican woman who did the chores, made some meals under a very watchful eye, and sat back in the afternoons for a lot of TV.

Soon enough, Bruce struck up a friendship with this Jamaican. She started forgoing her programs, hanging out with him at the table, talking endlessly about the meals she'd made. It was the mid-eighties. New York City was going down the toilet, crime was rampant, and unemployment was through the roof. There wasn't much to do but sit around and reminisce about food.

One day, she mentioned she'd just made a jerk goat stew at home. He was more than intrigued. "I'd love some," he told her.

If you listen carefully, you can hear the word *some* land at the exact moment his grandmother gasped from behind her newspaper.

"Brucie, darling, you don't want any of that."

"Goat can be kosher," he said.

She looked at him, looked at the Jamaican woman, looked back at him.

"Can," she said. She had him there. But he did want some. So he talked his way into it as the health aid was leaving for the day.

Sure enough, the next week, she brought over a foil packet of jerk goat.

Sure enough, his grandmother was apoplectic.

"Again with the food in my apartment," she said. "I still miss my Tupperware."

It was a complicated play for guilt, best attempted by a pro. A few years before, he'd stayed in her apartment while she was in Florida. He was always careful to make sure the meat and dairy dishes didn't get mixed up.

For her return home, he'd made her a pot of vegetable soup. She called him the minute she walked in the door. He claims her coat was still hanging off her back, the cab driver still waiting to be paid at the front door.

"Brucie, darling, what a nice thing to do. A pot of soup."

"It's vegetable," he said, trying to be helpful. "No dairy, no meat."

"And you put it in my Tupperware. But what pot did you make it in?"

Innocently, he said something about one of the saucepans in the cabinet below the stove.

There was that familiar gasp and the phone dropped. He'd made the neither-meat-nor-dairy soup in a meat pot but had put it in dairy Tupperware. Ever since, at any meal, the mere mention of leftovers brought on groans about the long-gone contaminated container.

This time, he knew to be more careful—although the fiery aroma of the Jamaican jerk stew was intoxicating. "Maybe I should eat it in the hallway," he said.

"Brucie, darling, whatever have I done that my grandson should eat in the hallway?"

"It's OK to eat it here?"

She was flattered he'd asked. "Of course." She turned to get a cup of coffee. "With a plastic fork."

He located the disposable implement and cracked open the foil. The chunks of tender goat were nestled in a still-warm chile-laced sauce.

He was about to set it down on the table when he heard that gasp behind him.

"Brucie, darling, put some paper under it." And then as if not to bear watching her own grandson descend to such wanton sinfulness, she walked out of the kitchen.

He spread out a sheet of newspaper, set the packet on top, and dived in. The meat was tender, moist, delicious. He savored every bite—while his grandmother watched TV. With the volume way up.

He carefully folded everything up in the newspaper and headed out to the incinerator shoot to discard the offense as quickly as possible.

His grandmother met him at the door. "Brucie, darling, that newspaper under that food. It was the *Post*?"

"No, *The Jewish Daily Forward*."

He claims it was the largest gasp he ever heard.

SHANKS WITH
CABBAGE, PORT, AND VANILLA

FOUR BRAISED SHANKS. ONE PER SERVING, I'D SAY.

This is the first of Bruce's four recipes for shanks—which can be from either the front or the back legs. His only caveat is that you need to buy shanks that are similarly sized, so they'll cook evenly. In any case, they're smaller than lamb shanks, and definitely leaner. Don't let them go too long, or they can turn tough. However, by the time these shanks are tender, the cabbage will have melted into the sauce, dyeing it red and turning it delectable.

MORE TO KNOW

Pink peppercorns are not pepper-corns, not in the strict sense. They're not from the flowering vine *Piper nigrum* (which gives us most other varieties of so-called peppercorns), but are instead the dried berries from a small South American tree, *Schinus terebinthifolius*, the Baies rose, related to the cashew tree. Pink peppercorns have a citrusy bite, acidic like all berries, but with pep-pery overtones.

Many recipes in this book call for a Dutch or French oven. Some people think the difference is one of shape (a Dutch oven is round; a French oven, oval). Not necessarily. In general, a Dutch oven is made of a metal like stainless steel or cast iron; a French oven is comprised of an enamel coating over some sort of metal, usually cast iron. Either will work—provided it's heavy, sturdy, and efficient. The most important part of the whole contraption? The lid. It should fit tightly. If not, steam will escape, thereby slicking the walls of your kitchen with flavor but otherwise doing no one much good.

1 tablespoon goat butter (or unsalted cow butter, if you must)

6 ounces (170 g) bacon, diced

Four 12- to 16-ounce (four 340- to 455-g) goat shanks

1 medium yellow onion, chopped

3 cups (680 g) shredded red cabbage (about 1 small head, halved, cored, the outer leaves removed, and the remainder chopped into long threads)

4 medium garlic cloves, minced

1 tablespoon pink peppercorns

1 teaspoon fennel seeds

½ teaspoon ground allspice

1 cup (240 ml) port

1½ cups (360 ml) reduced-sodium chicken broth

2 tablespoons reduced-sodium tomato paste

1 fresh rosemary sprig

One 4-inch (10-cm) cinnamon stick

1 vanilla bean (do *not* split it in half, or the flavor will be far too strong)

1 bay leaf

½ teaspoon salt

½ teaspoon freshly ground black pepper

1. Position the rack in the oven so a large Dutch or French oven with its lid can fit inside with about 3 inches (7.5 cm) of headspace. Get the oven heated up to 350°F (175°C).

2. Heat that pot over medium heat, then add the butter. Plop in the bacon and frizzle until crisp, stirring occasionally, about 4 minutes. Transfer to a plate or cutting board, using a slotted spoon so all that smoky fat stays behind.

3. Add the shanks and brown them well on all sides. If you have to do this in batches to avoid crowding, so be it. Don't gray the meat. Let it get good and caramelized. It'll probably take 8 to 10 minutes per batch. When done, transfer the shanks to the plate or cutting board with the bacon.

4. Add the onion to the pot; cook, stirring often, until softened and translu-cent, about 4 minutes. Then dump in the cabbage; stir for 3 to 4 minutes, until wilted.

5. Stir in the garlic, pink peppercorns, fennel seeds, and allspice. Cook just until aromatic, about 15 seconds or so; then pour in the port. As it simmers, scrape up any browned bits in the pot. Keep simmering until the amount as been reduced by half. No reason to measure—just make a good guess.

6. Pour in the broth; stir in the tomato paste, as well as the rosemary, cinnamon stick, vanilla bean, bay leaf, salt, and black pepper.

7. Finally, return the shanks, bacon, and any accumulated juices to the pot. Line the shanks up on their sides if necessary so they'll fit. They'll shrink as they cook and you'll have more playing-around room after things heat up. If, however, they still overlap, shift them around a bit as they cook. Bring the sauce to a simmer, then cover the pot and shove it into the oven. Leave it be until the shanks are meltingly tender, 2½ to 3 hours. Here's how Bruce tells if they're tender: He sticks a meat fork in one. If the shank comes up out of the pot with the fork, it's not ready; if the fork just slips out of the meat, leaving the shank behind with no hesitation, it's perfect.

One more thing: remove the cinnamon stick, vanilla bean, and bay leaf before serving.

NORMANDY-INSPIRED SHANKS WITH BUTTER, APPLES, AND CREAM

CALL IT DINNER FOR FOUR.

Normandy is heaven for butter lovers, a part of France where dairy is celebrated as the elixir of the gods. And goat milk, too. But why no goat milk in this recipe? Sometimes, life just calls for cow cream. For body, for taste, for texture. Often, in fact. Neither Bruce nor I could stomach the notion of using anything else in this classic French dish. See, we have our limits. But get this: The secret to a good cream sauce is not using too much cream. There's nothing worse than an overwhelming tongue-coater pretending to be a balanced sauce.

1 tablespoon goat butter (or unsalted cow butter, if you must)

4 ounces (115 g) bacon, cut into small pieces

Four 12- to 16-ounce (four 340- to 455-g) goat shanks

2 large leeks (white and pale green parts only), halved lengthwise, washed carefully for any grit in the inner chambers, then thinly sliced

1 tablespoon chopped fresh sage

1 teaspoon ground allspice

3 fresh rosemary sprigs

2 bay leaves

½ cup (120 ml) Calvados or apple brandy

One 750-milliliter bottle white wine, preferably a Sancerre or light white from the Loire Valley

2 large apples, peeled, cored, and quartered

½ cup (120 ml) cow cream

½ teaspoon salt

½ teaspoon freshly ground black pepper

1. Position the rack in the oven so a large Dutch or French oven can fit inside with about 3 inches (7.5 cm) of headspace when covered. Preheat the oven to 325°F (165°C).

2. Melt the butter in that pot over medium heat, then add the bacon. Crisp for about 3 minutes. Use a slotted spoon to transfer the bacon bits to a plate, leaving the fat behind.

3. Now brown the shanks. To do so, set them in the pot, leave them alone, let them get good and brown; then turn them over, after at least 4 or 5 minutes. If you try to turn them too soon, they'll stick. The sugars have to break down and caramelize for the things to release again from the pan. That's when you can get a flat spatula underneath them and pop them loose.

4. Once they're browned, transfer them to the plate as well, then add the leeks. Cook, stirring once in a while, until softened, about 4 minutes.

5. Add the sage, allspice, rosemary, and bay leaves. Stir a few times, then pour in the Calvados. There's a very slight chance the booze will ignite. If it does, carefully cover the pot and take it off the heat. Wait a couple of minutes, remove the lid, and set the pot back over the heat. Let it get hot again before proceeding.

6. Scrape up any browned bits in the pot as the Calvados simmers. Continue simmering until it reduces to a thick glaze, one you can make a line in with a wooden spoon, the line's demarcation not instantly giving way as the liquid flows back into place.

7. Pour in the wine, then add the shanks, bacon, and any of their accumulated juices to the pot. Tuck the apple quarters into the simmering sauce, then cover the pot and place it in the oven.

8. Bake until the shanks are crazy tender, until the meat is falling apart when prodded with a fork, about 2½ hours.

9. Using a large spoon, transfer the shanks to four serving bowls. Set the pot over medium-high heat; bring the sauce to a full simmer. Stir in the cream, then the salt and pepper. Reduce the heat and simmer slowly for a couple of minutes, before removing the bay leaves and spooning the sauce over the shanks. Try to get the bowls to the table before you dive into one.

MORE GOATY
GOODNESS

You could make this same braise with about 4 pounds (1.8 kg) of shoulder chops—but browning them will be a bit of a challenge, since they have more surface area and the fat can begin to burn. Work quickly and efficiently to get a good caramelization on them before continuing with the recipe—and braise them in the oven for about 2 hours, stirring occasionally so that they all get a chance to sit in the sauce.

On Bill Niman's Ranch

Pork king Bill Niman is on a mission again. You can tell it from his eyes. They dance and then suddenly stop, holding you in their gaze.

The day Bruce and I dropped by his ranch, it was as if we'd interrupted him, although we'd set an appointment.

"Nobody arrives early," he said, already walking away from us. It was the view of Bill I remember most: his straight back, on his way elsewhere.

He led us inside to the kitchen table. "You want to talk about goat," he said.

Yes, we did, while he sipped coffee from an enamel-over-tin mug and hitched his jeans where they tended to grab.

But we didn't get to it at first. Instead, we talked about grass, about rain, about soil—all of which were his ideas of goat ranching. He takes care of the land; the goats take care of themselves.

After thirty minutes or so, he'd clearly had enough. "Best if I just show you," he said, standing up, already walking away.

We headed up the steep hill behind his house, just south of Point Reyes National Seashore.

"Like I told you, I first brought goats to this place to manage the pastures," he said, not a whit winded by the climb.

We on the other hand were huffing and puffing, trying to get questions out, trying to seem somewhat knowledgeable. Mostly trying to avoid heart attacks. You don't work your way through all these goat recipes and then run up a steep hill. At least not in the same six months.

Fortunately, Bill didn't need our prompts as we climbed ever higher.

"Goats are browsers," he said, explaining that cows are grazers—and picky, too, eating certain plants to the ground, leaving the wiry thistle and bad weeds untouched. By contrast, goats pick and choose, the pasture their buffet. "I first brought them here to tend the land for the cows."

As he explained it, the goats eat here, eat there, move on, eat a little more, never all, thereby keeping the weeds under control. They don't pull the grass up by its roots. And the cows are happier for it.

Except goats have taken over Bill's life. The cows now stand in a small paddock on one bump, while the goats have the full range, a thousand acres of California heaven.

We caught up with Bill at the top of the hill. He was already talking. "Too often, the milking goats end up in the slaughterhouse along with the culls." (That is, the goats in poor health or poor stature, the ones no one wants.) "And so people get the idea that goat tastes bad. No wonder. Under those conditions, it does."

Bill is trying to change all that. He's trying to do for goat what he did for pork. He's building herds that are content, happy, grassfed, brought to slaughter with minimal fuss, given a stress-free life, even a stress-free death.

As we wandered the hills, we quickly saw that these goats were not milkers. Dairy goats are comfortable with humans. They run up to you, wanting to be petted like a dog.

These ran away. We didn't represent food or comfort or relief from full utters. Instead, these goats browsed on grass. And didn't need us.

Moving among them were tall, stately llamas. Bill explained they could kill a coyote with one kick, had been trained to do just that.

"Besides, they're browsers, too," he said. "So it all works out."

Indeed, it might. Because Bill's real passion was clearly the land. The animals were almost a secondary concern. Except when it came to their death. There, Bill was adamant. "It has to be clean, fast, and stress-free," he said. "And we still control that because the market is so small. We don't do anything special. No misting the carcasses so they take on water. We just hang them dry. Slaughter on Thursday, hang until Monday, and then off to the stores."

It sounded so simple. But it's not. It's a matter of careful ranching. And another culinary revolution in the making.

ITALIAN-INSPIRED SHANKS WITH WHITE BEANS AND LEMON

IT'LL FEED FOUR.

Bruce added gin to this classic Italian-style braise. Mostly because he could. And because it adds the lovely taste of juniper to the meat. If you want your shanks in a less potted state, substitute a dry white wine. In any event, you'll discover that the shanks are surprisingly lean, so the beans don't soak up too much fat, the way they can with lamb shanks.

1½ tablespoons olive oil

Four 12- to 16-ounce (four 350- to 455-g) **goat shanks**

6 medium carrots, peeled and cut into 1-inch (2.5-cm) pieces

2 small leeks (white and pale green parts only), halved lengthwise, washed carefully for any grit in the inner chambers, then thinly sliced

1 medium garlic clove, minced

2 tablespoons minced fresh sage leaves

2 teaspoons finely grated lemon zest

½ teaspoon salt

½ teaspoon freshly ground black pepper

¼ cup (60 ml) gin

2 cups (480 ml) reduced-sodium chicken broth

1½ cups (360 ml) canned white beans, drained and rinsed

1. Position the oven's rack so that a big Dutch or French oven will fit with still a couple of inches to spare at the top once covered. Preheat the oven to 350°F (175°C).

2. Heat that pot over medium heat, then swirl in the oil. Add the shanks and brown them on all sides, turning occasionally but letting them get good and caramelized—not crusty, but certainly sizzling, well beyond mere "golden." Maybe 8 to 10 minutes? Transfer the shanks to a plate.

3. Stir the carrots and leeks into the pot. Keep cooking and stirring until the leeks turn a bit translucent, about 4 minutes. Add the garlic, sage, lemon zest, salt, and pepper. Stir for about 15 seconds.

4. Pour in the gin. If it ignites, cover the pot quickly and take it off the heat. After several minutes, uncover the pot and return it to the heat, letting it come back to a simmer. In any case, let it bubble for 1 minute, then pour in the broth and beans. As the mixture comes to a simmer, scrape up any browned bits in the pot, then nestle the shanks into the sauce. Pour in any accumulated juices on their plate.

5. Once the sauce is at a full simmer, cover the pot and place it in the oven. Bake until the shanks are meltingly tender, about 2½ hours, stirring a couple of times (but not right toward the end, when the shanks can begin to come apart). Serve them in individual bowls with the sauce drenching each. Make sure there's some crusty bread on hand, too.

RIDICULOUSLY AROMATIC VIETNAMESE-INSPIRED SHANKS

THIS WILL MAKE A MEAL FOR FOUR.

In truth, Bruce's recipe includes Vietnamese flavorings, but it's assembled with a traditional Western technique. Goat is relished across Southeast Asia, but the tendency is to cut the meat into stewing or braising chunks, even the shanks. Here, Bruce honors the basic flavors of the region but also leaves the shanks intact for more at-the-table gnawing. There aren't even any vegetables to get in the way of this carnivore's empyrean.

1 tablespoon ancho chile powder (see More to Know)

1 teaspoon five-spice powder

1 teaspoon packed dark brown sugar

Four 12- to 16-ounce (four 340- to 455-g) goat shanks

2 tablespoons peanut oil

2 medium yellow onions, chopped

3 medium garlic cloves, minced

2 tablespoons minced peeled fresh ginger

2 cups (480 ml) reduced-sodium chicken broth

¼ cup (55 g) chopped fresh cilantro leaves

2 tablespoons rice vinegar

2 tablespoons fish sauce (see More to Know)

1 tablespoon honey

1 tablespoon soy sauce

Cooked white or brown rice, preferably a short-grain variety

1. Mix the chile powder, five-spice powder, and brown sugar in a medium bowl. Massage this mixture into the shanks, coating them well. Drop them back into the bowl, cover it, and place it in the refrigerator for 24 hours.

2. Position the oven's rack so that a Dutch or French oven can get in there with still a few inches of headspace when the pot is covered. Preheat the oven to 325°F (165°C).

3. Heat that pot on top of the stove over medium heat, then swirl in the peanut oil. Place the shanks in the pot, two at a time if necessary to prevent crowding; brown on all sides, taking care to let the sugars caramelize. Transfer the shanks to a bowl.

4. Add the onions; cook, stirring often, until softened, about 3 minutes. Add the garlic and ginger; cook, stirring constantly, for 30 seconds.

5. Dump in the broth, cilantro, rice vinegar, fish sauce, honey, and soy sauce. As it comes up to a simmer, make sure you scrape up any browned bits on the pot's bottom. Nestle the shanks into the sauce; pour in any juices on the plate.

6. Cover the pot, place in the oven, and bake until the shanks are meltingly tender, 2½ to 3 hours. Serve the shanks over the rice in bowls.

MORE TO KNOW

Although chili powder is indeed made from ground chiles, it's in fact a blend in most bottlings, one that includes dried oregano and ground cumin. However, there are other varieties, many considered *pure chile* powders—ancho chile powder (very aromatic), chipotle chile powder (nicely smoky)—made only from ground dried chiles. Check the recipe to see what kind is called for.

Fish sauce—*nam pla* in Thailand, *nuoc mom* in Vietnam, *teuk trai* in Cambodia, and sometimes *fish gravy* in Hong Kong—is a Southeast Asian condiment made from fermented fish. As you'd expect, it smells rather pungent but mellows to perfection over the heat.

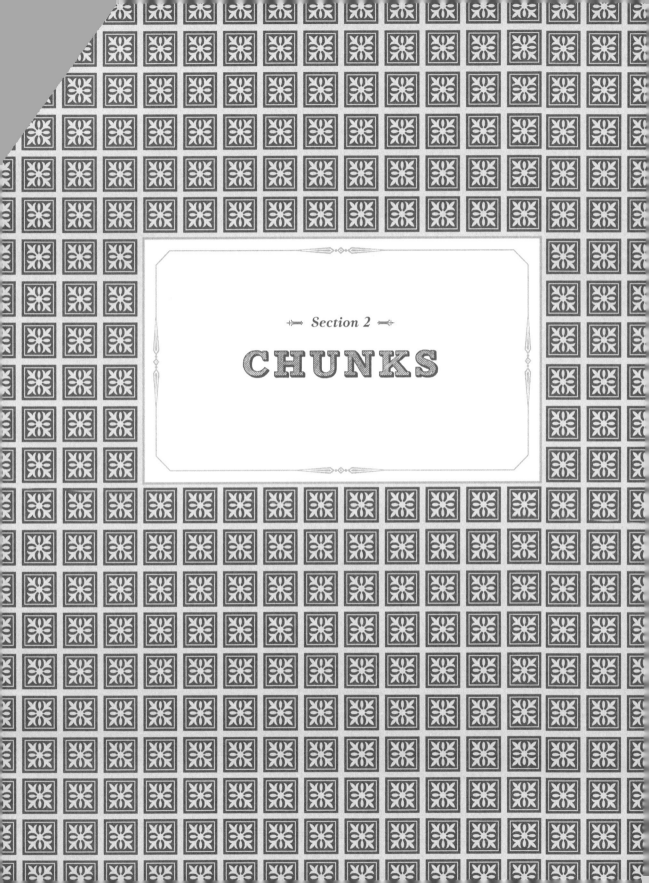

Section 2

CHUNKS

MOST PEOPLE DON'T PRACTICE their careers on their friends. When was the last time you were invited to a dinner party and told to bring your tax statements so "we can do a little accounting over dessert"?

Not so with Bruce. He foists his recipe-testing on our friends.

There were no problems with our other books. Everyone was happy to chow down on the leavings. I remember one particular night in New York City: I watched our publisher and her husband, a gym trainer and his wife, plus Bruce and me polish off 5 pounds (2.3 kg) of foie gras, two stuffed geese, a rack of lamb thrown in for good measure, and a whipped cream cake.

But goat?

All our friends were game for the legs, shanks, and such. Still, I'm a tad neurotic. You'd be, too, if you'd grown up as I did, surrounded by cotillions and Civil War reenactments. Those things morph and fuse into many different situations—most of them disastrous.

I imagined our friends were game only because the hunks were recognizable. But the chunks and bits? I feared that might be another matter entirely.

Most goat stew meat is cut from pieces off the back of the animal, around the belly, or under the breast—or even from some of the stringier bits around the front ribs. Delicious, no doubt; deeply flavored, too. But not necessarily the place you want to start. So I always stopped Bruce from testing these recipes on our friends.

"I think I'll try the tagine for the tasting party this weekend," he'd say.

"Really?" I'd quiver. "How about another roast leg?"

I should have timed things out better. Because I saved back testing many of these chunk recipes until Christmas. Right when my parents came up from Texas.

I had to warn them. I called my mother before they arrived. "Will you eat goat?"

"I'm fine, dear. How are you?"

I should add that we don't really do the niceties anymore.

"Will you?" I insisted.

"I've never had anything at your house I didn't eat."

For you who don't speak Southern, that's not a ringing endorsement. It's more along the lines of *Why in the world did you move to New England? Oh, because you're being a writer right now, aren't you, dear? And doing that gay thing.*

"I just wanted to make sure," I added.

"I'll be fine. I need to lose a little weight."

You don't have to speak Southern to hear that one.

Anyway, they came forewarned—and got a mess of goat stews. Which they slurped down—although I did notice that on the first night, my mother upended two glasses of wine before dinner. For a Baptist, that's the equivalent of pulling up the drawbridge, filling the moat, and arming the towers.

One afternoon, I followed her down to the basement, where she and Bruce checked out the remaining bits of stew meat in the chest freezer. She held up one frost-rimed package. "Honestly, Bruce, you can make anything taste good."

Need I continue translating? We take our victories where we can.

GOAT AND QUINCE STEW

**IT FEEDS FOUR COMFORTABLY, SIX IF YOU'VE GOT RICE
IN THE BOWLS AS WELL.**

Bruce and I actually had a fight about this one. I roused the collie one afternoon and walked into the kitchen as he was making it, only to see him adding red currant jelly to the pot. I freaked out. "That's absurd," I said. "People don't want to buy so many ingredients—and besides, this thing already has quince in it." Then I said something that began with "You know what your problem is . . ." and it didn't go well from there. Once we were finally eating a reheated dinner, I had to admit that the red currant jelly was just the thing: a little sweet accent underneath the more complex flavors. Score one for the chef.

MORE TO KNOW

Related to apples and pears, quince are indigenous to central Asia, although now grown in Europe and (more extensively) in South America. The flesh is quite hard and can be grated, even when ripe. Look for sweet-smelling, perfumy, yellow-gold quince without mushy spots or brown splotches. If they're quite firm, you can tuck one into a dresser drawer to use as a scented sachet. Just don't forget it's in there or in a month or so, you'll have a mushy mess among your dainties.

The basic flavoring of gin, juniper berries are a favored spice with game meats, adding a sharp, somewhat sour touch to stews and braises. Oddly, they're not berries at all, but cones from various juniper trees, like pinecones, only smaller and spherical.

2 pounds (910 g) boneless goat stew meat, preferably cut from the leg and into 1-inch (2.5-cm) cubes

2 medium yellow onions, sliced into very thin rings

3 medium garlic cloves, peeled and smashed on a cutting board with the side of a heavy knife or put through a garlic press

1 teaspoon caraway seeds

1 teaspoon salt

½ teaspoon saffron threads (see page 38)

8 juniper berries, crushed on a cutting board with the side of a heavy knife

One 4-inch (10-cm) cinnamon stick

2 bay leaves

2 cups (480 ml) sweet white wine, such as a Riesling

3 tablespoons goat butter (or unsalted cow butter, if you must)

2½ tablespoons all-purpose flour

1 cup (240 ml) reduced-sodium chicken broth

1 tablespoon red currant jelly

3 ripe quince, peeled and cored, then cut into 1-inch (2.5-cm) chunks

1. Mix the meat, onions, garlic, caraway seeds, salt, saffron, juniper berries, cinnamon stick, and bay leaves in a big bowl until the meat is coated. Pour in the wine, stir well, then cover and refrigerate for 24 hours.

2. Transfer the meat chunks from the marinade to a separate bowl. In truth, doing this is a pain in the neck, sorting the meat from the rest of the things. Ah, well.

3. Once the meat chunks are out and in their own bowl, strain the marinade in a colander set over a big bowl, reserving both the spices and vegetables in the colander and the liquid in the bowl. So now you have three bowls of things: meat, spices/vegetables, and liquid.

4. Melt the butter in a large Dutch or French oven over medium heat. Add the spices/vegetables from the colander. Stir over the heat occasionally until the onions are sweet and golden brown, about 6 minutes. Transfer all the vegetables and spices to a big bowl. It helps to use a slotted spoon to catch the onions, but it won't work on the spices—which are best fished out with a flatware tablespoon.

5. Use paper towels to pat the meat chunks dry. This is not a throwaway bit of advice. The meat won't brown properly unless you pat the chunks dry. Dump them all into the pot and brown well on all sides, maybe up to 10 minutes.

6. Once all the chunks have been browned, dust them with the flour and stir over the heat for 3 to 4 minutes, just until the flour browns a bit, coats all the chunks, and loses its raw look (and thus its raw taste).

7. Stirring all the while, add the broth in dribs and drabs to make sure the flour dissolves slowly without clumping. Once you get the flour mixture to a pastelike consistency, you can start adding the broth more quickly, in a steady stream and stirring all the while.

8. Now pour in all that reserved marinade liquid. Continue stirring over the heat until the sauce is thickened a bit and bubbling.

9. Stir in the red currant jelly as well as all the spices/vegetables in their bowl. Bring the sauce to a full simmer, stirring occasionally.

10. Cover the pot, reduce the heat to low, and simmer slowly for 1 hour, stirring occasionally.

11. Add the quince, stir well, and continue simmering slowly, stirring once in a while, until the meat is gorgeously tender, about 1 to 1½ hours. Remove the cinnamon stick and bay leaves before ladling the stew into bowls.

GOAT, POTATO, ARTICHOKE STEW

YOU'LL GET SIX BOWLFULS.

Delicate and sweet, this is a winter warmer or a springtime pleasure. It's also not really based on other dishes or morphed from classic techniques. Creativity run rampant!

¼ cup (60 ml) **olive oil**

5 medium **garlic cloves, slivered**

Two 5-inch (two 5-cm) **fresh rosemary sprigs**

2½ pounds (1.2 kg) **boneless goat stew meat, cut into ½-inch (1.25-cm) cubes**

½ teaspoon **salt, plus more as needed**

½ teaspoon **freshly ground black pepper**

½ cup (120 ml) **dry Marsala, dry Madeira, or dry vermouth**

1½ cups (360 ml) **reduced-sodium chicken broth**

2 **bay leaves**

1 pound (455 g) **yellow-fleshed potatoes, such as Yukon gold, cut into ½-inch cubes**

1 teaspoon **finely grated lemon zest**

Two 9-ounce (two 255-g) **boxes frozen artichoke hearts (do not thaw—the extra moisture will become part of the stew)**

MORE TO KNOW

Goat stew meat is usually taken from the neck, breast, shoulder, or front legs—with this caveat: The breast meat will be far fattier. If you really want to get obsessive, it's probably best to get all the stew meat from one cut (the shoulder, for example); but that's an almost impossible task unless you're willing to do some butchering on your own—that is, buy a boneless shoulder roast and cut it into ½-inch (1.25-cm) cubes—or buy 5 to 6 pounds (2.3 to 2.7 kg) of bone-in shoulder chops and cube the meat off the bones.

1. Pour the oil into a large Dutch or French oven. Add the garlic and rosemary sprigs, *then* set the pot over medium heat. Cook for 2 to 3 minutes as the oil heats, lightly infusing it with those flavors.

2. Add the meat, in batches as necessary; brown each chunk on all sides. Once some of the chunks are well browned, stack these up along the inside rim of the pot and add more to the center. Stack the garlic and rosemary sprigs among the pieces of meat as well, so they don't burn. Every once in a while, stir everything, so that nothing sticks at the sides. That all said, you don't want blackened goat, so if it helps to transfer them to a plate as you go along, do so. Just have all the meat back in the pot before you start the next step.

3. Sprinkle the salt and pepper over the meat, stir well, then pour in the Marsala or one of its substitutes. As it boils, scrape up all the browned stuff in the pot. Keep boiling until the added liquid has reduced from its original amount by about a third.

4. Tip the broth into the pot and tuck in the bay leaves. When the stew is simmering again, cover the pot, reduce the heat to low, and simmer slowly for 1 hour.

5. Stir in the potato cubes and lemon zest. Continue cooking, stirring occasionally, for about 1 hour more, or until the goat pieces are tender.

6. Stir in the artichoke hearts. Cover and cook for 10 more minutes, or until the artichoke hearts are heated through. Remove the bay leaves and taste for salt before serving.

GOAT RAGÙ with PAPPARDELLE

IT MAKES SIX SERVINGS—OR UP TO TEN FIRST-COURSE SERVINGS.

Years ago, I was married to an Italian (don't ask; I won't tell) and I learned to make real ragù *by morphing her aunts' recipe through Marcella Hazan's techniques. This is also that hybrid technique— except there's no milk in this* ragù. *Beef and pork need a little help to get them creamy and sweet; goat, not so much.*

¼ cup (60 ml) olive oil

2¼ pounds (1 kg) boneless goat shoulder meat or other stew meat, cut into big, 2-inch (5-cm) chunks

1 large yellow onion, chopped

4 medium garlic cloves, minced

1 teaspoon ground allspice

½ teaspoon ground coriander

½ teaspoon fennel seeds

½ teaspoon salt

1 cup (240 ml) dry red wine

3½ cups (840 ml) canned reduced-sodium diced tomatoes, drained

2 cups (480 ml) reduced-sodium chicken broth

2 tablespoons chopped fresh sage leaves

1½ pounds (680 g) fresh pappardelle, boiled a minute or two and drained; or 1 pound (455 g) dried pappardelle, cooked according to the package instructions

Aged goat cheese, such as a hard cheese or a house-aged crottin (see page 199)

MORE TO KNOW

Pappardelle are wide noodles, the better to catch the larger bits of goat in this deep, long-simmered ragù.

1. Heat a large Dutch or French oven over medium heat. Swirl in the oil, then add the goat chunks, in batches as necessary so the pot isn't crowded. Brown them well on all sides—maybe 7 minutes per batch.

2. Transfer all the goat bits to a bowl or platter, then add the onion to the pot. Cook, stirring often, until it softens, about 4 minutes. Stir in the garlic, allspice, coriander, fennel seeds, and salt. Cook for about 1 minute.

3. Pour in the wine. As it simmers away, use a wooden spoon to scrape up any browned bits in the pot. Simmer until reduced by half.

4. Pour in the canned tomatoes. Stir well, then cook until they begin to break down into a sauce, about 8 minutes, stirring occasionally.

5. Pour in the broth, then stir in the sage. Also add all the goat chunks and any juices from their bowl or platter.

6. Bring the whole thing back to a full simmer; then cover the pot, reduce the heat to low, and cook until the goat pieces are meltingly tender, between 2 and 2½ hours, stirring occasionally. If you think the ragù is too thin, uncover the pot and raise the heat a bit, letting the whole thing boil away for, say, 5 minutes to thicken it.

7. To serve, ladle a little of the ragù into a serving bowl. Top it with the cooked pappardelle, in a nestlike mound. Then pour the rest of the ragù on top. Finally, grate a little hard goat cheese over the whole bowl.

MORE GOATY GOODNESS

I'm scared to tell you this, lest you run away: Bruce sometimes makes goat ragù with a combination of goat heart and goat stew meat. If you want to go all out, you'll need to get a heart or two. They weigh between ½ and ¾ pound (225 and 340 g). Substitute one or two hearts for a similar amount of meat—in other words, a ragù made with one ½-pound (225-g) goat heart plus 1¾ pounds (800 g) goat stew meat. Oh, and this: You'll need to grind the heart. Bruce uses the grinding attachment to his stand mixer. Or you can ask the butcher to do it for you. Trust me: The process is like a *Saw* sequel for goats, but the result is incredible—rich and satisfying.

DAUBE DE CHÈVRE

Call this dohb-duh-shevr, *a goaty version of beef bourguignon—except the meat's on the bones for even more flavor, like making stock and stew all at once. Because bone = flavor, Bruce says he'd use beef this way in the classic stew, too, except that beef bones are usually too big and short ribs, just too fatty, an overkill for the other flavors in the dish. Lean, goaty shoulder chops to the rescue!*

4 pounds (1.8 kg) bone-in goat shoulder chops, each cut in half depending on how the bone lies, a bit of bone in each piece if possible

4 large carrots, peeled and cut into 2-inch (5-cm) pieces

1 large yellow onion, thickly sliced

4 large garlic cloves, peeled

3 fresh oregano or rosemary sprigs, depending on your proclivities

3 fresh thyme sprigs

2 bay leaves

One 750-milliliter bottle red wine, preferably from grapes that have suffered, like those in Vacqueryas, Sablet, or other Côtes du Rhône bottlings

3 tablespoons goat butter (or unsalted cow butter, if you must)

¼ cup (30 g) all-purpose flour

6 ounces (170 g) pancetta (or *ventrèche*, if you really want to get French), diced into small bits

2 cups (455 g) peeled pearl onions, or 2 cups (455 g) frozen pearl onions (no need to thaw or peel)

1 pound (455 g) brown or white mushrooms, sliced

½ cup (115 g) pitted small green olives

1. Stir the goat chops, carrots, onion, garlic, herb sprigs, and wine in a large bowl. Cover, then refrigerate for 24 hours, stirring two or three more times.

2. Take the bowl with the meat and marinade out of the fridge and set it on the counter for 20 minutes before you begin to make the stew.

3. Pick the meat out of the marinade and put the pieces on a cutting board, reserving the marinade separately. Blot the pieces of meat dry.

4. Melt the butter in a large Dutch or French oven set over medium heat. Add the chunks, in batches as necessary to prevent crowding. Too many in the pot and they'll just stew in their own juices, graying hideously. Brown on both sides, taking care to let the meat get beyond a light brown and begin to caramelize, about 6 minutes, maybe more. Reduce the heat a bit if the butter darkens too much. Transfer the browned meat to a platter.

5. Add the carrots, onion, and garlic from the marinade to the pot. Cook, stirring often, for 5 minutes; then sprinkle the flour over them. Brown the flour a bit, about 3 minutes, stirring all the while.

6. Pick the herbs out of the marinade, then pour the liquid into the pot. Stir constantly until bubbling and a little thickened, the flour fully incorporated into the wine. Return the meat and any juices on its platter to the pot; cover, drop the heat to low, and simmer slowly for 1 hour, stirring occasionally. Meanwhile, position the rack in the oven so the covered pot can fit inside with about 3 inches (7.5 cm) of headspace; preheat the oven to 325°F (165°C).

7. Remove the meat from the pot. Now here's the tough part: You have to strain the stuff left in there—and it's hot. Set a big strainer, sieve, or chinois over a big bowl in the sink, then pour the contents of the pot into it. (It sometimes helps to have a second set of hands to hold the strainer in place.) Discard the vegetables, set the strained liquid aside, and return the pot to the stove, this time over medium-high heat.

8. Add the pancetta (or *ventrèche*) bits and fry until crisp, stirring occasionally, about 4 minutes. Now add the pearl onions and cook, stirring more often, until lightly browned, just a couple of minutes.

9. Dump in the mushrooms, stir well, and keep cooking, stirring once in a while, until they release their liquid, collapse a bit, and that liquid reduces to a thick glaze, about 7 minutes.

10. Stir in the olives, then pour in the reserved, strained liquid. Add all the meat and any juices back to the pot. Bring the whole thing to a simmer. Then cover, shove the pot into the oven, and braise until the meat is falling-off-the-bone tender, about 2 hours.

GO ALL OUT! GO ALL OUT! GO ALL OUT! GO ALL OUT! GO ALL OUT!

To complete the sybaritic feast, Bruce serves this stew over big, crunchy croutons. Cut a baguette or a loaf of crunchy Italian bread into big cubes, then leave these out on the counter overnight to get stale. For the best results, make the chunks of bread fairly large, about the size of the chunks of goat in the stew. Position the rack in the center of the oven and preheat the oven to 400°F (205°C). Pour all the cubes into a big bowl and add a couple of tablespoons of olive oil. Toss well, then pour the bread cubes out onto a large baking sheet. Bake them, tossing occasionally, until brown and crisp, about 15 minutes. If making the croutons in advance, lay them on a wire rack and cool completely before storing for a day in a zip-sealed plastic bag.

CHILI

SIX CAN MAKE A MEAL OUT OF IT.

This chili is made from chiles and meat. Period. Add beans and it's bean soup. Add tomatoes and it's a stew. The only culinary complications come from what you put on top of the chili once it's in the bowls: sour cream, minced scallions, and the like. One note: The coconut here is Bruce's whimsy. I'll give it to that Yankee: It's a brilliant notion— sweet, mellow, a nice contrast to the meat.

MORE TO KNOW

Bruce doesn't brown the meat in this recipe. He's not looking to complicate the flavors with burned bits on the bottom of the pot. Instead, he wants the fresh, light, bracing taste of those chiles to shine through— then he builds equally bright flavors with the herbs and coconut. In other words, he's lightening up an otherwise heavy dish.

Chili needs a hefty set of garnishes for the bowls: shredded cheese, minced scallions, diced tomatoes, diced tomatillos, chopped pickles, diced radishes, and even diced mangoes.

6 guajillo chiles (see page 59)

4 dried New Mexico red chiles (see page 59)

2 dried chipotle chiles (see page 59)

Boiling water

¼ cup (55 g) packed fresh oregano leaves

¼ cup (55 g) shredded unsweetened dried coconut

2 teaspoons ground cumin

3 medium garlic cloves, minced

1 teaspoon salt

2 tablespoons almond oil

1 medium yellow onion, chopped

1 medium green bell pepper, stemmed, seeded, and chopped

3 pounds (1.4 kg) goat stew meat, cut into ½-inch (1.25-cm) cubes

1 cup (240 ml) reduced-sodium chicken broth

12 ounces (360 ml) beer, preferably a sweet beer such as Thai Singha or Indian Kingfisher

1 tablespoon yellow cornmeal (optional)

1. Remove the stems from all the chiles, then slit the chiles open. Scrape out and discard the seeds and any membranes, then tear the chiles into large pieces.

2. Dry-fry them in a skillet set over medium heat, turning the pieces occasionally, until lightly browned and aromatic, working in batches to avoid crowding if necessary. Transfer them to a bowl and cover with boiling water. Set aside for 20 minutes.

3. Drain the chiles in a colander set over a bowl in the sink to catch the soaking liquid. Place the softened chiles in a food processor fitted with the chopping blade or in a large blender.

4. Dump in the oregano, coconut, cumin, garlic, and salt. Process until a paste, scraping down the inside of the canister as necessary. If you find that the mixture is not blending well, add a little of the soaking liquid, perhaps no more than a tablespoon or two, just to get the whole thing spinning.

5. Heat a large Dutch or French oven over medium heat. Swirl in the oil, then dump in the onion and bell pepper. Stir occasionally over the heat until the onion turns translucent, about 4 minutes.

6. Scrape the chile paste into the pot. Stir over the heat for 2 minutes as it turns aromatic—and volatilizes the chile oil. Step back to avoid getting any in your eyes.

7. Add the meat and cook, stirring often, for 2 minutes. Then pour in the broth and beer. The beer will foam, of course. Pour slowly to avoid the rabid-dog look in your pot.

8. Once the chile is simmering, cover the pot, turn the heat down to low, and simmer, stirring occasionally, until the meat is meltingly tender, almost velvety. It'll take about 2 hours, maybe a little more if you're working with stew meat from an older goat.

9. One last step, if you want: You can thicken the stew by stirring in the cornmeal and letting the whole thing bubble, uncovered, for a couple of minutes as you continue to stir. It's a matter of taste, frankly. Some people like a thicker chile; some, thinner.

DRIED CHILES 101

Dried chiles should still be pliable, like fruit leather. When you squeeze a package, they shouldn't crackle, snap, or break. Indeed, when you take the seeds off the inner membranes, your hands should be a little sticky from the residual moisture. If not, their flavors may have dulled to a meaningless burn. Here are the ones used in this book:

Ancho: a dried poblano; moderately hot but with raisin, coffee, and licorice accents.

Chipotle: a smoked and dried red jalapeño; chocolaty but banging hot (sometimes also canned in fiery adobo sauce).

Guajillo: cinnamon and nutmeg notes, somewhat sweet and a little grassy, with a low-grade heat.

Mulato: like the ancho, a dried poblano but with a low-grade heat, nicely balanced sweet and sour notes, quite smoky.

New Mexico reds: woodsy cherries and blackberries, with moderately low but on-the-tongue heat.

Pasilla: a dried chilaca; notes of grassy herbs and raisins, with moderate heat.

TAGINE with PRESERVED LEMON

YOU'LL GET ABOUT SIX SERVINGS.

This is a traditional Moroccan dish, made in a shallow round pan with a conical lid. Both the pan and the resulting dish are called a tagine. *That high-hat lid lets every molecule of steam condense on its inside and drip into the pot. One note: Fava beans are often cooked and then peeled so they don't fall apart. Here, they're peeled* before *they're cooked so they almost melt, creating a thicker sauce.*

MORE TO KNOW

Moroccan preserved lemons are a delicacy, indeed: sour lemons, preserved in salt (which eventually leaches moisture from the fruit, creating its own brine, as it were). Some bottlings include saffron for flavor, which would be a welcome addition here, too. Remove the lemon from the brine and chop it into tiny bits, flesh and rind, discarding any seeds. It'll be soft, like a very mushy tomato in August, so use a sharp knife and be prepared to make a bit of a mess. Some people don't eat the flesh, finding it too squishy; but it simply dissolves in this tagine, adding yet another spike of flavor.

LESS TO DO

You can make this stew in a Dutch or French oven, no new kitchen gadget necessary—but you might also have a problem with not stirring the tagine, particularly if the pot is thin. The meat and other ingredients can stick and burn. For better results, if you're working with a gas flame, make sure it is very even under the pot, not shooting up on one side or the other. Better yet, make the dish through step 6, cover the pot, and put it in a preheated 300°F (150°C) oven for 3½ to 4 hours, until the meat is quite tender.

12 ounces (340 g) **dried fava beans**

2 pounds (910 g) **goat stew meat, preferably cut into 2-inch (5-cm) chunks from the leg, although boneless shoulder meat or neck meat will work just as well, if a little fattier**

2 teaspoons **ground coriander**

2 teaspoons **ground cinnamon**

½ teaspoon **ground turmeric**

½ teaspoon **freshly ground black pepper**

3 tablespoons **olive oil**

3 small **shallots, chopped**

¼ cup (55 ml) **minced peeled fresh ginger**

3 medium **garlic cloves, minced**

1 **Moroccan preserved lemon, seeded and chopped**

1 tablespoon **honey**

1 cup (240 ml) **reduced-sodium chicken broth**

½ cup (115 g) **green olives, preferably Picholines or other small, tart olives**

1. The day before, place the fava beans in a large bowl, cover with cool water to a depth of 2 inches (5.1 cm), and set aside for 24 hours.

2. At the same time, mix the meat, coriander, cinnamon, turmeric, and pepper in a second big bowl. Cover and refrigerate for 24 hours.

3. The tedious part comes the next day: skinning those fava beans. Drain them in a colander set in the sink, then squeeze each one out of its hull.

4. Now build the dish. Heat the bottom of a large tagine over medium heat. Swirl in the oil, then add the shallots. Stir until softened, about 3 minutes.

5. Pour in the meat and any juices that might be in that bowl, taking care to scrape out any recalcitrant spices as well. Cook, stirring often, until nicely browned on all sides, about 6 minutes. Once that's done, add the ginger and garlic; stir over the heat for 30 seconds.

6. Dump in the preserved lemon and the honey; again, stir over the heat for 30 seconds. Then stir in those peeled soaked fava beans, the broth, and the olives. Stir well as the mixture comes up to a simmer.

7. Put the lid on the tagine, reduce the heat to low, and simmer slowly until the meat is tender, between 2 and 2½ hours. Keep the heat low enough that you never have to stir the mixture. The fava beans will soften and melt. Don't touch it before you serve it. Bring the tagine to the table, set it on a trivet, and open the thing up. Oohs and aahs will abound.

MAKFOUL

SERVE UP SIX BOWLFULS OVER RICE.

Here's another Moroccan wonder, this time named for its topping: the makfoul, a spiced onion and tomato ragout. Like Bruce's chili (see page 58), this one's not based on classical, French technique—which is to brown the meat, take it out, build a sauce from what's in the pot, put the meat back in, and simmer. (There's a thousand years of Gallic culinary tradition in a nutshell. Add a Chanel suit and a foofed-up poodle, and you've got the whole deal.) Here, the meat and spices are cooked together, blending slowly, not as layers of flavors, but rather as an aromatic mouthful—topped with makfoul, *of course.*

LESS TO DO

Makfoul is traditionally made with *ras el hanout*, a heady spice blend that includes nutmeg, cloves, and many other spices, sometimes even dried rose hips. It's available as a bottled blend at Middle Eastern or East Indian markets. To use it, omit all the spices with the meat and add a couple of teaspoons, even up to a tablespoon. Check to see if your bottling includes salt—you'll know whether you need to add extra.

2 pounds (910 g) **boneless goat stew meat, cut into 1-inch (2.5-cm) cubes**

1 teaspoon ground ginger

1 teaspoon ground turmeric

1 teaspoon ground cloves

1 teaspoon salt

1 teaspoon freshly ground black pepper

½ teaspoon saffron threads (see page 38)

¼ teaspoon freshly grated nutmeg

3 tablespoons olive oil

4 large yellow onions, 2 of them chopped, 2 of them halved and thinly sliced (to be used at different points in the recipe)

3 medium garlic cloves, minced

¼ cup (55 g) packed, stemmed, and chopped parsley leaves

¼ cup (55 g) packed, stemmed, and chopped fresh cilantro leaves

One 4-inch (10-cm) cinnamon stick

2 cups (480 ml) water

2 tablespoons goat butter (or unsalted cow butter, if you must)

3 tablespoons honey

1 pound (455 g) plum or Roma tomatoes, halved, seeded, and diced

½ teaspoon ground cinnamon

Cooked rice, especially a brown or red rice

1. Mix the meat, ginger, turmeric, cloves, salt, pepper, saffron, and nutmeg in a big bowl. Set aside at room temperature as you begin to prepare the stew.

2. Heat a large Dutch or French oven over medium heat. Swirl in the oil, then dump in the 2 chopped onions. Cook, stirring often, until translucent, about 5 minutes. Stir in the garlic and cook for 20 seconds.

3. Scrape the meat and all its spices into the pot. Stir over the heat once in a while until the meat loses its raw, pink color, about 5 minutes.

4. Add the parsley, cilantro, and cinnamon stick. Stir a few times, then pour in the water. Bring to a full simmer, scraping up those precious browned bits in the pot.

5. Cover, reduce the heat to low, and simmer slowly until the meat is incredibly tender, between 2 and 2½ hours, stirring occasionally. If the mixture begins to dry out because of too much evaporation (and a lid that doesn't fit the pot tightly enough), add a little more water so that it stays like a really thick stew (and write out a budget to buy better cookware).

6. Meanwhile, melt the butter in a large skillet over low heat. Add the 2 sliced onions, reduce the heat even further, and cook very slowly, stirring occasionally, until the onions turn golden, soft, and wonderfully sweet, 30 to 40 minutes. Stir in the honey and keep cooking, stirring constantly, for about 5 minutes, to let the sugars caramelize.

7. Add the tomatoes to the skillet as well as the ground cinnamon. Raise the heat to medium-low and cook, stirring frequently, until thick and dark, 20 to 30 minutes.

8. To serve, remove the cinnamon sticks and ladle the stew into bowls over rice; then top each with a portion of the *makfoul*—that is, the tomato and onion ragout.

GOAT SKEWERS
WITH A VINEGARY HERB SAUCE

**YOU'LL END UP WITH FOUR SKEWERS.
ONE PER PERSON, MAYBE? DOUBLE OR TRIPLE THE RECIPE AT WILL.**

Some of the best chunks come from the goat leg, the meat sweeter and subtler. We've already considered that meat in the Goat and Quince Stew (page 52), but here it's more elemental, less adorned, a real pleasure on its own. Bruce's sauce here is sort of like chimichurri (page 111) but skewed more to the Middle East, less to South America.

MORE TO KNOW

This is the conundrum of the leg: A cow's leg is fatty and tough; a goat's, quite tender, even though a goat uses its legs to rear back and support its entire weight for head-butting games. Here's the deal: The meat off a goat leg is tender *if* thinly sliced and quickly seared over high heat. Much more cooking, and it turns tough. It will then only retenderize if cooked slowly for a couple of hours, as in our various roasted or braised whole legs (pages 30–40).

¼ cup (55 g) minced fresh chives or the green bits of a scallion

¼ cup (55 g) stemmed, packed fresh cilantro leaves

¼ cup (55 g) stemmed, packed fresh parsley leaves

3 tablespoons red wine vinegar

½ teaspoon freshly ground black pepper

¼ teaspoon salt

⅔ cup (165 ml) olive oil

1½ pounds (680 g) goat meat chunks from the leg, cut into 1-inch (2.5-cm) cubes

1 teaspoon mild paprika

½ teaspoon ground cardamom

4 metal kebab skewers

1. Whir the chives, cilantro, parsley, vinegar, pepper, and salt in a food processor fitted with the chopping blade. While the machine is running, pour the olive oil through the open feed tube in a slow dribble to make a light sauce.

   ☞ No food processor? Mince the chives, cilantro, and parsley on a cutting board, then mash them with the other ingredients in a mortar with a pestle until pasty. Drip in the oil, grinding the mixture into a sauce as the oil is added in dribs and drabs. It won't be as smooth as that from a food processor, but it'll do in a pinch.

   ☞ No food processor, no mortar, no pestle? (Are you sure you wanted to buy a goat cookbook?) You can make this sauce by rocking a knife through the herbs on a cutting board until they're minced, almost pureed, then adding coarse-grained salt and wiping the side of the knife's blade across the mess, using the grainy salt to further mash the herbs into a pulp. Scrape all this into a bowl, stir in the vinegar and pepper; then whisk in the olive oil in a slow, steady stream.

2. Place half of this herb sauce in a large bowl (reserve the remainder in a separate bowl in the fridge for a garnish). Add the meat cubes, paprika, and cardamom. Stir well, cover, and refrigerate for at least 4 hours or up to 12 hours.

3. Thread the meat cubes onto the skewers and set them aside at room temperature while you prepare the grill, either heating a gas grill to high heat (about 550°F [288°C]) or building a high-heat coal bed in a char-

coal grill. If you don't want to use the grill outside, heat a large, heavy grill pan over medium-high heat until smoking. As the grill is heating up, take the reserved sauce out of the fridge so it comes back to room temperature. You can even nuke it for a few seconds to take the chill off (but don't get it too hot or the taste will become too pronounced, almost bitter).

4. Set the skewers directly over the heat (or in the grill pan). Grill for 6 minutes, turning occasionally, until browned on all sides and an instant-read meat thermometer inserted into a cube without touching the skewer registers 160°F (71°C). Serve the skewers with the reserved sauce on the side.

CHICKEN-FRIED GOAT with GOAT MILK GRAVY

YOU'LL MAKE DINNER FOR SIX.

Hands down, this is my favorite way to eat the leg meat. But I'm a Texan and chicken-frying is in my blood. (Or along my arteries, as the case may be.) When we first met, Bruce wasn't too familiar with the whole chicken-fried thing. It's not a common preparation among the urban sophisticates. And darn hard to explain. Chicken-fried doesn't mean there's any chicken in it (although I've had chicken-fried chicken in my life). Instead, it means something's fried up the way chicken is sometimes fried up in the South: pounded thin, batter-coated, submerged in hot oil. No wonder Bruce was soon a convert. No, a zealot. I've watched him chicken-fry everything over the years. *See, his grandmother was right: You marry a goy and the next thing you know, you're eating dicey foods. And putting up a Christmas tree.*

2 pounds (910 g) **thinly sliced goat leg meat**

2 teaspoons **salt, plus more as needed**

1 teaspoon **freshly ground black pepper, plus more for the gravy**

1 cup (125 g) **all-purpose flour**

3 large **eggs**

¼ cup (60 ml) **peanut oil, plus a little more if necessary**

2 cups (480 ml) **reduced-sodium chicken broth**

½ cup (120 ml) **goat milk (don't even think about the low-fat stuff)**

Freshly grated nutmeg and freshly ground black pepper, for garnish

MORE TO KNOW

This recipe asks you to use slices of meat off the goat leg. Here's how to make them yourself: Look for the biggest, meatiest muscle on the leg. Set the leg on the cutting board so this part is facing you. Start slicing with a thin, sharp knife, making flat pieces about ¼ inch (.6 cm) thick, about what you'd get if you were running a carpenter's plane over the meat. It's irrelevant whether you slice with or against the grain, because (1) the meat won't fall apart when raw and (2) you're going to pound it tender. But heed this: Don't use stew meat or other cuts. Only the leg meat can be cut this way and remain tender when cooked quickly.

1. Lay the goat slices on a large cutting board, working in batches as necessary, giving them some room to be flattened out. Use the pointy side of a meat mallet to pound the slices into thin scaloppini-like strips, about ¼ inch (.6 cm) thick. Don't take out your marital frustrations (see a therapist, please)—instead, pound evenly and firmly without whacking needlessly. In the end, the strips should look like bits of a wool sweater, not pieces of velvet. You're trying to make nubbly ridges, even a few holes, so that the coating gets inside and the things fry from the inside out—or fry on the inside and outside at the same time. Season both sides of the flattened strips with a little of the salt and pepper. If you're working in batches, peel these off the cutting board, put them on a plate, and do the whole thing again with a new bunch.

2. Set up the two-bowl dip line. First, put the flour in a wide bowl, like a soup serving bowl. Then beat the eggs until creamy and light in a second, wide bowl, no random bits of egg white scumming the mixture.

3. Slip a slice of meat in the flour, coat both sides, shake off the excess, and dip the meat into the egg—then back into the flour and back into the egg a second time to get a nice, thick coating—and then finally back into the flour one more time. In other words, flour-egg-flour-egg-flour. Place

the coated piece on a platter and continue with the rest, making a single layer. Once you're done, set the platter in the refrigerator for 10 minutes. Reserve the remaining flour.

4. Meanwhile, pour the oil into a large, high-sided sauté pan or skillet; heat it over medium heat until waggles of heat run across the surface of the oil.

5. Slip enough cold, coated strips into the skillet to form one layer without crowding. Fry for about 6 minutes, turning once, until lightly browned and crisp. (In the meantime, set the remainder of the strips on their platter back in the fridge.) Transfer the golden bits to a wire rack set over paper towels (to make the cleanup of the inevitable drips easier) and continue frying more until you're done.

6. When all the strips are crisp and on the rack, add some more oil to the skillet so that it has 3 tablespoons of fat in it. Obviously, you can't try to measure the scalding oil with a measuring spoon. Eyeball it and do your best. However, because of ambient humidity and the flour's uptake of it, you may also have more oil in the skillet than you need. If so, pour off oil until you've got 3 tablespoons. But if you're pouring off oil, make sure you leave behind the browned bits. That's the flavor!

7. Whisk 3 tablespoons of the flour from the dredging bowl into the oil in the skillet; keep whisking for 30 seconds. Then pour in the broth in a thin, steady stream, whisking all the while to dissolve the flour. Whisk in the milk as well (no need to go slowly here because the flour will have dissolved in the broth). Cook, whisking constantly, until bubbling and thickened. Remove the skillet from the heat and check for salt. To serve, put the chicken-fried goat pieces on a platter and ladle the gravy over them—or offer the gravy on the side for dunking. In any case, grate a little nutmeg over the gravy and give it a grind or two of black pepper.

LESS TO DO

I, a good Texan, don't eat cream gravy on chicken-fried things. Never have. I save cream gravy for ham steaks. I douse all things chicken-fried with ketchup. But then again, I moved away to Manhattan, so take my advice for what it's worth. But I'm clearly not alone in my lack of orthodoxy. In my time, I've also seen chicken-fried things eaten with mustard, with barbecue sauce, with mayonnaise—and with a combo of fifty-fifty barbecue sauce and mayonnaise. Let's just say I've spent some time in Oklahoma. Anyway, any of these solutions may keep you from making cream gravy. No guarantees, though.

CURRIES

ALTHOUGH GOAT IS EATEN around the world, there are pockets of culinary culture where it truly comes into its own—perhaps none more than in India, the original slow food nation.

Take the bold meat, usually cubed or in chunks; add a sweet, sometimes fiery, but always fragrant palette of flavors; and feel little compulsion about getting dinner on the table in the next 5 minutes. Voilà: great curries.

Which are most often made in a *kari*, a flat-bottomed, heavy pan with a dome-shaped lid. You needn't have such fancy equipment—that ol' heavy Dutch or French oven will do as well, so long as you remember the point: to keep every drop of steam in the pot, condensing back and bringing elegant intensity to the dish as the flavors meld. Or as Huck Finn says of his favorite kind of cooking: "The juice kind of swaps around and the things go better."

Truth be told, to say you're making a curry is to say nothing. *Curry* simply means "blend," as in a mash-up of spices, usually dried (although wet pastes are used in India and preferred in Southeast Asia, where curries have spilled into the local cuisine and been morphed by indigenous braising traditions).

Given that curry is simply a blend and given that a mind-boggling array of herbs and spices is available worldwide, there are probably as many curries as there are cooks who make curry. Some blends are passed down as family traditions; others, adapted from this or that chef's recipe. Some are bottled; the best aren't.

Despite the apparent freedom in this open-ended arrangement, it all works out about as well as an open marriage. In other words, it doesn't. All that freedom gives way to earnestness. That's also the thing about swingers: They're so damn serious about being swingers.

In terms of curries, questions of authenticity swamp the open-ended creative process. Soon enough, someone gets up on a pedestal somewhere to proffer their curry as the ur-dish, the one from which all the others sprang.

All cooking is interpretation. Go out on any cooking Web site and read the responses to the posted recipes. Everyone morphs and changes ingredients. In other words, they interpret. Did they make the original? Not exactly. But did they make *an* original? You bet. And that's the spirit of curries: an interpretation, with lots of spices. Bruce's are a collection of somewhat similar techniques, all astounding with goat, the juices being swapped around a bit. About the way it should be.

With this advance notice: You'll need a good spice drawer. Remember when Marge Simpson found a spice rack at the town's flea market? "Eight bottles?" she asked, puzzled. "Some must be repeats."

Curries take a full rack, bigger than the one Marge found. And even dried, the spices should be "fresh." Dried spices do indeed have a shelf life, sometimes as little as six months if there are chiles in the mix, perhaps up to a year or so with dried herbs. In no case should the dried spice have a tealike tang or dusty aroma. Smell your bottlings and determine which are beyond the pale.

But don't be deterred. With lots of spices on hand, you'll start down a road to real food, to real flavors, far from the processed, bland stuff that all too often passes as dinner. You'll always have plenty of spices at the ready, for more flavor in every bite—and more curries, too.

And one more thing: As we go through these five curries, watch to make sure you've got the right sort of stew meat: bone-in or boneless.

SALI BOTI

CALL IT DINNER FOR FOUR.

This traditional curry with dried apricots is sweet and savory, a comfort-food delight. Bruce calls for Turkish apricots, rather than the more familiar California variety, because the Turkish ones are a little sweeter, a better foil to the many spices. These apricots also hold up well during long stewing. Admittedly, there are about a million ingredients to this thing; but in reality, it's just a dump-and-stir.

2½ pounds (1.2 kg) **bone-in goat stew meat, preferably shoulder chops or neck slices** (see page 17)

¼ cup (60 ml) **cider vinegar**

2 teaspoons **ground coriander**

2 teaspoons **ground cumin**

1 teaspoon **ground cardamom**

1 teaspoon **ground cinnamon**

1 teaspoon **freshly ground black pepper, halved and used in two places in the recipe**

3 tablespoons **peanut oil**

2 teaspoons **cumin seeds**

1½ teaspoons **fennel seeds**

1 teaspoon **whole cloves**

¼ teaspoon **saffron threads** (see page 38)

1 large **yellow onion, halved, then sliced into very thin half-moons**

1 tablespoon **minced peeled fresh ginger**

2 large **garlic cloves, minced**

½ cup (120 ml) **reduced-sodium chicken broth**

3 tablespoons **reduced-sodium tomato puree**

1 tablespoon **packed dark brown sugar**

½ cup (115 g) **sliced almonds**

12 **dried apricots, preferably Turkish apricots, halved**

1 teaspoon **salt**

Cooked long-grain brown rice, like brown basmati

1. Combine the meat, vinegar, coriander, cumin, cardamom, cinnamon, and ½ teaspoon of the black pepper in a big bowl until the meat is well coated in the spices. Set aside at room temperature.

2. Heat a large Dutch or French oven over medium heat. Swirl in the oil, then add the cumin seeds, fennel seeds, whole cloves, and saffron. Stir over the heat until the seeds are fragrant and popping, about 2 minutes.

3. Dump in the onion slices; cook, stirring to break them up into individual rings, until translucent, about 3 minutes. Stir in the ginger and garlic; cook for about 15 seconds.

4. Pour the meat into the pot. Make sure you scrape all the spices and juices out of the bowl into the pot as well. Cook, stirring often, until lightly browned, about 10 minutes.

5. Pour in the broth, then stir in the tomato puree and the brown sugar. Keep stirring over the heat until the latter two are fully dissolved, also getting up any stuck-on spices or browned bits along the pot's bottom.

6. Once the mixture is at a good simmer, cover the pot, drop the heat to low, and simmer slowly for 1 hour, stirring once or twice.

7. Stir in the almonds, apricots, salt, and the remaining ½ teaspoon black pepper. Set the lid back in place and continue simmering slowly until the meat is gorgeously tender, no need for a knife whatsoever, about 1 more hour for shoulder chops, 2 more for neck slices, stirring a couple of times. When done, set the pot off the heat, covered, for 10 minutes, so the flavors can come to their full fruition without a final blast of heat. Serve it over cooked brown rice.

GO ALL OUT! GO ALL OUT! GO ALL OUT! GO ALL OUT! GO ALL OUT!

Want to take these goat dishes over the top? Make your own goat stock. Buy 4 pounds (1.8 kg) of goat bones, like back ribs and other gnarly cuts without too much meat on them. Set them on a lipped tray in a preheated 400°F (205°C) oven for about 20 minutes, or until they begin to brown nicely. Dump them into a big pot; scrape any browning goodness from the tray into the pot as well. Add a couple of quartered small onions, a few chunked-up carrots, and some celery leaves (those inner feathery bits from the head), as well as a couple of bay leaves and a teaspoon or so of whole black peppercorns. Fill the pot with water, bring it to a boil over high heat, then reduce the heat to low and continue cooking at the slightest bubble until reduced, golden, and absolutely irresistible, 7 to 8 hours.

Want it all to go faster? Then do it in a pressure cooker: Seal everything up, bring the pot to full pressure over high heat, then drop the heat to medium and go for 50 minutes; take the pot off the heat and let the pressure drop naturally back to normal, following the manufacturer's instructions. In either case, strain the stock, toss out the spent bones and vegetables, and freeze that stock in 2-cup (480-ml) containers until you're ready to use them.

DOPIAZA

IT MAKES SIX SERVINGS.

It means "double the onions." Boy, is it accurate. All those onions are caramelized into nothingness, like French onion soup, but spicier, more herbaceous. If that's not enough for you, the bowls are topped with bits of cashews and sunflower seeds fried in butter. Just make sure both are not salted, to avoid a salty zap on this fine stew.

4 tablespoons (¼ cup [60 ml]) clarified goat butter (see page 81)

3 medium yellow onions, halved and thinly sliced

2 tablespoons minced peeled fresh ginger

5 medium garlic cloves, minced

1 teaspoon cayenne pepper

2½ pounds (1.2 kg) boneless goat stew meat, cut into 1-inch chunks

1½ cups (360 ml) reduced-sodium chicken broth

⅓ cup (76 g) stemmed, chopped fresh mint leaves

⅓ cup (76 g) stemmed, chopped fresh cilantro leaves

½ teaspoon ground cinnamon

½ teaspoon ground coriander

¼ teaspoon ground cardamom

¼ teaspoon ground cloves

¼ teaspoon ground cumin

¼ teaspoon freshly grated nutmeg

½ cup (115 g) chopped roasted unsalted cashew

2 tablespoons unsalted sunflower seeds

1. Melt 3 tablespoons of the clarified butter in a big Dutch or French oven over low heat. Add the onions and cook, stirring occasionally, until golden and super-soft, 40 to 45 minutes. Be patient. If the onions brown, drop the heat further and stir more often.

2. Add the ginger, garlic, and cayenne. Stir over the heat for a few seconds, just until aromatic, then add all the meat. Cook, stirring often, until it browns on all sides. There should be no raw spots anywhere.

3. Pour in the broth and scrape up any browned bits on the pot's bottom. Then cover the pot, reduce the heat to low, and simmer slowly until the meat is quite tender, 2 to 2½ hours, stirring occasionally.

4. Stir in the mint, cilantro, cinnamon, coriander, cardamom, cloves, cumin, and nutmeg. Cover and turn the heat to the lowest setting you have, just to keep the stew warm.

5. Melt the remaining 1 tablespoon clarified butter in a large skillet over medium heat. Add the cashews and sunflower seeds. Fry until lightly browned and a little crisp, about 3 minutes. To serve, dish the stew into bowls and sprinkle the nuts and seeds on top.

DALCHA GOSHT

A MEAL FOR FOUR TO SIX.

Of all the curries, this may be the most rib-sticking, the most substantial. It's a garlicky yogurt-based mélange, made with channa dal—*that is, split chickpeas without their hulls. Look for them in east Indian markets or order from online suppliers. They pack a wallop of earthy flavor as well as lots of fiber (something you may need after all this goat). Serve the stew over long-grain basmati or jasmine rice, with some minced mint or cilantro for a garnish.*

MORE TO KNOW

Split chickpeas suck up moisture, continuing to dry out in storage. Depending on how long they've been stored, yours may be wetter or drier than Bruce's. In other words, you've got to eyeball this stew as it cooks to make sure it keeps simmering away, thickening up, and turning luscious without going dry and scorching.

¼ cup (60 ml) **clarified goat butter (see page 81)**

1 large onion, halved and sliced into paper-thin rings

13 medium garlic cloves: 3 minced and 10 slivered and saved for later

1 tablespoon minced peeled fresh ginger

½ teaspoon ground turmeric

½ teaspoon coriander seeds

¼ teaspoon ground mace

3 small fresh hot red chiles, stemmed, cut lengthwise, and seeded if you're sane, left unseeded if you're nuts

One 4-inch (10-cm) cinnamon stick

6 cardamom pods

5 whole cloves

1 bay leaf

1¾ pounds (800 g) **boneless goat stew meat, cut into 1-inch (2.5-cm) chunks**

3 cups (720 ml) **reduced-sodium chicken broth, plus more as needed**

2 cups (480 ml) **plain goat yogurt**

1 cup (250 ml) *channa dal*

1 tablespoon peanut oil

1 teaspoon salt

2 tablespoons lemon juice

1. Melt the clarified butter or ghee in a large pot over medium heat. Add the onion and cook, stirring occasionally, until the slices turn translucent, about 3 minutes.

2. Stir in the 3 minced garlic cloves, the ginger, turmeric, coriander seeds, mace, chiles, cinnamon stick, cardamom pods, cloves, and bay leaf. Keep stirring over the heat until ridiculously aromatic, about 1 minute.

3. Add all the stew meat and stir over the heat until lightly browned, certainly without a single bit of raw color, about 10 minutes.

4. Pour in the broth and scrape up any browned bits on the pot's bottom as the liquid comes to a full simmer. Then stir in the yogurt and the *channa dal.*

5. Once the mixture is bubbling away, cover the pot, reduce the heat to low, and simmer slowly until the meat is tender and the stew has thickened with the melting lentils, between 2 and 2½ hours. You'll need to check it occasionally: Stir a few times and add broth in ¼-cup (60-ml) additions if the thing is drying out.

6. Toward the end of the stew's cooking, heat the peanut oil in a large skillet over low heat. Add the 10 slivered garlic cloves, then stir over the heat until they're crisp and a little brown at the edges.

7. To serve, stir the salt and lemon juice into the stew, then take the pot off the heat and let it sit, covered, for 10 minutes to blend the flavors. Remove the cinnamon stick and bay leaf; then ladle it up, topping each bowlful with some of the fried garlic.

By the way, the whole cloves in the stew are a pain to remove—and often aren't removed in traditional preparations. They'll soften but will indeed provide a pop of flavor in some bites. The choice is yours: to drive yourself batty fishing them out or to enjoy the bold bang they'll provide.

MASAMAN CURRY

IT'LL SERVE FOUR TO SIX, DEPENDING ON HOW HUNGRY EVERYONE IS.

Not all curries are Indian. Masaman—a.k.a. Moslem—curry is a Southeast Asian dish, a blend developed when the trade routes between India and Indochina intersected, bringing spices into contact with other culinary traditions. In this stew, the curry is a coarse, wet paste, not a dried blend, stocked with lots of aromatics, some perhaps a little unfamiliar. They'll melt into each other, forming an extravagant range of flavor undertones. Be cautious if you decide to substitute one of the ready-made bottlings of Masaman curry paste; these are often ridiculously hot without any sweet and savory balances to develop the nose.

MORE TO KNOW

When you're buying cilantro, you can sometimes find the plants with the dirty roots still attached, particularly at farmers' markets or higher-end grocery stores. Wash these white roots well, then slice them into thin disks. If you can't find cilantro roots, use only the cilantro stems, not the leaves, for the paste.

Shrimp paste—*kapi* in Thailand, *mam tom* in Vietnam, and *belacan* in Malaysia—is available at Asian markets and from online suppliers. Made from fermented shrimp, usually left out in the sun to liquefy, it's notoriously pungent, like old socks filled with moldy cheese and wrapped in seaweed. Shrimp paste does mellow over the heat, but not as much as fish sauce. It's strictly for the adventurous. If in doubt, leave it out.

Both tamarind paste and tamarind puree are made from the slightly unripe fruit of the tamarind tree. It's the sour in Worcestershire sauce. Look for it at gourmet, Asian, east Indian, Middle Eastern, and Latin American markets.

2 dried New Mexico red chiles, stemmed, seeded, and torn into large bits (see page 59)

Boiling water

2 large shallots, peeled and quartered

1 lemongrass stalk (tender white part only), very thinly sliced

One 2-inch (5-cm) piece of fresh ginger, peeled and diced

6 medium garlic cloves, peeled and slivered

½ cup (115 g) thinly sliced cilantro roots

1 teaspoon shrimp paste

½ teaspoon freshly grated nutmeg

5 whole cloves

30 (or so) tiny black seeds from green cardamom pods

One 4-inch (10-cm) cinnamon stick, broken into two pieces

2 tablespoons goat butter (or unsalted cow butter, if you must)

3 pounds (1.4 kg) bone-in goat-neck slices (see page 17), shoulder chops, or even back rib slices

1 cup (240 ml) coconut milk

1 cup (240 ml) reduced-sodium beef broth

3 tablespoons fish sauce (see page 49)

3 tablespoons grated palm sugar or dark brown sugar

3 tablespoons tamarind puree, or 1 tablespoon tamarind concentrate

½ cup (115 g) roasted unsalted peanuts

1½ pounds (680 g) yellow-fleshed potatoes, such as Yukon gold

1. Drench the chile pieces with boiling water in a small bowl. Steep for 10 minutes, then drain in a colander set in the sink.

2. Place those soaked chiles, the shallots, lemongrass, ginger, garlic, cilantro roots, shrimp paste, nutmeg, cloves, and cardamom seeds in a food processor fitted with the chopping blade. Pulse, then process until smooth, scraping down the inside of the canister a few times to make sure everything is getting minced up.

This Masaman curry paste is enough for two pots of stew. Save back half in the fridge in a nonreactive covered container for a couple of weeks—or in the freezer for a couple of months. Bruce discovered that to make less was to make so little that it wouldn't blend right in the food proces-sor, even in a mini food processor. So since it freezes well, he thought it better to make a double batch and get the right consistency.

3. Place the broken cinnamon stick in a large Dutch or French oven set over medium heat. Toss the pieces around in there a few times with a wooden spoon until they start to get fragrant.

4. Plop in the butter and let it melt, then pour in half the Masaman curry paste. Stir this over the heat for a couple of minutes before adding all the meat. Stir until the pieces are well coated and have lost their red, raw color, about 4 minutes.

5. Pour in the coconut milk, beef broth, and fish sauce. Stir a couple of times, then add the palm sugar and the tamarind puree or concentrate. Stir until they dissolve, then add the peanuts and bring the mixture to a full simmer. Cover the pot, reduce the heat to low, and simmer slowly for 1 hour, stirring once in a while.

6. Peel and cut the potatoes into 2-inch (5-cm) pieces. Drop them into the stew, stir well, cover the pot again, and continue simmering until the meat is fork-tender, another 1 to 1½ hours for shoulder chops, another 2 to 2½ hours for neck slices or back rib bits. Remove the cinnamon stick pieces before serving.

GOAT VINDALOO

IT'LL SERVE SIX.

Vindaloo is often some weird excuse for chile-induced machismo. Instead, it should be fragrant, almost fruity, as well as hot. Unfortunately, as foods cross oceans or other boundaries, the flavors tend to become more pronounced, less subtle, less layered. (Just think of Chinese food in American restaurants.) Although this recipe offers you Bruce's interpretation, you can morph the curry to your taste, adding more cayenne for more heat, or more mace for more nose, or more cardamom just because. Note that there's no broth; the wine or vermouth will provide the requisite sweetness so that the spices come forward.

6 medium garlic cloves, peeled, then mashed with the side of a heavy knife or put through a garlic press

2 tablespoons cider vinegar

1 tablespoon minced peeled fresh ginger

1 teaspoon cayenne pepper

1 teaspoon ground coriander

1 teaspoon ground cumin

1 teaspoon dry mustard

1 teaspoon salt

½ teaspoon ground cardamom

½ teaspoon ground cloves

½ teaspoon ground mace

¼ cup (60 ml) clarified goat butter or ghee (see More to Know)

3 large yellow onions, halved and thinly sliced

2½ pounds (1.2 kg) boneless goat stew meat, cut into 1-inch (2.5-cm) cubes

¾ cup (180 ml) dry white wine or dry vermouth

Cooked long-grain white rice, such as jasmine or basmati

1. To make a vindaloo paste, use a fork to mash together the garlic, vinegar, ginger, cayenne, coriander, cumin, dry mustard, salt, cardamom, cloves, and mace in a small bowl. Then spread this paste out onto a cutting board and use the side of a heavy knife to wipe it back and forth across the board until fairly creamy.

2. Melt the clarified goat butter in a large Dutch or French oven over medium-low heat. Add the onions, reduce the heat further, and cook, stirring often, until the onions are golden and soft, about 20 minutes.

3. Raise the heat to medium and scrape in the vindaloo paste. Stir over the heat for 30 seconds, then raise the heat to medium-high and add all the meat at once. Stir occasionally until the meat has browned and is simmering in its own juices, about 5 minutes.

4. Pour in the wine, scraping up any browned bits on the pot's bottom as the liquid first simmers. Cover the pot, drop the heat to low, and simmer slowly until the meat is fork-tender, between 2 and 2½ hours. Serve the stew over cooked rice.

MORE TO KNOW

To make clarified goat butter, place 8 tablespoons (½ cup [120 ml]) goat butter in a small saucepan and melt it on the stove over very low heat without disturbing it. Once it's melted (you can swirl it gently to tell), take a flatware spoon and pull the white solids gently to the side of the pan, lifting them out to discard them, leaving the yellow, now-clarified fat behind. There may still be a few bits of white floating at the pan's bottom. If so, slowly pour the clarified butter on top into a small bowl, leaving those solids behind. It can be stored, covered, in the fridge for up to 1 month.

LESS TO DO

If you really don't want to make your own vindaloo spice mixture, consider skipping the bottled brands, often quite unbalanced, and instead using 1 tablespoon Madras curry powder along with 6 pressed garlic cloves, 1 teaspoon ground cumin, ½ teaspoon ground cloves, and ½ teaspoon salt. But know this: The stew will still be chair-arm-grippingly hot.

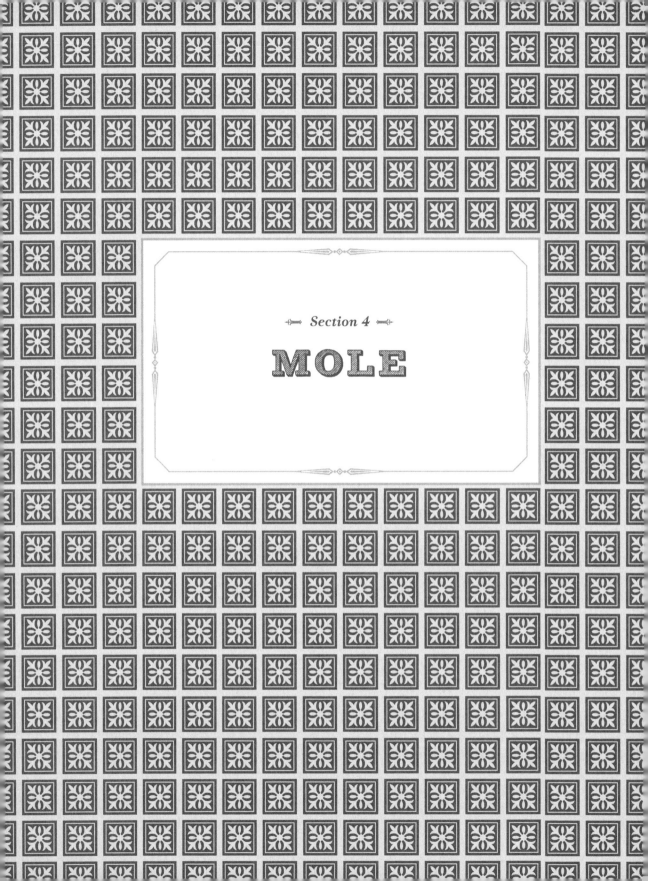

Section 4

MOLE

WHEN I MET BRUCE in the mid-nineties, I was an academic in Texas and he was a creative director in New York. We played the long-distance, back-and-forth game for as long as we could stand it.

On one of my trips to see him, I couldn't figure out what to bring. After all, he was a trained chef who now worked on some pretty crazy ad accounts. He put in a zillion hours a week and still cooked at home every night just for the fun of it.

I thought I'd met an urban sophisticate. Instead, his Manhattan apartment was a frickin' country store: shelves of homemade pickles, chutneys, and sauces. I had Proust; he had apricot preserves.

He also didn't leave Manhattan, except to go to Queens for the Jewish holidays. "Why should I go anywhere else?" he asked once. "It'll all come here eventually."

Because of all that, I brought him *mole* (that is, *MOH-lay*, from an Aztec word meaning "sauce" or "mixture"—as in *guacamole*, or "avocado mixture"). It was the best thing I could imagine. Mostly because he didn't know what it was.

Stocked with spices, nuts, and fruits, moles are the curries of Mexico. They aren't faux Tex-Mex, the stuff I'd grown up with. Moles are complex and textured. Like Proust.

As you can see, I, the non-Manhattanite, was the true snob. Which as far as I was concerned meant I knew where to get the best mole.

Not from a restaurant, mind you. Every Christmas, I bought the dark, chocolaty variety: a Crisco can full of *mole negro* from a woman in east Austin. Once she'd used most of the shortening—and I mean most, because there was always some ringing the inside or floating like white chips in the sauce—she'd fill the cans and sell them off to waiting Austin liberals for a hefty profit.

For my part, I froze it in chunks, the better to use it all year.

And that's how I came to bring him a bag of mole chunks, slowly thawing on the flight from Austin to New York. (These were simpler times. People didn't question you when you brought bags of chile sauces on planes.)

Right off the jetway, I straight-armed the bag at him.

"What is it?" he asked, a little cautious.

Ha! I'd caught a New Yorker off guard. But admittedly, the stuff wasn't at its best: icy bits of mushy brown ooze. Still, I had to put a good face on it.

"Mole," I chirped, opening the bag. "Try it."

Without a moment's hesitation, he stuck his finger in there.

That he did so will tell you everything about Bruce.

And that he did so at LaGuardia because I was so excited about the stuff may explain how we ended up together.

Ever since, he's been perfecting his moles, slowly shifting and changing the recipes.

These three are his grail. He's never had a chance to show them off. But goat is definitely the right moment. Because moles are often served with goat below the Rio Grande, a magnificent pairing.

Although I'll admit I'm a little miffed. Because he was right. It all eventually did come to him. He didn't have to leave home.

New Yorkers. You can't beat 'em even when you try.

GOAT MOLE NEGRO

EIGHT WILL SLURP IT UP.

Here's a classic, often (but not always) made with chocolate for a rich, sweet, elegant finish—but with one Bruce-induced twist: roasted cashews. They offer a rich balance to the chiles and spices, already so presently fragrant in the dish. There's really not much else you need, except tortillas, as well as some shredded lettuce, chopped tomatoes, and grated hard goat cheese for garnishes.

MORE GOATY GOODNESS

You can substitute up to 3½ pounds (1.6 kg) bone-in goat neck slices (see page 17) for the stew meat, but the resulting mixture will need to cook longer, up to 3½ hours. To prevent the sauce's scorching, add a little extra broth—perhaps ½ cup (120 ml)—at the start and then watch the pot to make sure it doesn't dry out during the long cooking.

4 dried ancho chiles, stemmed and seeded (see page 59)

4 dried mulato chiles, stemmed and seeded (see page 59)

4 dried pasilla chiles, stemmed and seeded (see page 59)

¼ cup (60 ml) chopped golden raisins

Boiling water

3 large tomatillos, any papery hulls removed, halved

2 large plum tomatoes, halved

2 cups (480 ml) reduced-sodium chicken broth, plus a little additional if necessary

¼ cup plus 2 tablespoons (85 g) chopped roasted cashews (do not use salted cashews)

2 tablespoons white sesame seeds

3 medium garlic cloves, minced

2 teaspoons ground cinnamon

1 teaspoon salt

½ teaspoon freshly ground black pepper

¼ teaspoon ground allspice

¼ teaspoon ground cloves

One 8-inch (20-cm) corn tortilla, torn into bite-size bits

2 tablespoons lard, rendered duck fat, or unsalted goat butter

2 pounds (910 g) boneless goat stew meat, cut into 1- to 1½-inch (2.5- to 4-cm) cubes

1 ounce (30 g) unsweetened chocolate, chopped

1 ounce (30 g) semisweet chocolate, chopped

1 teaspoon honey

1. Tear the chile flesh into big pieces, then toast the fragments in batches in a dry skillet set over medium heat, just a couple of minutes. They should become aromatic with little brown marks—not too far, or they'll turn bitter.

2. Place the toasted chile fragments in a big bowl along with the chopped raisins. Cover with boiling water and set aside for 20 minutes.

3. Meanwhile, position the rack about 4 inches (10 cm) from your broiler's heat source and preheat the broiler. Set the tomatillos and tomatoes, cut side down, on a lipped baking sheet and broil, without turning, until pretty well charred, perhaps 3 to 5 minutes, depending on how hot your broiler gets.

Alternatively, you can do this operation on a grill, setting them, skin side down, on the grate over high heat.

4. Place the charred tomatillos and tomatoes in a food processor fitted with the chopping blade. Add the broth, cashews, sesame seeds, garlic, cinnamon, salt, pepper, allspice, cloves, and the torn-up tortilla. Drain the chiles and raisins in a colander set in the sink, then add these to the food processor as well. Process, scraping down the sides of the canister a few times to make sure everything takes a spin on the blades.

If you don't have a food processor, you can use a blender, but you may have to help the contents along by turning off the machine and pushing everything down onto the blades occasionally.

In either case, if you find the mixture is too thick (your dried chiles may be even drier than Bruce's), thin it out with a little more broth, usually no more than a couple of tablespoons. You can make the *mole negro* to this point, then scrape it into a nonreactive container, cover, and store in the refrigerator for up to 4 days or in the freezer for up to 3 months.

5. Heat the lard, duck fat, or butter in a large Dutch or French oven over medium heat. (Isn't that a glorious sentence?) Add all the *mole negro* and fry it in the fat for about 4 minutes, stirring constantly.

6. Plop in the goat stew meat, both kinds of chocolate, and the honey. Bring to a simmer, stirring until the chocolate has melted; then cover the pot, reduce the heat to low, and cook, stirring occasionally, until the meat is fork-tender, 2 to 2½ hours.

GO ALL OUT! GO ALL OUT! GO ALL OUT! GO ALL OUT! GO ALL OUT!

Great mole needs great corn tortillas. You can make a dozen from just three ingredients. Mix 2 cups (455 g) instant masa harina (often marked *for tamales* on the package) and 1 teaspoon salt in a medium bowl; stir in ½ cup (120 ml) water, then continue stirring in water in 1-tablespoon increments until a soft dough forms (you'll probably use a little less than 1 cup (240 ml) water in all, but the amount depends entirely on the day's humidity and the moisture content of the masa harina). Divide the dough into 12 balls, each about 2 inches (5 cm) in diameter. Roll each ball between sheets of plastic wrap into circles 6 inches (15 cm) in diameter and ⅛ inch (.3 cm) thick. Alternatively, use a tortilla press, following the manufacturer's instructions, to press the balls into tortillas. In either case, keep the tortillas between the sheets of plastic wrap after they've been flattened. Set a medium skillet, preferably nonstick, over medium heat until a drop of water sizzles in the pan. Slip a flattened disk into the skillet and cook until speckled brown and slightly puffed, about 1 minute. Turn and cook until mottled on the other side, a little less than 1 minute. Transfer to a plate lined with a clean kitchen towel; fold the towel closed. Continue making the tortillas, stacking them in the towel one on top of the other.

GOAT MOLE ROJO

FOUR PEOPLE WILL DO IT JUSTICE.

MORE TO KNOW

Ripe plantains are not yellow. They are quite brown, best with lots of black splotches across the skin. If the peel sticks to the flesh inside, the thing's not ripe enough and will have an unpleasant, alumlike taste that won't balance the chiles' kick.

LESS TO DO

As to the fat in the recipe, Bruce and I went round and round on this one. Bacon fat? Really? I asked him how many people had rendered bacon fat in their refrigerators. He said, "They should just fry up a couple of slices and make their own." Sigh. We're just lucky he didn't insist on rendered smoked pork jowl fat. If you want to cheat, use 3 tablespoons almond oil and 1 tablespoon smoked paprika (see page 28). You'll get a smoky flavor without having to fry up bacon in advance.

Red mole is not necessarily as complex as the black stuff—no chocolate and no blend of chiles—but it's also made with oregano and thyme for a more herbaceous finish.

6 ancho or dried New Mexico red chiles, stemmed and seeded (see page 59)

Boiling water

4 tablespoons (¼ cup [60 ml]) rendered bacon fat, divided

1 small yellow onion, chopped

4 medium garlic cloves, chopped

1½ pounds (680 kg) boneless goat stew meat, cut into 1-inch (2.5-cm) cubes

1 tablespoon Worcestershire sauce

1 teaspoon dried thyme

1 teaspoon dried oregano

½ teaspoon ground cloves

½ teaspoon freshly ground black pepper

1 bay leaf

1 cup (240 ml) reduced-sodium chicken broth

1 tablespoon red wine vinegar

2 ripe plantains, peeled and cut into 1-inch (2.5-cm) pieces

1. Tear the chiles into large pieces, then cook them in a dry skillet set over medium heat until lightly browned and very aromatic. Transfer them to a large bowl, cover with boiling water, and set aside for 20 minutes.

2. Meanwhile, melt 2 tablespoons of the bacon fat in a large Dutch or French oven over medium heat. Add the onion and garlic; cook, stirring often, until wilted, about 3 minutes.

3. Push the onion and garlic to the sides of the pot, then add the meat chunks in batches, browning them well in the residual fat. As they brown, transfer them to a plate and add more until all are nicely done.

4. Take the pot off the heat. Scoop out the onion and garlic and place them in a blender or in a food processor fitted with the chopping blade. Drain the chiles in a colander set in the sink, then add them to the blender or food processor. Also add the Worcestershire sauce, thyme, oregano, cloves, pepper, and bay leaf. Blend or puree until smooth.

5. Melt the remaining 2 tablespoons bacon fat in the pot set back over medium heat. Scrape the chile paste into it and fry for 3 minutes, stirring almost constantly.

6. Return the meat and any juices on the plate to the pot. Also add the broth and vinegar. Bring to a simmer, stirring occasionally; then cover, reduce the heat to very low, and cook, stirring occasionally, for 1 hour.

7. Add the plantains to the pot and continue cooking, stirring once in a while, until the meat is falling-apart tender, 1 to 1½ additional hours.

GOAT MOLE VERDE

CALL IT DINNER FOR SIX.

This one is a coarse green sauce, made from pepitas, a.k.a. *green pumpkin seeds. You might want to double the sauce, then freeze half for another day. It does make a killer condiment at an outdoor barbecue, heated up in a little saucepan right on the grill and used like barbecue sauce. The trick to this dish is to get the meat thoroughly cooked before* adding it to the sauce.

6 cups (1½ L) water

Two 2-pound (910-g) bone-in goat shoulders

2 large carrots, cut into hunks

1 large yellow onion, quartered

8 whole cloves

2 whole garlic cloves, peeled

1 cup (225 g) *pepitas* (green pumpkin seeds)

3 tablespoons goat butter (for a heavier taste) or olive oil (for a lighter one)

12 ounces (340 ml) tomatillos, any papery hulls removed, the flesh chopped

4 ounces (115 g) shallots, chopped

2 fresh jalapeño chiles, stemmed, seeded, and chopped

3 medium garlic cloves, chopped

¼ cup (55 g) stemmed, packed, fresh cilantro leaves

½ teaspoon ground cinnamon

½ teaspoon ground cumin

½ teaspoon freshly ground black pepper

¼ teaspoon ground cloves

3 tablespoons lime juice

Cooked white rice

MORE GOATY GOODNESS

You can also make this recipe with 5 pounds (2.3 kg) bone-in breast of goat, although the resulting stew will be fattier.

---

1. First off, you have to cook the meat: Place the water, bone-in goat pieces, carrots, onion, cloves, and whole garlic cloves in a big pot. Bring the water to a boil over high heat. Cover, reduce the heat to low, and cook at a slow simmer until the meat is gorgeously tender, between 2 and 2½ hours, maybe even a little longer. The meat should fall apart. If you pick up a shoulder and it holds together about as it did when you got it out of its packaging a couple of hours ago, you haven't let it go long enough.

2. Transfer the falling-apart meat to a large cutting board. Remember: Those shoulders are quite hot with melted interstitial fat. Let them cool until you can get your hands on them, shredding the meat and any cartilage off the bones. Keep all this stuff, every last bite; but discard the bones and strain out all the vegetables and spices in the pot, saving back the broth separately. You can make this recipe ahead to this point. Cover and refrigerate the pot with the broth—and cover the meat on its plate and refrigerate it as well, both for up to 3 days.

3. To make the green mole, place the *pepitas* in a dry skillet set over medium heat and toast them until they begin to pop. And pop they will. Don't be tempted to cover the skillet to keep them in place. They'll steam and turn gummy. Instead, be prepared and let them go.

4. Transfer them to a big blender or a food processor fitted with the chopping blade; add 1 cup (240 ml) of strained reserved broth. Puree until fairly smooth. It'll never be completely so, more like green wet sand—but just don't let any *pepita* hunks stay in the mix. Scrape all this into a bowl and clean the blender or food processor.

5. Heat 2 tablespoons of the butter or olive oil in a large skillet over medium heat. Drop in the tomatillos, shallots, jalapeños, and chopped garlic. Cook, stirring often, until the tomatillos have begun to soften, about 5 minutes.

6. Scrape everything in the skillet into the blender or food processor. Add the cilantro, cinnamon, cumin, pepper, and cloves—along with ¾ cup (180 ml) of strained reserved broth. Puree until very smooth.

7. Now bring it all together. Throw out any remaining broth in the pot and wash the pot. Heat the remaining 1 tablespoon fat in that pot over medium heat. Add the *pepita* paste and fry for 4 minutes, stirring almost constantly. Scrape the tomatillo puree into the pot as well as all the shredded meat. Bring to a full simmer, then continue cooking, stirring often, until the meat is heated through, about 10 minutes. Stir in the lime juice just before serving over bowls of rice.

GO ALL OUT! GO ALL OUT! GO ALL OUT! GO ALL OUT! GO ALL OUT!

Mole verde is best with flour tortillas. To make about a dozen and a half, put 2½ cups plus 2 tablespoons all-purpose flour, 1 teaspoon baking powder, 1 teaspoon salt, and ½ teaspoon sugar in a food processor. Pulse to combine, then add 3 tablespoons lard. Pulse again until the mixture is grainy and coarse, the lard in little bits throughout. With the machine running, pour 1 cup (240 ml) warm water through the feed tube and process until a soft dough forms. Turn the dough out onto a dry, clean work surface and knead for 30 seconds. Gather into a ball, cover with plastic wrap, and set aside for 15 minutes. Then divide the dough into 16 balls, each about the size of a ping-pong ball. Roll each ball between sheets of plastic wrap to circles about 6 inches (15 cm) in diameter and ⅛ inch (.3 cm) thick. (The thickness is more important than the diameter; they needn't be perfectly round, just roundish.) Finally, set a nonstick skillet over medium heat until a drop of water skitters across its surface. Reduce the heat to medium-low and add one tortilla; cook until blistered with brown speckles and slightly puffed, about 1 minute. Turn and continue cooking until the other side is speckled, about 1 more minute. Keep the tortillas warm as you make more by wrapping those cooked in a clean kitchen towel or a cloth napkin.

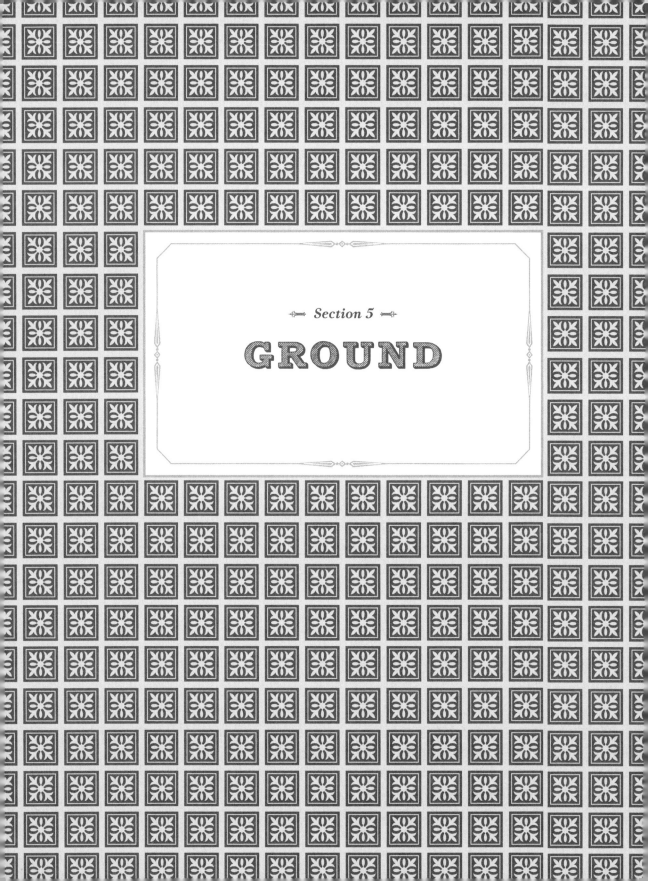

Section 5

GROUND

WHEN WE FIRST STARTED testing the ground goat recipes, we wanted to check out all the local sources. The first that jumped to mind was a halal market in West Hartford, a leafy suburb, just down the road from where Mark Twain used to titter at Harriet Beecher Stowe from behind the hedges.

We pulled up out front and sat in our car, both quiet. All the windows were covered with pasteboard. We couldn't see inside. Was it open?

"You go and ask them about goat," Bruce said.

"But you're doing the recipe testing," I said. "You're working in the kitchen. You know what you want."

"Weinstein," he said, pointing to himself. Then: "Halal," pointing to the store.

He had me there. I got out of the car—and hesitated, my hand still on the door. I'm not proud of it. I'm as liberal as the next guy. (Well, assuming there are any liberals left. I'm waving. If you see me, wave back.) But halal?

I walked in and disturbed the guys at a game of checkers. Like the country store on Green Acres, but with Mr. Drucker and Uncle Joe in tunics.

They couldn't have been nicer. They were so intrigued that I would want ground goat. I explained that it was for a book.

"We'll have to order it," the butcher said. "Two, maybe three, weeks."

"You don't keep it in stock?"

He saw the pleading in my eyes. "In Hartford?"

I nodded, as if I knew what he meant. I thanked them roundly—and they walked me to the door, telling me how great the olive oil was, the pastries, the lahmajoon. "You come back soon," they said, probably just glad for the promise of business in these turbulent times.

"How'd it go?" Bruce asked.

"It didn't. Any kosher butchers around?"

He didn't know.

So we drove back home, mostly quiet, listening to people on NPR blather about Islamofacism. I tried to imagine these pundits: pasty white faces, in a gleaming studio, talking into silver microphones.

We had to make one stop: our weekly pickup at the CSA we belong to in Falls Village, Connecticut. In exchange for buying shares in the farm, we get a once-a-week supply of organic fruits, berries, and vegetables.

As the sun was setting, we walked into the red ramshackle barn. Lo and behold, Bruce spotted a sign-up list on the table for "local goat." It was through Naf, who worked at the Isabella Freedman Jewish Retreat Center near us.

"It's our ram in the bush," I said.

He just stared at me. I still haven't figured out that he doesn't get the references. I lob Torah at him, only to be met with a glazed stare. This is what happens when a Southern evangelical marries a New York Jew. Among other things.

Anyway, he signed us up.

A few weeks later, we still hadn't heard from Naf. But as luck would have it, we saw him out weeding the fields of our CSA one afternoon: tzitzit among the broccoli.

"Hey, where's our goat?" Bruce called across the fields.

"I can't sell you any," Naf called back.

Don't tell Bruce he can't buy something. "What do you mean?" he hollered.

Naf seemed to duck his head. "You're not kosher."

After a ham book, we're undoubtedly suspect. But Bruce was undeterred. He headed out across the muck.

When we finally got to Naf, he was leaning on his spade. "I just can't," he said. "My kosher meat is all spoken for. And I can't sell nonkosher meat to another Jew."

"But I'm not religious," Bruce said.

"He doesn't get references to Abraham and Isaac," I added, as if that helped.

"Doesn't matter," Naf said, and turned back to weeding.

Bruce was not to be outdone. "Can you sell it to Mark, my partner?"

Naf cocked his head, furrowed his brow.

"Gentile," Bruce said, thumbing at me.

Naf snapped his fingers. "You found the Jewish loophole!"

Sure enough, we ended up with lots of ground meat, all because I was willing to sign the check.

Now who says Middle Eastern politics are so complicated?

BURGERS

This may be the simplest way to experience ground goat at home: lightly spiced patties, best for burger buns or pita pockets. For condiments, err on the side of vinegary, piquant ones—harissa, as follows, or deli mustard, or even chutney.

1½ teaspoons caraway seeds

1 teaspoon coriander seeds

1 teaspoon cumin seeds

1½ pounds (680 g) ground goat

½ teaspoon salt

½ teaspoon freshly ground black pepper

1 tablespoon peanut oil, if cooking in a skillet

4 hamburger buns, pita pockets, or split, toasted English muffins

Crunchy lettuce leaves, such as romaine leaves

1. Dry-toast the three kinds of seeds in a small skillet over low heat until they begin to sizzle and pop. Then grind them by

☞ dumping them into a spice grinder or a mini food processor and whirring until a powder,

☞ putting them in a mortar and mashing them with the pestle until quite powdery,

☞ or scattering them on a big cutting board and crushing them to a powder with the bottom of a heavy saucepan or a rolling pin.

Why not use ground spices, rather than going to all this trouble? Because that slight toasting will deepen the flavors, offering a darker, richer taste against the ground goat.

2. Mix half the ground spice mixture with the ground goat, salt, and pepper in a large bowl, working the spices into the meat without its becoming mush. The second half of the spice mixture should be saved back for a second round of goat burgers—or a batch of *harissa*.

3. Form the ground meat mixture into 4 patties, flattening each one, then putting a thumb-shaped indentation on the top side of each. This little well will help the patties stay flat over the heat, keeping the burgers from curling up into balls.

4. You can cook them in one of several ways:

☞ Heat a gas grill to high heat (550°F [288°C]) or build a high-heat coal bed in a charcoal grill.

☞ Heat a grill pan over medium-high heat.

☞ Heat the oil in a large skillet set over medium-high heat.

In any event, place the patties (on the grill grate right over the heat or in the grill pan or skillet) and sizzle, turning once, until an instant-read meat thermometer inserted into the center of one of the patties registers 150°F (66°C) (Bruce's preference for medium—beyond the life expectancy of most pests), about 6 minutes, or 165°F (74°C) (the USDA's approved number—for well done, and starting to dry out a bit too much in Bruce's opinion), about 8 minutes.

All that said, these timings are ridiculously inaccurate, given that ground goat varies so widely in terms of its fat content. The less marbled the ground meat, the more quickly it will cook. Use an instant-read meat thermometer to be sure.

Serve the patties in the hamburger buns, pita pockets, or English muffins with the lettuce leaves and the *harissa* as a condiment.

GO ALL OUT! GO ALL OUT! GO ALL OUT! GO ALL OUT! GO ALL OUT!

Harissa is a spicy Middle Eastern sauce that pairs well with these sweet, aromatic burgers. There's more here than you'll need. Store it, covered, in the fridge for up to a week—or freeze it for up to a couple of months. However, freezing will no doubt throw a little water on the chiles' fire. Once the sauce is thawed, stir in a little more lemon juice to brighten the flavors, if not the heat.

To make *harissa*, stem, seed, and tear up 8 guajillo chiles (see page 59) and 8 dried New Mexico red chiles (see page 59). Set the fragments in a big bowl and cover with boiling water. Set aside for 20 minutes. Then drain in a colander set in the sink and transfer the pliable chile pieces to the canister of a food processor fitted with the chopping blade. Add 5 quartered medium garlic cloves, 3 tablespoons toasted walnut oil, 2 tablespoons lemon juice, 1 teaspoon salt, and the rest of the spice powder from the burger recipe. Pulse a couple of times, then process until a thick paste, scraping down the inside of the canister with a rubber spatula once or twice to make sure everything gets well blended.

DOWN-HOME STEW

IT'LL BE DINNER ON THE TABLE FOR SIX.

You can also make this stew in a Dutch or French oven. However, you may need to cook the stew uncovered in step 5 for 10 to 15 minutes, since the pot's higher sides will not allow the liquid to reduce as quickly.

LESS TO DO

Omit the carrots, corn, okra, and lima beans and instead add 7½ cups (1.7 kg) frozen mixed vegetables.

GO ALL OUT! GO ALL OUT!

Make dumplings for the stew: Stir 1½ cups (185 g) flour, 1 tablespoon baking powder, 1 teaspoon dry mustard, ½ teaspoon salt, and ¼ teaspoon nutmeg in a large bowl. Cut in 3 tablespoons shortening or lard with a pastry cutter or a fork, working the fat into the flour mixture until the whole thing resembles coarse sand. Use a fork to stir ⅔ cup buttermilk into the flour mixture. With your clean, dry hands, form this into 12 balls and set them into the stew after it has cooked for 20 minutes in step 5. Continue simmering for 20 minutes. Cool, uncovered, for 5 minutes to let the flavors meld and the dumplings dry out just a little.

- ¼ cup (60 ml) **peanut oil**
- 2 pounds (910 g) **ground goat**
- 1 large **yellow onion, finely chopped**
- 3 **celery ribs, thinly sliced**
- 2 medium **carrots, peeled and thinly sliced**
- ¼ cup (30 g) **all-purpose flour**
- 1½ tablespoons **minced fresh sage leaves**
- 1½ tablespoons **minced fresh oregano leaves**
- 1½ tablespoons **stemmed thyme leaves**
- 1 teaspoon **salt**
- 1 teaspoon **freshly ground black pepper**
- Several dashes of **hot red pepper sauce, such as Tabasco sauce**
- 3 cups (720 ml) **reduced-sodium chicken broth**
- 1 cup (240 ml) **dry white wine or dry vermouth**
- 3½ cups (840 ml) **canned reduced-sodium diced tomatoes, with juice**
- 1 to 2 tablespoons **Worcestershire sauce**
- 2 cups (455 g) **fresh or frozen corn kernels**
- 2 cups (455 g) **fresh or frozen sliced okra**
- 2 cups (455 g) **frozen lima beans**

1. Heat a high-sided sauté pan over medium heat. Pour in the oil, then crumble in all the ground meat. Brown for about 10 minutes, stirring frequently.

2. Add the onion, celery, and carrots. Stir over the heat with the ground meat until the onion begins to turn translucent, about 4 minutes.

3. Sprinkle the flour over everything, stir well, then continue stirring over the heat for 2 minutes as the flour browns a bit.

4. Add the herbs, salt, ground black pepper, and several dashes of the hot sauce. Stir over the heat for a few seconds; then stir in the broth and wine or vermouth, pouring these liquids into the pan in a slow, steady stream. The slower, the better, since the flour has to dissolve. Once it has indeed done so, pour in the diced tomatoes and Worcestershire sauce. Bring to a full simmer; then cover, reduce the heat to low, and simmer slowly for 10 minutes.

5. Stir in the corn, okra, and lima beans. Cover again and continue simmering for about 40 minutes, until the stew is thick and luscious.

GOAT MEAT LOAF

THIS MAKES ONE MEAT LOAF. HOW MANY CAN THAT SERVE? FOUR
WITH LEFTOVERS FOR SANDWICHES? SIX? WHO KNOWS?

Meat loaf needs a binder of some kind, something to absorb the mois-
ture and keep the loaf juicy as the ground meat bakes to higher temper-
atures than you might want for a burger. Goat is so lean that it requires
two of these moisture-hording binders: bread crumbs and (for Bruce's
recipe) lentils, an earthy, hearty flavor in this comfort food. Why the
higher temperature for a meat loaf than for, say, a hamburger? First,
the mixed-in egg must be cooked to a safe temperature. Second, the
slightly higher temperature allows for a more luxurious set, thanks to
that melting collagen. And third, the higher temperature allows a little
more crust, always a boon to pickers and nibblers.

⅔ cup (150 g) small green lentils,
 sometimes called French lentils

1½ pounds (680 g) ground goat

8 ounces (225 g) carrots, peeled and
 shredded through the large holes of
 a box grater or with the shredding
 blade of a food processor

¾ cup (170 g) fresh bread crumbs

1 large egg

1 tablespoon Dijon mustard

1 tablespoon Worcestershire sauce

2 teaspoons dried marjoram or dried
 chervil

1 teaspoon dried thyme

½ teaspoon salt

½ teaspoon freshly ground black
 pepper

1. Place the lentils in a large saucepan, cover them with water, and bring to
 a boil over high heat, stirring occasionally.

2. Reduce the heat to low and cook until they're tender, about 20 minutes.
 Don't undercook the lentils. Better to go longer so that they're really
 soft, easily mashed into mush. Drain in a colander set in the sink; cool
 to room temperature, about 1 hour. Meanwhile, position the rack in the
 center of the oven and preheat the oven to 350°F (175°C).

3. Mix everything—even the cooled lentils—in a big bowl, taking care not
 to turn the meat's fibers into puree. The best way to do this? With your
 cleaned and dried hands. Yes, you'll get a little goat under your finger-
 nails. Did you buy a book on goat because you thought you'd miss that
 opportunity?

4. Form the mixture into an oblong lump in a 9 x 13-inch (23 x 33-cm) baking dish, sort of like the dome on the new Dallas Cowboys stadium. (I
 have no idea what I'm talking about, but I did a Google search for oblong
 domes and this came up.) Bake until an instant-read meat thermometer
 inserted into the center of the meat loaf registers 165°F (74°C), about 1
 hour. Cool in the baking dish for a few minutes before slicing.

KOFTA

EIGHT SKEWERS PROBABLY EQUALS FOUR SERVINGS.

There are about a million ways to spell the name of this dish: kufta, cofta, quftah. They're all derived from a Farsi word for to grind— and thus refer to ground meat, or these meatballs, common across the Middle East and Southeast Asia. They can be round, or tubular, as Bruce has made them, sort of like sausage-shaped meatballs. Serve them in pita pockets (off their skewers!) with lettuce, mustard, and chutney. Or serve them in hot dog buns with ketchup and pickle relish. (No fatwas, please.) Or simply serve them drizzled with a lemon tahini sauce (page 34) and a salad on the side.

1¼ pounds (570 g) **ground goat**

¼ cup (55 g) **chestnut flour, chickpea flour, fine-ground semolina, or fine-ground cornmeal**

1 very small **yellow onion, minced**

¼ cup (55 g) **fresh parsley leaves, minced**

¼ cup (55 g) **fresh cilantro leaves, minced**

2 medium **garlic cloves, minced**

2 teaspoons **minced peeled fresh ginger**

2 teaspoons **ground sumac (see More to Know)**

1 teaspoon **ground cumin**

1 teaspoon **salt**

½ teaspoon **ground cinnamon**

½ teaspoon **freshly ground black pepper**

1. Mix all the ingredients in a big bowl until there are no traces of flour in the mixture and the spices are evenly distributed throughout. Divide the mixture into 8 balls. (It helps to divide the whole lump in half first, then each of these halves into quarters.) Form the balls into sausagelike shapes, shaping each one around a metal skewer. If you don't have 8 metal skewers, just form them into long, tubular sausages.

2. Heat a gas grill to high heat (550°F [288°C]) or prepare a high-heat coal bed in a charcoal grill. Alternatively, heat a seasoned cast-iron grill pan over medium-high heat until smoking.

3. Place the kofta, either on the skewers or not, directly over the heat on the grill grate or in the grill pan. Turn on the vent if you're working at the stove. Or open a window. The house is about to get smoky. Cook, turning once or twice, until browned on all sides and an instant-read meat thermometer inserted into one without touching the skewer registers 150°F (66°C) (Bruce's preference for medium) or 165°F (74°C) (the USDA's recommendation), between 6 and 9 minutes (they'll cook faster on the metal skewers).

MORE TO KNOW

Made from ground chestnuts, chestnut flour has a distinct smokiness—an intense hit of flavor—and is best used in moderation. It's not as authentic as the chickpea flour alternative in this recipe but certainly better with goat. In a pinch, any of the substitutes will work.

Sumac is a dark red spice, ground from the berries of a variety of sumac common around the eastern Mediterranean as well as the Middle East. It adds a nutty but tart taste, a terrific combo for goat. One warning: The sumac that grows in North America is poisonous. Don't go spice-gathering along the interstate.

BRAISED MEATBALLS WITH ARTICHOKES AND FENNEL

IT'LL SERVE FOUR, MAYBE SIX, IF YOU'VE GOT A COUPLE OF SIDES LIKE WILTED CHARD AND MASHED POTATOES.

Meatballs are one comfort food trend among many, all of which seem to have been with us since the nineties for no obvious reason. Maybe we've all gotten so very tired of politics and obstructionists and pundits and sign-wavers and bad times and bank bailouts and . . . OK, comfort foods aren't going away any time soon. So try this Greek-inspired dish, the flavors based on those from the eastern part of the Mediterranean.

1 pound (455 g) **ground goat**

1 large **egg white**

3 tablespoons **fresh bread crumbs** (see page 96)

2 medium **shallots**, minced

1 teaspoon **dried oregano**

1 teaspoon **dried dill**

1 teaspoon **salt**, halved and used in two places in the recipe

1 teaspoon **freshly ground black pepper**, halved, same as with the salt

½ cup (225 g) **whole wheat flour**

2 tablespoons **olive oil**

1 large **yellow onion**, chopped

1 large **fennel bulb**, any stems and fronds removed, the tough root end sliced off and discarded, then the bulb itself chopped

1 large **tomato**, chopped

1 pound (455 g) **fresh baby artichokes**, trimmed; or one 12-ounce (one 340-g) **package whole or quartered frozen baby artichokes** (no need to thaw)

1⅓ cups (360 ml) **reduced-sodium vegetable broth**

1½ tablespoons **reduced-sodium tomato paste**

2 teaspoons **lemon juice**

1 teaspoon **ground cinnamon**

MORE TO KNOW

If you've never worked with fresh baby artichokes, take this warning to heart: You may need to lose a little more than half of each before they're ready to go in the stew. Cut the top third off the artichoke, getting rid of any spiky points, even inside. Then pull off the outer leaves until you get down to a small pale green, sometimes yellowish, teardrop-shaped vegetable. The choke inside (the hairy bits in a bigger artichoke) is still edible in these small ones, so there's no need to remove it. Or buy frozen baby artichokes and be done with it.

1. Mix the ground meat, egg white, bread crumbs, shallots, oregano, dill, ½ teaspoon of the salt, and ½ teaspoon of the pepper in a medium bowl until uniform—that is, until the spices are spread evenly throughout; the bread crumbs, too; and the egg white is no longer visible as a scummy film. Form this mixture into 12 golf balls.

2. Heat a large pot over medium heat. Meanwhile, spread the flour on a plate. Swirl the oil into the pot, then roll half the balls in the flour. Put them in the pot and brown on all sides. (OK, geometry teachers, balls don't have sides. But you know what I mean.) About 7 minutes will do it. Transfer them to a plate and repeat with the remaining balls.

3. Dump the onion, fennel, tomato, and artichokes into the pot. Stir over the heat until the onion begins to soften, about 3 minutes.

4. Pour in the broth; stir in the tomato paste, lemon juice, cinnamon, the remaining ½ teaspoon salt, and the remaining ½ teaspoon pepper. As the mixture begins to simmer, make sure you scrape up any browned bits in the pot. Then tuck the meatballs into the simmering sauce and pour any juices on their plate over everything. Cover, reduce the heat to low, and simmer slowly for 1 hour.

BAKED MEATBALL-AND-RICE CASSEROLE

YOU'LL END UP WITH ONE CASSEROLE THAT'LL SERVE SIX. THE ONLY THING MISSING IS A VINEGARY GREEN SALAD.

No doubt about it: There's a lot of saffron here. You can cut its amount by half, if you want. Just use enough so that the rice is incredibly aromatic, a way to "lighten it up" after the meatballs have leached their juice into it.

MORE TO KNOW

Necessity is not the only mother of invention. Laziness is, too. After all, Newton invented gravity when he was lollygagging under an apple tree. In the spirit of cosmos-altering discoveries, Bruce didn't want to dirty another bowl in an already complicated recipe, so he pushed those softening onions to the side of the pot in step 6. In the end, they got so caramelized that they added lots more flavor to the stew than they would have under "normal" cooking conventions.

3 cups (720 ml) reduced-sodium chicken broth

1 teaspoon salt, halved and used in two places in the recipe

1 teaspoon freshly ground black pepper, halved, same as with the salt

½ teaspoon saffron threads (see page 38)

1½ pounds (680 g) ground goat

¾ cup (170 g) fresh bread crumbs (see page 96)

1½ teaspoons mild paprika

1 teaspoon ground cumin

1 teaspoon ground ginger

½ teaspoon ground turmeric

3 tablespoons olive oil

2 medium yellow onions, chopped

1¼ cups (280 g) long-grain rice, such as basmati, jasmine, Carolina, or patna

3 medium garlic cloves, minced

½ cup (115 g) cilantro leaves, chopped

⅓ cup (76 g) chopped pitted green olives

1 cup (240 ml) dry white wine or dry vermouth

1 to 2 tablespoons lemon juice

1. Position the rack in the center of the oven and preheat the oven to 325°F (165°C).

2. Stir the broth, ½ teaspoon of the salt, ½ teaspoon of the black pepper, and the saffron in a medium saucepan over medium heat. Keep the broth warm while you start the dish.

3. Mix the ground meat, bread crumbs, paprika, cumin, ginger, turmeric, the remaining ½ teaspoon salt, and the remaining ½ teaspoon black pepper in a big bowl. Form this mixture into 24 balls, each about 1½ inches (4 cm) in diameter.

4. Heat a large Dutch or French oven over medium heat. Swirl in the oil, then add the onions. Cook, stirring often, until sweet and soft, about 5 minutes.

5. Push the onions to the sides of the pot and add about half the meatballs, as many as will fit without crowding. Brown these lightly on all sides; then take them out of the pot, put them on a clean platter, and add more meatballs, browning these as well.

   Meanwhile, the onions will continue to cook. Yes, some will darken considerably. Don't worry. They're going to add flavor to the dish. Just avoid too many blackened bits by stirring them occasionally.

6. Once all the meatballs have been browned, add the rice, garlic, cilantro, and olives to the pot. Stir well, incorporating the onions back into the mixture, for about 1 minute.

7. Add the wine and scrape up the browned gunk in the pot as it comes to a full simmer. Now pour in the warm broth. Put the meatballs and any accumulated juices from their platter into the pot. Stir well, then cover the pot and put the whole thing in the oven.

8. Bake for 50 minutes, or until the rice is tender when fluffed with a fork (and tasted, of course).

9. Remove the pot from the oven and let it stand at room temperature, covered, for 5 minutes to blend the flavors fully. Drizzle the lemon juice over the top of the pot just before serving—or over each serving at the table.

MOUSSAKA

Call it a goat festival in a 9 x 13-inch (23 x 33-cm) pan. In Bruce's version, the thick ground goat ragout is layered with eggplant slices in the baking dish, sort of like a lasagna with eggplant rather than noodles. The whole thing is then topped with the béchamel (a thickened cream—or in this case, goat milk—sauce). When I got a plateful, I didn't come up for air.

2 medium eggplants

2 tablespoons plus ½ teaspoon salt, divided

½ cup (120 ml) olive oil, used in tablespoon amounts here and there throughout the recipe

1 large yellow onion, chopped

4 medium garlic cloves, minced

2 pounds (910 g) ground goat

¼ cup (60 ml) reduced-sodium tomato paste

1 tablespoon minced fresh oregano leaves

1 teaspoon freshly ground black pepper

½ teaspoon ground cinnamon

2 cups (480 ml) dry red wine

1 cup (240 ml) reduced-sodium chicken broth

1½ tablespoons goat butter (or unsalted cow butter, if you must)

1½ tablespoons all-purpose flour

3¼ cups (780 ml) regular or low-fat goat milk

1 large egg yolk, whisked until smooth in a small bowl

¼ teaspoon freshly grated nutmeg

2 ounces (55 g) hard, aged goat cheese, like a goat Gouda, or even a crottin you've aged in your own fridge (see page 199)

1. Slice the eggplants into ¼-inch-thick (.6-cm) rounds. Salt them on both sides with 2 tablespoons salt; put them on a big wire rack set over some paper towels for 20 minutes. (The paper towels will catch the drips.) Meanwhile, position the rack in the middle of the oven; preheat the oven to 400°F (205°C).

2. Rinse the slices and blot them dry. Really dry. Lay them on a large baking sheet and brush them with 2 tablespoons of the oil. Turn them over and brush with another 2 tablespoons of the oil. Bake the slices until softened, turning once, about 20 minutes.

3. Meanwhile, heat a large skillet over medium heat. Swirl in 3 tablespoons of the oil, then add the onion. Cook, stirring often, until softened—then keep going until lightly browned, about 6 minutes in all. Stir in the garlic; cook for 10 seconds or so.

4. Add the ground meat and stir over the heat until it loses its raw, pink color throughout, maybe 4 minutes. Stir in the tomato paste, oregano, pepper, and cinnamon. Keep stirring over the heat until the tomato paste dissolves, about 2 minutes.

5. Stir in the wine and broth, then bring the sauce to a simmer. Reduce the heat a bit and simmer, uncovered, until the mixture is thick and most of the liquid either has been absorbed or has evaporated, about 25 minutes, stirring occasionally. In the end, you want a thick sauce, closer in consistency to that in Sloppy Joes, certainly not a soupy mess.

6. Melt the butter in a medium saucepan over medium-low heat. Whisk in the flour and continue whisking over the heat just until you have a creamy paste, about 1 minute or so. Starting with a few dribbles, then slowly adding more, whisk in the milk. It's important you incorporate those first few bits really well to keep the flour from clumping, long before you start adding the milk in a steady if thin stream. Continue whisking the mixture until it's bubbling and thick, about 3 minutes.

7. Whisk about a cup of the hot milk mixture into the egg yolk until smooth, then whisk this combined mixture back into the saucepan. Take the saucepan off the heat and whisk in the remaining ½ teaspoon salt and the nutmeg.

8. Use the last tablespoon of olive oil to grease a 9 x 13-inch (23 x 33-cm) baking dish. Put a third of the eggplant slices in the dish, layering them as you would lasagna noodles. Top these with a third of the meat sauce; then make two more similar layers of eggplant and sauce, ending with the last of the meat sauce. Pour the goat milk béchamel over the casserole and (to take the whole thing into realms of culinary indulgence undiscovered until now) grate the cheese over that.

9. Bake until golden and bubbling, about 1 hour. Cool for 10 minutes before cutting into squares to serve.

GO ALL OUT! GO ALL OUT! GO ALL OUT! GO ALL OUT! GO ALL OUT!

A nice accompaniment would be a jicama salad with a blood orange vinaigrette. To make about eight servings, peel and quarter two 1-pound (455-g) jicamas, then shred them through the large holes of a box grater or in a food processor fitted with the shredding blade. Set the shreds in a serving bowl, then squeeze the juice from 2 blood oranges over them. Also stir in 3 tablespoons red wine vinegar, 1 tablespoon chile powder, and ½ teaspoon salt. Add 2 cups (455 ml) baby arugula leaves (stemmed if fibrous or tough), then stir in ⅓ cup (75 ml) olive oil. Taste for salt and serve at once.

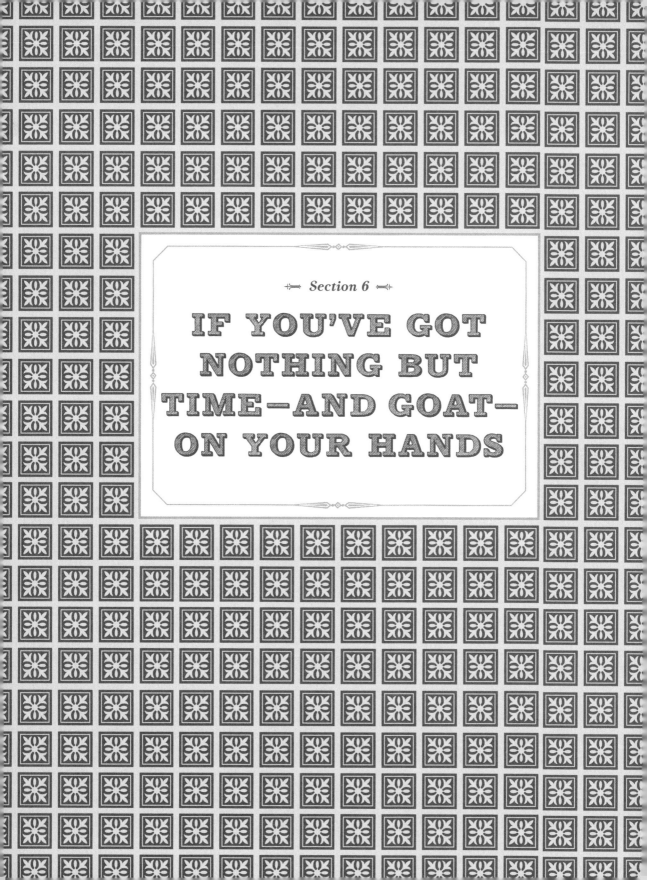

Section 6

IF YOU'VE GOT NOTHING BUT TIME—AND GOAT— ON YOUR HANDS

BRUCE AND I HAVE BEEN at this cookbook career for a while: eighteen or so books in twelve years. Naturally, we've seen a few changes. Time was, everybody was nuts for fast meals. Do you remember Pierre Franey's television series from the eighties, *The Sixty-Minute Gourmet*?

Seems almost laughable these days. Over the last decade or so, a meal's preparation time has collapsed further and further—until somebody finally came up with five-minute meals.

Then came the Internet. It took care of the problem. Because all those fast recipes went out into cyberspace.

Don't get me wrong: I blog quick recipes all the time at our site, www.realfoodhascurves.com. But the Internet seems the natural home for solid recipes with few ingredients, recipes that someone can glance at on a smart phone and get done in a matter of minutes.

Which means that cookbooks in the past few years have gotten more expansive. All that pressure to get dinner on the table with four ingredients in three and a half seconds has been siphoned off.

Bruce has never been happier. He's not a five-minute gourmet. He loves to tinker and toy. It's like play, only with food. Even when he was still racing with the other rats in ad agencies, he'd plain if I made dinner at night. "But I wanted he'd say.

I did, too. Back in the day, when I was an academic, a nice dinner seemed the only way to wash endless faculty meetings out of my brain. And not the eating of the meal (although that helped). The cooking of it, mostly.

Let's face it: We all work repetitive jobs. We all do the same thing day in and day out. And that incessant repetition bleeds into our cooking, too. How many times can you face the stove to make another boneless, skinless chicken breast? Or another salmon fillet, the chicken breast of today?

Cooking is a way to fight back, to be creative. And being creative is the very essence of being human. We draw pictures, create dance, write books—and make food.

So here are four recipes for those moments when you've got time to practice the very essence of your being.

With goat? OK, maybe I'm pushing it a bit. But these recipes are ways to stretch yourself, push your boundaries, and come up with something marvelous.

Listen, that's about as human as it gets.

PÂTÉ DE CAMPAGNE

YOU'LL END UP WITH A 6-CUP (1.5-L) TERRINE OF THE STUFF, PROBABLY
ENOUGH FOR A STARTER AT A DINNER PARTY PLUS SEVERAL LUNCHES IN
THE DAYS FOLLOWING, SLICED FOR SANDWICHES ON CRUNCHY BREAD WITH
COARSE-GRAINED MUSTARD. (IF YOU PUT MAYONNAISE ON PÂTÉ, I'M GOING
TO MAKE A SPECIAL TRIP TO YOUR HOUSE TO STRAIGHTEN YOU OUT.)

*A pâté de campagne (French, pah-TAY duh kahm-PAHN-yuh) is a
coarse terrine, usually made with pig liver and other bits of pork-
ish goodness. For Bruce's recipe, you'll need a goat liver as well as
an unsmoked pork (not goat) jowl. In other words, you'll need to go
to a farmers' market to search out local producers—or you'll need to
explore small farms in your area through networks on the Web.*

1½ tablespoons goat butter or lard

1 small yellow onion, chopped

12 ounces (340 g) goat liver

12 ounces (340 g) unsmoked (a.k.a. fresh) pork jowl, any rind removed

10½ ounces (295 g) boneless goat shoulder meat, cut into 1-inch (2.5-cm) chunks

1 large egg, well beaten in a small bowl

1 medium garlic clove, minced

1½ tablespoons port

1 tablespoon salt, preferably kosher salt or a mineraly sea salt

1 teaspoon freshly ground black pepper

½ teaspoon ground allspice

½ teaspoon ground cloves

Parchment paper, aluminum foil, waxed paper, and cardboard

1. Melt the butter or the lard in a medium skillet over medium heat. Add the onion and cook, stirring often, until softened a tad, about 3 minutes. Scrape the contents of the skillet into a small bowl and put it in the refrigerator to chill for 1 hour.

2. Set the rack in the center of the oven and preheat the oven to a mere 300°F (150°C).

3. Grind the goat liver, pork jowl, and goat shoulder meat. Use the coarse blade if you have that option on your grinder—and put the meat through that grinder twice. If you only have a fine blade, run the meat through it only once (the consistency will still be much smoother). Let the ground meat fall into a big bowl.

   Without a meat grinder at hand, you can get this job done in a food processor fitted with the chopping blade, provided (1) you cut all the meat (the liver, jowl, and shoulder) into very small cubes first, probably about ¼ inch (.6 cm) each, and (2) pulse the processor only a few times, rearranging everything after each pulse, so you don't end up with a puree.

4. Stir the chilled onion and any fat (but, of course!) into the bowl with the ground meat, as well as the beaten egg, garlic, port, salt, pepper, allspice, and cloves. Spoon and spread this mixture into a narrow, heavy, 6-cup

(1.4-L) terrine mold with a lid. If you don't have that nifty bit of kitchen gadgetry, use a 6-cup (1.4 L) loaf pan. Put a piece of parchment paper over the terrine mold, then put a piece of aluminum foil over the top—and seal it closed. Set the lid in place. If you're working with a lidless loaf pan, cover the terrine with the parchment paper and then a double thickness of foil to make sure not a drop of moisture can escape.

5. Bake until the internal temperature of the pâté registers 165°F (74°C) when an instant-read meat thermometer is put into the center of the loaf without touching the bottom or sides of the pan, about 1 hour. As you can tell, this is a ridiculous step—because you've gone to the trouble of sealing the thing in its mold, only to have to unseal it to take its internal temperature. Ah, well.

6. Remove the terrine from the oven and let cool for 10 minutes or so. Take the lid off the mold and remove the foil and parchment paper. Don't faint: The meat will not be form-fitting, the pan its girdle. Instead, the pâté will have shrunk and the intervening space filled with juices (mostly fat). Mercy, don't throw them out.

7. Cut a piece of heavy cardboard to fit the top of the terrine. Place a piece of wax paper right on top of the pâté, then put this piece of cut cardboard on top of the wax paper. Weight the thing down with a couple of heavy cans (like of diced tomatoes) turned on their sides. Refrigerate for at least 12 hours or up to 36 hours.

For the best taste, the *pâté de campagne* should be served at room temperature, so let it sit out a bit before slicing off wedges for appetizers—or even for dinner with a salad on the side. Oh, and red wine. Lots of red wine. May I suggest one from Gigondas?

GO ALL OUT! GO ALL OUT! GO ALL OUT! GO ALL OUT! GO ALL OUT!

A *pâté de campagne* is usually served with cornichons (French, *cohr-NEE-chawnz*), sour little pickles. However, this one is particularly great with sweet and sour prunes preserved in red wine. To make them, bring 1 pound (455 g) pitted prunes to a simmer in a big saucepan set over medium-high heat with 1½ cups (360 ml) red wine, 1 cup (200 g) sugar, ⅔ cup (165 ml) red wine vinegar, and ½ teaspoon salt, stirring all the while until the sugar dissolves. Once the whole thing is bubbling away, reduce the heat to low and simmer slowly for 10 minutes, just a few bubbles at a time. Remove the saucepan from the heat and cool to room temperature, about 2 hours. Pour into a big jar and refrigerate for up to 3 weeks, fishing out the preserved prunes one at a time to serve with slices and hunks of the pâté.

DOLMADES

THERE'LL BE TWENTY-FOUR STUFFED GRAPE LEAVES.

These stuffed grape leaves (Greek, dohl-MAH-days*) are goaty and ter-rific, a real treat, and without a doubt something that will make your dinner guests sit up and take notice. "Where'd you get these?" they'll ask. "Oh, I made them," you'll say. (Practice the appropriate head toss in the mirror before they come over.)*

2 tablespoons olive oil

2 medium yellow onions, minced (and seriously minced—not diced or finely chopped)

1 pound (455 g) ground goat

¼ cup (55 g) long-grain white rice (like basmati)

½ cup (115 g) fresh parsley leaves, chopped

2 tablespoons fresh dill fronds, chopped

2 tablespoons fresh mint leaves, chopped

½ teaspoon salt

½ teaspoon freshly ground black pepper

24 bottled large grape leaves, any thick stems removed (there will be more leaves than this in a large jar—keep all the extras and any stems, as you'll see why)

2 cups (480 ml) reduced-sodium chicken broth

1 cup (240 ml) dry white wine or dry vermouth

¼ cup (60 ml) lemon juice

2 tablespoons reduced-sodium tomato paste

MORE TO KNOW

When the stuffed leaves are finally done, there will inevitably be some of the grape leaves used to line the pot that have burned a bit and gotten stuck. Don't despair. Fill the pot with water and leave it to soak overnight. The next day, bring the water to a boil over high heat. Boil for at least 10 minutes before you reach in there with a long-handled wooden spoon and lift the leaves off the bottom.

1. Heat a large skillet over medium-low heat. Swirl in the oil, then add the onions. Reduce the heat to low and cook, stirring often, until the onions are golden, some even starting to melt into a sauce, about 30 minutes. If you notice any browning, reduce the heat even further, or take the skillet off the heat for a bit to calm it down. Once the onions are right, take the skillet off the heat and cool to room temperature, about 30 minutes.

2. Do not put the skillet back over the heat. Instead, stir in the ground goat and the rice. Then stir in the parsley, dill, mint, salt, and pepper. Now you've got a raw goat filling for the grape leaves.

3. Rinse the grape leaves one by one to get rid of any adherent, too-salty brine. Set one on your work surface, vein side up. Put about 1½ table-spoons of the filling in the center of the leaf, fold the sides to the right and left of you over the filling, then roll the leaf up. Set it aside, seam side down, and continue making the rest of the filled grape leaves, 24 in all.

4. Line a large, heavy pot such as a Dutch or French oven with the remain-ing grape leaves from the jar as well as any reserved stems. Stack the stuffed grape leaves on top, all seam side down.

5. Whisk the broth, wine, lemon juice, and tomato paste in a bowl; pour this mixture over the grape leaves. Set a heat-safe plate on top of the stuffed leaves, thereby submerging them in the liquid. The plate should be just about the diameter of the pot you're using.

6. Cover the pot and bring the sauce to a simmer slowly over medium-low heat. Reduce the heat to low and cook at a very slow simmer for 1 hour.

7. Turn off the heat and let the pot cool down for 10 minutes. Use tongs to remove the plate inside. Carefully remove the *dolmades* and put them in a bowl, on a plate, or in a plastic container. Cover with plastic wrap (or the container's lid, if using that sort of storage device) and refrigerate for at least 2 hours or up to 1 week. By the way, they're best at room temperature, not right out of the chill.

MEAT EMPANADAS ᴡɪᴛʜ CHIMICHURRI

YOU'LL COME OUT WITH SIXTEEN EMPANADAS,
WITH THE SAUCE ON THE SIDE.

We'd been working on this book for a while when we got booked to teach cooking classes on a Holland America cruise from Chile around Cape Horn to Brazil. We made an overnight, two-day stop in Buenos Aires—and sort of fell head over heels for the place, mostly because of goat empanadas with chimichurri, *a traditional herb-laced sauce. When we got home, Bruce set about to re-create what we'd had with beers one long, hot afternoon.*

For the filling:

2 tablespoons olive oil

1 small yellow onion, minced

2 medium garlic cloves, minced

1 pound (455 g) ground goat

¼ cup (55 g) fresh cilantro leaves, chopped

½ teaspoon ground allspice

½ teaspoon ground cinnamon

½ teaspoon red pepper flakes

2 tablespoons red wine vinegar

½ cup (120 ml) reduced-sodium chicken broth

¼ cup (60 ml) red wine

¼ cup (55 g) chopped pitted green olives

¼ cup (55 g) dried currants

½ teaspoon salt

½ teaspoon freshly ground black pepper

1 tablespoon reduced-sodium tomato paste

For the chimichurri:

½ cup (115 g) packed fresh parsley leaves

¼ cup (60 ml) red wine vinegar

3 tablespoons packed fresh oregano leaves

2 teaspoons red pepper flakes

1 teaspoon salt

½ teaspoon freshly ground black pepper

4 medium garlic cloves, quartered

½ cup (120 ml) olive oil

For the dough:

2½ cups (315 g) all-purpose flour, plus more for dusting your work surface

½ cup (115 g) instant masa harina (labeled *for tamales* on the package)

2¼ teaspoons baking powder

½ teaspoon salt

¾ cup (170 g) lard or solid vegetable shortening

⅔ cup (165 ml) sweet dessert wine or sweet vermouth (sometimes called *red vermouth*), plus more as needed

¼ cup (60 ml) regular or low-fat goat milk

1. Make the filling by first heating a large skillet over medium-low heat. Swirl in 2 tablespoons olive oil, then add the minced onion. Reduce the heat to low and cook, stirring often, until the onion is softened and sweet, about 5 minutes. Stir in the garlic and cook for 20 seconds.

2. Raise the heat to medium and crumble in the ground goat. Cook, stirring frequently, until it loses its raw, pink color and browns slightly, about 6 minutes.

3. Stir in the cilantro, allspice, cinnamon, and ½ teaspoon red pepper flakes. Cook for 1 minute, then pour in the vinegar and scrape up any browned bits on the skillet's bottom as the vinegar boils away.

4. Stir in the broth, red wine, olives, currants, ½ teaspoon salt, and ½ teaspoon black pepper. Continue cooking for 5 minutes, boiling down the liquid to a thick glaze.

5. Stir in the tomato paste, then continue cooking, stirring constantly, until no liquid remains, 2 to 3 minutes. Set the skillet off the heat and cool the mixture to room temperature, about 1 hour. You should have about 3 cups (720 ml) of filling. You can make it in advance and then store it in a covered bowl in the fridge for up to 3 days.

6. To make the *chimichurri*, place the parsley, red wine vinegar, oregano, 2 teaspoons red pepper flakes, 1 teaspoon salt, ½ teaspoon black pepper, and the 4 quartered garlic cloves in a food processor fitted with the chopping blade. Pulse until coarsely ground, then pour in ½ cup (120 ml) olive oil in a thin stream through the feed tube with the machine running until everything is minced but not smooth, less than 1 minute of processing.

If you don't have a food processor, grind all the ingredients except the olive oil in a mortar with a pestle. Once it's coarsely ground, scrape this mixture into a bowl; then stir in the olive oil in small dribs and drabs, letting each addition get incorporated before adding the next.

The *chimichurri* can be made in advance. Store it in a covered bowl in the refrigerator for up to 1 week—but let it come back to room temperature before serving with the hot empanadas.

7. To make the dough, whisk the flour, masa harina, baking powder, and ½ teaspoon salt in a large bowl. Add the lard or shortening and cut it in with a pastry cutter or a fork, pushing the fat through the tines repeatedly, in all directions, cleaning those tines often, and working at it until the whole thing looks like coarse sand.

8. Stir in the ⅔ cup (165 ml) sweet wine or sweet vermouth to form a dough. Sometimes, because the flour or the masa harina has dried out too much, you may need a little more wine to get a soft, pliable dough. If so, add more in 1-tablespoon increments. You don't want a wet dough, but it should definitely be soft and silky, easy to work with. Scrape it all together in the bowl, cover with a clean kitchen towel, and set aside to rest for 1 hour at room temperature.

9. Position the rack in the center of the oven and preheat the oven to 350°F (175°C). Pour the milk into a shallow bowl, like a soup bowl from your dishware set. Divide the dough mixture into 16 golf balls. (If you want to be obsessive, they should be about 1½ ounces [40 grams] each.)

10. Dust a clean, dry surface with a little flour, then set a ball in the center. Flatten the ball a bit, then use a rolling pin to roll the dough into a circle about 6 inches in diameter. You'll need to work the pin in various directions to make sure the circle is uniform in shape and in thickness.

11. Place 2 heaping tablespoons of the meat filling in the center of the circle. Fold the circle into a half-moon, sealing the filling inside without any big air pockets. Use the tines of a fork to seal the open edge, pressing down into the dough all the way around the curve to seal it. Brush the empanada top with some of the milk, then set on a large baking sheet.

12. Repeat steps 10 and 11, to make the remaining 15 empanadas.

13. Bake until golden and hot, about 35 minutes. Cool on the baking sheet for a couple of minutes, then transfer the empanadas to a wire rack to cool for at least 10 minutes before you start to wolf them down. Put them on serving plates and drizzle the *chimichurri* over them.

If you like, you can freeze the baked empanadas. Cool them completely on a wire rack, about 2 hours; then store them in zip-sealed bags. They'll keep in the freezer for up to 4 months. Put them straight from the freezer onto a baking sheet and warm them in a preheated 325°F (165°C) oven for about 15 minutes before serving.

KIBBEH

IT'LL MAKE A DINNER FOR EIGHT. HAVE LOTS OF STUFFED GRAPE
LEAVES, BABA GANOUSH, OLIVES, AND COLD SALADS AS SIDES.

*The city of Aleppo, Syria, brags that it's the birthplace of seventeen
varieties of kibbeh! (And a darn fine pepper, as you'll see on page 189.)
Still, kibbeh is a strange dish for many North Americans: a dough made
with meat and bulgur—that is, parboiled, debranned whole wheat.
The dough is then used to encase a meat filling, sort of like a* picadillo,
*that Latin American staple of ground meat and aromatics. In fact, if
formed into traditional little ovals and fried, kibbeh morphs into (1) a
British staple from various wars in the Middle East, sometimes called*
Syrian torpedoes, *and (2) a popular Latin American dish,* quipe *(kee-
peh), probably brought to the region by Lebanese and Syrian immi-
grants. In any case, it's incredibly delicious: herby, full flavored, and
a crazy-great way to experience goat. For the best taste, serve it with a
lemon tahini sauce (page 34) on the side.*

MORE TO KNOW

In North America, bulgur is sold with
a numerical marking to indicate how
finely it's been ground (that is, the
size of the individual kernels): #1
through #4. It's important you work
with only #1, the finest, for this
dish. All other types will not work.
And do not use cracked wheat,
sometimes mistakenly called *bulgur*
in the United States. Search for the
real thing at health food stores,
high-end markets, online suppliers,
and Middle Eastern or east Indian
supermarkets.

**8 ounces (or 1½ cups [350 ml]) #1 fine
bulgur (see More to Know)**

1½ cups (360 ml) boiling water

¼ cup (55 g) pine nuts

2 pounds (910 g) ground goat, divided

**2 medium yellow onions, finely
chopped, divided into two equal
parts for the recipe**

**3 teaspoons salt, a third of it used at
one point in the recipe and the rest
at another**

1 teaspoon dried sage

1 teaspoon ground allspice

1 teaspoon ground coriander

1 teaspoon ground cumin

**½ teaspoon freshly ground black
pepper**

**2 tablespoons olive oil, plus more if
you're making a kibbeh loaf**

**1 tablespoon ground sumac (see
page 97)**

**Peanut oil, if you're deep-frying
kibbeh balls**

1. Put the bulgur in a medium mixing bowl, pour the water over it, and set
   it aside for 1 hour. Don't be impatient. The bulgur has to absorb all the
   water. And sometimes, because it's already doped with water from ambient humidity, it may not take in the whole amount. If not, you've got to
   squeeze it dry in small handfuls over the sink.

2. While the bulgur soaks, toast the pine nuts in a dry skillet set over
   medium-low heat, stirring often, until very lightly browned, about 3
   minutes. Pour them into a small bowl and set aside until step 7.

3. When all the water has been absorbed into the bulgur, fluff it with a fork,
   separating it into grains. Pour into a food processor fitted with the chopping blade, then add 1 pound (455 g) of the ground meat and half the
   chopped onions. Process until smooth and doughlike, scraping down
   the inside of the canister as necessary with a rubber spatula.

4. Dump this mixture into a bowl; add 2 teaspoons of the salt, the sage, allspice, coriander, cumin, and black pepper. Knead these in with your cleaned, dried hands, about the way you'd work seasonings into a meat loaf mixture. Set this meat dough aside.

5. Heat a large skillet over medium heat, then swirl in the 2 tablespoons olive oil. Add the remaining onions and cook, stirring often, until soft and sweet, about 4 minutes.

6. Add the remaining 1 pound (455 g) ground meat; cook, stirring often, until well browned and thoroughly cooked through, about 10 minutes.

7. Stir in the toasted pine nuts, the sumac, and the remaining 1 teaspoon salt. Let this mixture cool for 15 minutes. And now you've got the two parts of the kibbeh: the dough and the filling. There are two ways to proceed—by baking a kibbeh loaf or deep-frying kibbeh balls.

To bake a kibbeh loaf:

1. Position the rack in the center of the oven and preheat the oven to 350°F (175°C). Lightly grease a 9 x 13-inch (23 x 33-cm) baking dish with some olive oil dabbed on a paper towel.

2. Using half the meat dough, press it into a thin, even layer across the bottom of the baking dish. It's easiest to put little lumps everywhere, then smoosh these together with moistened fingers.

3. Spread the cooked ground meat mixture over this in an even layer.

4. The remaining dough will become the top crust. Pick up some of it, not too much, and flatten it into a thick crust between your palms. It's important to keep your hands damp throughout this whole process. Place this flattened bit on top of the casserole; then make another, and another, filling in the spaces. Begin to pinch and join the pieces together to form a solid top crust across the baking dish—it should be covered completely to all the sides and the corners. Brush the top of the casserole generously with olive oil.

5. Now cut the kibbeh into squares *before* it's baked. The traditional pattern is a set of diamonds, sort of like baklava. Cut 5 or 6 lines across the baking dish, equidistant from each other and parallel to the short sides. Cut all the way through to the bottom, making sure the cuts also go to both sides of the dish. Next, starting at one corner, cut parallel, diagonal lines across the baking dish, working your way to the opposite corner, thereby creating a diamond pattern across the top of the kibbeh.

6. Bake until brown and crisp, 25 to 30 minutes. Cool in the baking dish on a wire rack for 10 minutes before lifting the pieces out one by one.

To deep-fry kibbeh balls:

1. Pick up about ⅓ cup (76 g) of the meat dough and form it into a ball with moistened hands. Use your wet thumb to open up one side of the ball, starting with an indentation, then working it into a little hole, and then bigger and bigger, cupping the ball so that it begins to look like a large, hollow egg, open at one end. Fill this ball with about 2 tablespoons of the ground goat filling, then seal the opening closed—tightly so no filling can leak out. Set aside and make more, about 16 balls.

2. Pour peanut oil into a large, high-sided sauté pan until it comes about 1 inch (2.5 cm) up the sides. Clip a deep-frying thermometer to the inside of the pan and heat the oil over medium heat until the thermometer registers 350°F (175°C).

3. Add the stuffed kibbeh balls, about 4 at a time, and fry them until deeply golden brown on all sides, about 6 minutes. Transfer them to a wire rack set over some paper towels to catch any drips, and fry more. You may have to add a little more oil to fry the next batch.

Once they're all done, whether baked into squares or fried in balls, serve the kibbeh with a lemon tahini sauce (see page 34).

GO ALL OUT! GO ALL OUT! GO ALL OUT! GO ALL OUT! GO ALL OUT!

If you sample the meat and bulgur mixture raw out of the bowl—and we don't recommend it, but *if* you do—you're eating a dish popular in Syria, Lebanon, and even Iraq: *kibbeh nayya*. Minced garlic, mint leaves, olive oil, and lemon juice are added as toppers to a platter of *kibbeh nayya*. And if you take those fried balls and float them in a tomato-stocked vegetable soup, laced with warm spices like cardamom and cloves, plus a little lemon juice for pop, you've got *kubbeh matfuniya*, a staple of Sephardic cooking.

CHAPTER 2

MILK
&
YOGURT

It's not just goat meat. Goat milk is also consumed by more people than any other animal's milk.

So come along and cross a line. The farmer and the cowman might be friends, if my frontier smarts from Rodgers and Hammerstein hold true. But the goat rancher and the goat dairyman go their separate ways. A dairy farmer doesn't milk goats until they're ready for the abattoir.

For one thing, there's a different ethic. You handle someone's nipples and you tend not to want to kill them. (Unless their in-laws get involved.)

More importantly, dairy goats produce copious amounts of milk over the years. They get rather stringy and spent. They're not the best choice for butchering.

The goats' amazing milk production without any helping hormones, combined with their general lack of fussiness *and* their ability to manage pastures without stripping them bare, makes up only part of the story behind their global dominance. The rest lies with the milk's digestibility—or, more specifically, with the structure of the milk fat.

The individual fat molecules in goat milk are very small, a little more than half the size of the fat molecules in cow milk. Specifically, they're about two micrometers across, or 0.002 millimeter. For those of you who refuse to join the One World, United Nations conspiracy called the metric system, that's 0.0000788 inch. For those of you involved in Civil War reenactments, that's 0.000000794 rod.

Tiny, they can crowd in, like grandmothers at a free buffet. On average, 8 ounces (225 g) of whole goat milk has about 10 grams of fat.

More importantly, given the goat-fat globules' Lilliputian size, they're easy to digest. Put crudely, they break down quickly, passing on before fermenting.

They also don't clump—all because of a missing protein called *agglutinin*. Cows produce it; goats don't. It permits the fat in cow milk to gather into luscious clots of cream. Since goat milk lacks agglutinin, the fat rarely clots. It's evenly distributed throughout the milk. The cream may eventually rise to the top, but very slowly and not all of it.

The absence of agglutinin also explains why you'll rarely see fat-free goat milk at your supermarket. Making even low-fat goat milk is a chore. You can't just skim it. Rather, the milk has to be centrifuged—that is, spun in a high-speed chamber until the fat is pulled out of suspension. It's labor-intensive and costly, so you'll almost never see goat cream at your supermarket. What little can be extracted goes to goat butter.

But it's not just the fat. The proteins in goat milk are easy to digest because they are short- to mid-size in their strandlike chains. As such, they form a softer curd than those in cow milk. We'll get to more of this in the next chapter. For now, suffice it to say that a curd is a coagulated protein structure, trapping the fat globules almost by accident. The proteins ball up in the presence of an acid. Stir lemon juice into milk, and you'll see the curds forms. Add the acids in your stomach, and you've got a similar thing going on. Goat milk proteins, when combined with your stomach's acids, don't immediately seize into balls that take more effort to digest.

One other difference, while we're on the subject. Goat milk has 13 percent *more* calcium, 47 percent *more* vitamin A, and a whopping 137 percent *more* potassium than cow milk. Has your doctor told you that you need more potassium? Drink goat milk. (But in all fairness, cow milk has 500 percent more vitamin B-12 and 1,000 percent (!) more folic acid. Which is why goat milk, when given to infants, must then be supplemented with folic acid.)

Goat milk, cow milk—listen, they're both nutritional wonders. Yet when people first taste goat milk, they often have one reaction: *tangy*.

I forswear that word. First off, it's a cliché. But mostly, I don't know that it's true.

What is true is that goat milk has an expanded range of flavors—or to use the current culinary jargon, a bigger *flavor profile*. Taste it. Carefully. That is, a slow sip, held in your mouth a moment while you pull air over your tongue. You'll experience grass, spinach, meat, wheat, beer, and (yes) lemon.

Thus, goat milk and yogurt recipes have to be crafted with a broader range of flavors in mind.

Think of it this way: A good recipe is a five-sided piece of plywood, a pentagon, with *sweet, sour, bitter, spicy*, and *umami* as each of the points.

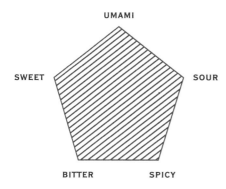

If you're not familiar with umami (Japanese, 旨味, *oo-MAH-mee*, meaning "flavor" or "taste"), it's the basic taste of meat, mushrooms, and good broth: savory, rich, and dense. Long a recognized taste profile in Japan, it's now been given research creds to prove its validity.

OK, now imagine our pentagon tipping one way or the other in any recipe based on the ingredients, then your having to rebalance it by loading flavors onto various other points.

For example, there's a lot of sour in a lemon meringue pie, so you have to balance that taste with sweet (the sugar) as well as some bitter undertones (the grated zest).

Or what about a stew with goat meat and sweet potatoes? You know automatically that you've got heavy weights on the umami and sweet points of that pentagon. Bitter is probably not the best counterbalance, although a little might help. A better place for the weight is the spicy corner, thereby pulling the stew back to an even keel.

Seems simple enough, right? It isn't. There's a complication. Our culinary pentagon isn't sitting on a flat surface. Instead, it tips this way and that

because it's sitting on a fulcrum—that is, the fat in the dish, the point on which the whole structure balances.

If the fat is a flavorless oil like safflower oil, the fulcrum is pretty much under the center of the pentagon, all things being equal. But if the fat is butter, then the fulcrum is no longer directly under the pentagon's center. Instead, it's skewed a little toward the sour point. If the fat is lard, the fulcrum is skewed quite a bit toward the umami point. (Which is why *sweet* fruit pies made with a *lard* crust are so *frickin'* irresistible.) If the fat is almond oil, the fulcrum moves just slightly toward the sweet point. And if it's solid vegetable shortening, the fulcrum is back to a neutral, center point.

Thus, when the fulcrum moves off center, the ingredients lying on top of our flavor pentagon have to be even more heavily weighted one way or another to compensate and balance the dish.

Without a doubt, the fat in goat butter, milk, or even yogurt skews that fulcrum toward a point somewhere more on an axis with the sour and umami points. So a balanced recipe weights the ingredients on the top of our pentagon toward the spicy, bitter, or sweet point—as in the Creamy Carrot-Dill Soup (page 137): lots of sweet (softened onions, carrots) and a little bitter (dill) for a counterpoint to the goat butter and goat milk.

In the end, recipes that use goat butter, milk, or yogurt require a more sophisticated balancing act than those that use relatively neutral, flavorless oils. And there's the real rub: In the United States, we're used to working with neutral tastes like boneless, skinless chicken breasts, all-purpose flour, and even diminished herbs and spices.

If there's one thing Bruce and I want to preach in this tour of the goatapedia, it's that neutral tastes and flavors are not to be commended. Nor are they to be condemned. Neutral is useful as a culinary tool. But rarely. It is not as powerful as deep, sophisticated flavors—like those found in goat milk and yogurt. Using them, we'll be forced to use bolder ingredients, so we'll discover more flavor in every bite. True satiety is found right there. Always has been. We've just forgotten it. Until now.

THE SMELL OF GOAT IN THE MORNING

WE WERE SUPPOSED TO MEET Paul Trubey at Beltane Farm by 7:00 A.M. to watch the morning milking. We'd set out on time but were soon foiled by this modern, it'll-make-your-life-easier, GPS technology.

We pulled up around 8:30. The yard in front of us bled out into the wider meadows. The grass all around was studded with rudbeckia, yellow petals ringing midnight cones, a celebration of all things summer. Across the driveway, a white farmhouse rose as tall as the sugar maples.

But the smell of the barnyard soon closed around me, wrapped me up, a scratchy sweater in August.

We headed up the rutted driveway toward the quintessential New England barn: not tarted up red for tourists, but workaday, sturdy, and weathered, the test of time passed and forgotten.

The big, slatted door stood open. We called out. Nothing. We stepped inside. The floorboards creaked. There was a partitioned room just to our right. A large window was fogged white, but darker shapes were moving inside. I could hear muffled voices. In front of us, hacksaws and axes hung on the wall. I started to wonder. Another creak on the floorboards, and someone smeared a hole in the fog on the window. She leaned her face right to it, pressing her nose to the side. She scowled, then said, "You're not allowed." She held up a huge white bag by its neck, a viscous milk dribbling off its heavy, rounded bottom. Was this some sort of Wes Craven nightmare but with milk?

Just then, Paul came around the corner. He's not a guy you'd mistake for brutal. Or sentimental. He's stocky from hard work, more rugby than soccer, given to flannel but soft-spoken.

"I'm embarrassed we're late," I said, ever the Southerner with an apology at the ready. One little war, and you spend the next hundred and fifty years being sorry.

"Didn't even notice," he said flatly, his hands jammed down into the front pockets of his grimed jeans. "You guys still want to see the goats?"

We both nodded. "I can sure smell them," I said.

"There's no them," he corrected. "There's him. You smell the buck. He's in rut."

Dairies have to keep at least one of the guys around. He mounts the does and thus gets the milk flowing. And he stinks. No doubt about it. Maybe that was the reason that old troll on the bridge didn't want those billy goats crossing over. How much air freshener can a troll keep on hand?

We wandered among the various pens set in the meadows where the grasses danced in the breeze. Back in the barn, his milking parlor was shockingly small, just a few stanchions. For the spring and fall shoulder seasons, when the does don't produce much, Paul does the work by hand.

"And in there?" I asked, pointing to the window that had fogged over again.

"Cheese. But we'll have to save that for another day. We're really under the gun."

As we stepped back out of the barn, we saw one goat outside a pen, lying against a ramshackle fence.

Paul actually stopped to introduce us, an unexpected bit of sentimentalism. "I'd like you to meet Matty."

She was an old goat, the first he'd ever gotten. She was long past milking, long past any usefulness whatsoever. Her teeth were snaggled, a serious underbite giving her a half-hearted smile, a *grande dame* reduced to negotiating the world with cloudy eyes and rickety legs. She had the run of Beltane Farm—if she could have run.

That Paul had hung on to her will tell you everything you need to know about the differences between dairy farms and goat ranches. Time and again as we toured goat dairies across the United States, we were shocked to see so many of the old milkers; long dry, just quiet and peaceful.

Several months later, we went back to see Beltane Farm. This time, it was deep winter, ice streaked across the driveway. I instantly asked about Matty. Paul met my gaze in that quiet New England way: no shrug, no apology. "She died a couple months ago," he said. He told us about the burial he'd given her one cold afternoon.

It's that relationship that makes good milk: the calm assurance among the goats that the world will stay on an even keel, that they will be cared for to the end.

It's pretty much the same with us. Except most of us don't have a Paul Trubey on our side.

WHEAT GERM–BANANA MUFFINS

YOU'LL GET ABOUT A DOZEN MUFFINS, BUT READ
THE CAVEAT IN THE FIRST STEP.

*To balance the goat milk in these healthy muffins, the bananas offer
a sweet, delicate richness, while the so-called warm spices (cinnamon
and nutmeg) lend a slightly bitter undertone. Rather than using goat
butter as the fat, Bruce went for walnut oil, a deeper taste and another
counterbalance in the overall equation. In other words, this is a great
place to start a culinary exploration of goat milk: not too assertive,
balanced, with some of those characteristic notes in the mix.*

MORE TO KNOW

Wheat germ—that is, the germ
removed from wheat kernels—is sold
toasted (and thus more flavorful) or
untoasted. The toasted variety offers
a deeper, richer taste. Once opened,
store it in the refrigerator.

¼ cup (60 ml) **toasted walnut oil, plus
more for greasing the muffin pan**

2⅓ cups (315 g) **all-purpose flour**

1 cup (225 g) **toasted wheat germ**

2 teaspoons **baking soda**

1 teaspoon **baking powder**

½ teaspoon **ground cinnamon**

½ teaspoon **salt**

¼ teaspoon **freshly grated nutmeg**

2 large **eggs, at room temperature**

½ cup (115 g) **packed dark brown
sugar**

½ cup (120 ml) **honey**

1½ cups (360 ml) **regular or low-fat
goat milk**

2 ripe **bananas, peeled and diced**

1 tablespoon **vanilla extract**

1. Make sure the rack is in the center of the oven; heat the oven to 400°F
   (205°C). Put a little walnut oil on a crumpled paper towel and grease the
   indentations of a 12-indentation muffin tin.

   One note: There's no standard-size muffin tin. That said, those with
   indentations that hold between ½ and ⅔ cup (120 and 165 ml) are considered "normal" in North America. Because of this lack of standard-
   ization—a curious failing in our otherwise puritanical country—muffin
   batters are inexact formulas. If this recipe makes more batter than your
   tin can hold in one baking go-round, just make a second batch. You can
   also make these muffins in mini muffin tins, but the baking time should
   be reduced by half, if not a little more.

2. Use a fork to mix up the flour, wheat germ, baking soda, baking powder,
   cinnamon, salt, and nutmeg in a large bowl, making sure the leavening
   agents and spices are evenly distributed.

3. Whip the eggs, brown sugar, and honey with an electric mixer at medium
   speed in a large bowl until pale brown and fluffy, about 5 minutes. Beat
   in the milk and bananas. When fairly smooth, do the same with the
   ¼ cup (60 ml) oil and vanilla.

4. Turn off the beaters, scrape any of the banana mixture on them back
   into the bowl, and dump in the flour mixture. No beaters this time. Just
   stir with a wooden spoon or rubber spatula until there are no pockets of
   undissolved flour.

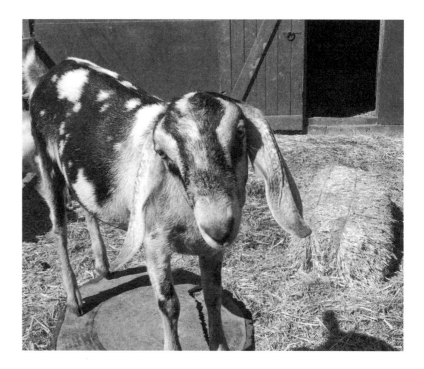

5. Divide the batter among the indentations of the prepared muffin tin, filling each about two-thirds to three-quarters full. If you've got any batter leftover, save it for a second baking. There's no need to grease the indentations a second time. However, cool the muffin tin for at least 10 minutes before using it again. A hot muffin tin can cause overrisen, malformed muffins.

6. Bake until the muffins are puffed, browned, and set, 18 to 20 minutes. Cool in the muffin tin for a couple minutes; then turn them out onto a wire rack, righting them so they look like little mushrooms. Continue cooling to room temperature. (See how many last. Especially if you've got some butter nearby.) The cooled muffins can be stored in a zip-sealed plastic bag at room temperature for a couple days—or in the freezer for several months.

GOAT CHEESE DANISHES

AFTER A GAZILLION HOURS IN THE KITCHEN, YOU'LL EMERGE COVERED
WITH FLOUR, HOLDING A PLATTER OF EIGHTEEN FILLED SWEET ROLLS.

Nothing sets up Christians like pastries. When I was growing up in Texas, danishes were our go-to treat before church. Of course, we never made them ourselves, what with getting the clip-on tie on straight and everything else that had to be done on Sunday mornings. But after I left the South, got involved with a New Yorker, and moved to New England, I actually learned how to make these particularly little bits of divine creation. Suffice it to say, they involve making a type of puff pastry, this time leavened with yeast, a task for a weekend when you want to play around in the kitchen, get your hands dirty, and expand your skills. You'll end up with light, crunchy pockets filled with sweetened goat cheese. You don't even have to be on your way to church to gobble them down.

For the dough:

½ cup (70 g) **cake flour**

16 tablespoons (that is, 1 cup [225 g] or 2 sticks) **cool goat butter, cubed**

¾ cup (180 ml) **plus** 1 tablespoon (15 ml) **regular goat milk (do not use low-fat)**

3 tablespoons **sugar**

2¼ teaspoons **active dry yeast**

2⅔ cups (330 g) **all-purpose flour, plus more for dusting your work surface**

1 large egg, well beaten in a small bowl

For the filling:

9 ounces (250 g) **fresh chèvre or soft goat cheese, at room temperature**

1 large egg, at room temperature

1 tablespoon **sugar**

1½ teaspoons **all-purpose flour**

½ teaspoon **freshly grated nutmeg**

LESS TO DO

Buy frozen puff pastry sheets, thaw them according to the package's instructions, and cut into squares as this recipe directs. Top the squares with the goat cheese filling, fold them as directed, seal them with an egg-and-water wash, and bake.

1. Put the cake flour in a big bowl, then drop in the cool butter cubes—that is, right out of the fridge, just now cut into little pieces. Use a fork or a pastry cutter to push the fat through the flour, continually working it all around the bowl, cleaning the tines often, then going at it again. There's way more fat here than flour, way more butter than you'd use for a pie crust, so the resulting mixture will be about the consistency of the stuff in a jar of elementary-school paste that's been left uncovered overnight.

You can also do this task in a food processor fitted with the chopping blade. Add the flour and butter, and process until the mass starts to adhere into a ball.

2. Line a clean, dry work surface with wax paper. Gather the dough together, then turn it out onto the wax paper. Set another sheet of wax paper on top. Roll the dough into a 9 x 12-inch (23 x 30.5-cm) rectangle. Note the missing words *about* or *approximately*. Don't cheat; use a ruler and make the rectangle exactly the right size by repositioning the rolling pin repeatedly and rolling just once or twice in each direction before changing and rolling in another set of directions. Once you've got the rectangle, pick it up still between its sheets of wax paper, set it on a large

baking sheet, and put the whole thing in the fridge for at least 1 hour or up to 24 hours.

3. Heat the milk in a large saucepan over low heat until the milk is between 100°F and 105°F (38°C and 41°C). It's important to be accurate. Use an instant-read meat thermometer to be sure, taking the milk's temperature without letting the probe touch the pan itself.

4. Once the milk is at the right temperature, take it off the heat and stir in 3 tablespoons sugar and the yeast. Set the pan aside for 5 minutes to proof the yeast—that is, to make sure it's bubbly, even foamy, starting to come alive and producing the fizzy carbon dioxide that will eventually make the pastry rise.

5. Dump in the 2⅔ cups (330 g) all-purpose flour and 2½ tablespoons of the beaten egg (reserve the rest of the beaten egg in the fridge for later in the recipe). Stir a bit; then once the stuff starts to form a dough, turn it out onto a clean, dry, lightly flour-dusted work surface and knead for 2 minutes, pulling it with one hand while twisting the stretched lump and at the same time digging the palm of your other hand into it. Basically, you want to create a smooth dough, not as silky as good bread dough, but still coherent and cohesive. Cover it with a clean kitchen towel and let it rest on the counter for 10 minutes.

6. Clean up your work surface so it's got no sticky bits of dough, dry it well, then dust it lightly with flour. Set the lump of dough in the center and use a rolling pin to roll it into a 14 x 20-inch (35.5 x 50-cm) rectangle.

7. Take the chilled butter dough out of the fridge and set it on top of and at one end of the flour dough so that the 12-inch (30.5-cm) side of the buttery rectangle is an inch (2.5 cm) or so from but also parallel to the 14-inch (35.5-cm) side of the larger sheet of dough. Turn the dough so that the buttery rectangle is farthest from you. Now fold the larger dough sheet up and over the buttery one, thereby encasing it. Work around the dough to seal all the edges.

8. Roll it out again into a large rectangle, about 14 x 20 inches (35.5 x 50 cm)—not exactly this time, just close enough. If you knead it during this step, you can dust your work surface with a little flour, but do so as infrequently as possible, using as little as possible. More flour = more gluten = the possibility of a tougher dough.

9. Take one short side of this rectangle and fold it over until it comes to the two-thirds mark on the rectangle's long side. Now take the other

exposed side and fold it over the other way, thus folding the piece of dough into three equal sections on top of each other. Roll this piece of dough out into a large rectangle, about 14 x 20 inches (36 x 51 cm). Then do this three more times: folding it into thirds and rolling it back out, and then again, and then again. Fold the dough into thirds one last time, then set it in the refrigerator to chill for 1 hour.

10. Meanwhile, prepare the filling: Mix the fresh chèvre or soft goat cheese, the large whole egg (not the reserved beaten egg), the sugar, all-purpose flour, and nutmeg in a bowl until creamy and smooth. Take out that remainder of the beaten egg from the fridge and whisk it with 1½ table-spoons water.

11. To make the danishes, take the chilled dough out of the refrigerator and slice it into 3 equal pieces. Clean and dry that work surface yet again. (Is it any wonder why pastry chefs are so irritable?) Give it a light dust-ing with flour. On that surface, roll each piece of the dough out to a 6 x 8-inch (15 x 20-cm) rectangle, about ¼ inch (.6 cm) thick. Be fairly precise but not obsessive—because once all 3 are rolled out, you will trim them to perfect 5 x 7½-inch (13 x 19-cm) rectangles with perfectly straight edges. (The excess dough can be thrown out or baked on its own for little puff pastry twists or braids.)

12. Cut each of these rectangles into six 2½ x 2½-inch (6 x 6-cm) squares. In other words, make one straight cut parallel to the 7½-inch (19-cm) sides, and two even cuts parallel to the 5-inch (13-cm) sides.

13. Place a heaping tablespoon of the filling in each square. Fold the corners of each square toward the center to meet in the middle over the filling. Dab a little of the beaten-egg-and-water mixture on the dough to seal it at the center point. Once all the little packets are made, line a large baking sheet with a silicone mat or parchment paper, and put the filled packets on a large baking sheet, cover them with a clean kitchen towel, and let them rest at room temperature for 30 minutes. Meanwhile, position the rack in the center of the oven and preheat the oven to 400°F (205°C).

14. Bake until the danishes are puffed and golden brown, about 20 minutes. Cool for a minute or two on the baking sheet, then transfer to a wire rack and continue cooling. Once they're at room temperature (if they make it that long), they can be stored on the counter in a zip-sealed plastic bag for a couple of days or in the freezer for several months.

YOGHURT BROT

Or call it yogurt bread. That is, YOH-guhrt BROAT *in German. Crack
that second* r *into a guttural, and you'll have the right pronunciation.
As its name implies, this recipe uses goat yogurt, a fairly complex flavor profile in these traditional German loaves, made with lots of seeds
and rye flour, to boot, all counterbalance against the yogurt's more
assertive taste. As I said, it's all about balance.*

1¾ cups (420 ml) **lukewarm water,
between 105°F and 115°F (41°C and
46°C [don't guess—take its tempera-
ture])**

5½ teaspoons **active dry yeast (two
¼-ounce [two 10-g] packages)**

½ teaspoon **sugar**

8 ounces (240 ml) **regular goat yogurt
(do not use low-fat), strictly at room
temperature**

1 cup (225 g) **rye flour**

1 cup (225 g) **pumpkin seeds**

½ cup (115 g) **white sesame seeds**

½ cup (115 g) **unsalted sunflower
seeds**

6 to 6½ cups (1.4 to 1.5 kg) **bread
flour, maybe even more, plus additional for dusting your work surface**

½ teaspoon **salt**

**Walnut or almond oil, for greasing
the bowl**

1 large **egg white beaten with 2
tablespoons water in a small bowl**

1. Whisk the water, yeast, and sugar in a large bowl. Set aside until fizzy,
   even foamy, about 10 minutes.

2. Whisk in the yogurt. Remember: It must be at room temperature. If it's
   cold, it will shock the yeast and the bread will not rise.

3. Stir in the rye flour, pumpkin seeds, sesame seeds, and sunflower seeds.
   Then stir in 6 cups (1.4 kg) bread flour to make a dough—or perhaps
   a little more—plus the salt. In the end, the dough will be firm, hard to
   work with, but still moist.

4. Dust a clean, dry work surface with bread flour, then turn the dough
   onto it. Knead for 10 minutes. It's tough on the fingers. It's one of the
   reasons old German grandmothers are notoriously impatient. Well, that
   and the Nazi thing. Anyway, twist the dough, digging the palm of one
   hand into it while turning the loaf with the other, all the while stretching
   it as you pull it. If your forearms get tired, you're actually not applying
   enough pressure. This is shoulder work, not arm work.

5. Lightly oil the inside of a large bowl, then turn the dough into it. Turn
   the dough over to coat with the oil. Cover the bowl with a kitchen towel
   and set it in a warm, dry place until the dough has doubled in bulk, 1½
   to 2 hours.

Bruce has a fancy setting on his tricked-out oven that lets the temperature hover at 100°F (38°C), so he uses the inside of the oven as a place for his dough to rise. You can also choose to put yours near a radiator in the winter, or in the laundry room if you're running the dryer, or in the basement boiler room, or even near a sunny window on a winter day (the summer sun is too intense). Failing all that, you can always run a large towel on high heat in the dryer for 10 minutes, then wrap it loosely around the bowl to create a warm, draft-free environment inside the bowl.

6. Divide the dough in half; form each half on a flour-dusted counter into a pointy, flat-bottomed oval loaf, like a football cut in half through the narrow ends, and set, flat side down, on your counter.

7. Line a large baking sheet with a silicone baking mat or parchment paper. Set the loaves on top. Cover them with that kitchen towel and set them back in that fabled warm, draft-free place until doubled again in volume, between 45 minutes and 1 hour.

8. Meanwhile, position the rack in the oven's middle and preheat the oven to 400°F (205°C).

9. Brush each loaf with the egg white mixture, then slide the tray into the oven. Bake until browned and the loaves sound resoundingly hollow when tapped on the bottom, about 35 minutes. Unless you want a nasty burn, don't pick them up with your bare hands when they're in the oven. Use oven mitts or a couple of clean kitchen towels to turn them on their sides before tapping gently. Once they're done, cool them on the baking sheet for 5 minutes before transferring them to a wire rack to cool completely. After that, put them in large, zip-sealed plastic bags to store at room temperature for up to 2 days; or freeze them in those bags for several months.

MORE TO KNOW

There are several reasons bread doughs don't rise:

1. Yeast is a living organism. Yours should be fresh. Check the expiration date.

2. Salt retards and even kills yeast. That's why it's added as late as possible in a recipe—so it's as diluted as possible among the other ingredients.

3. Yeast will meet its end in the presence of too-hot ingredients. And it will not wake up and do its work in the presence of cold ingredients. It thrives around 110°F (43°C), a little hotter than bath water.

4. The dough must be kneaded. Don't shortchange this step, although it's labor-intensive. Kneading develops the wheat's gluten, stretching it out so that it can trap that carbon dioxide created by the yeast and force the bread to rise.

5. The place where the dough rises cannot be cool. Between 75°F and 85°F (24°C and 29°C) is ideal.

SAVORIES

BY NOW YOU CAN SEE that being a goatherd is not an easy matter. These animals are both smart and independent, like a pet dog or cat. Images dealing with a herd of those. But let's say you were going to be a goatherd. Let's just say. You must first decide *why* you want to be a goatherd. You've got three options:

1. Meat These days, you're most likely going to go with the Boer goat, brought fairly recently to North America from South Africa. Although some of the Boers at 4-H shows are hulking creatures, most are small, more diminutive than the girls who stand on the milking line. Most Boers are also white with red or brown splotches, although some have splotchy red or brown coats. They're not skittish; however, they're also not terribly friendly. In the end, they just don't see humans as a source of food or udder relief.

Other popular meat breeds include the Kiko from New Zealand, with its broad, don't-mess-with-me horns; the Savanna, mostly white, with well-muscled haunches and (like a superhero gone to seed) loose skin at the neck; and the famed Myotonic goats, also called the Tennessee fainters—as if they were a bridge club prone to moral outrage. These pass out for up to ten seconds when startled.

2. Wool You're looking for soft hair and a calm disposition. You can't cuddle with well-muscled haunches. (Consider this relationship advice as well.) You might first consider cashmere goats and their near kin, the pashminas. Their wool is renowned, but separating the soft stuff from the coarse hairs is quite a job. So you'll probably end up going with Angoras, small goats that came out of Turkey to the delight of the knitting and spinning set. An Angora's hair—called mohair (a.k.a. my contact lens is killing me)—is lush and prolific: One of these babies can bring in 12 pounds (5.4 kg) of mohair a year. Although a bit athletic, an Angora will go in for quite a bit of brushing and grooming, much like the closet-case cheerleaders in your high school.

3. Milk (and thus yogurt and cheese, too)
You'll probably select from these five breeds:

⁂ **Nubians,** larger than Boers, bulky, almost the dairy cow of goats (in looks only, because the breed actually produces less milk than some others), with a short, glossy coat and long, dangling ears.

⁂ **Oberhaslis,** moderate milk producers from Switzerland with fairly big ears that stick straight out from the head like little wings; a little smaller than Nubians, with a reddish brown or black coat, but a bit aggressive (in mixed packs, an Oberhasli will most often be the goat queen).

⁂ **Alpines,** a smaller breed, from the French Alps, but a great dairy goat, producing a particularly fatty milk, best in cheeses and ice cream

⁂ **Saanens,** another breed from Switzerland, this one pure white, with ears like the Oberhaslis but an otherwise gentle, almost passive temperament; known for its high milk production and for the fact that both bucks and does have horns.

⁂ **La Manchas,** sturdy but limber, noted for their minuscule, sometimes almost missing, ears (no more than cartilage buds in some cases), as well as for their sweet, fragrant milk.

Although there are milking differences among these breeds, the real difference often lies with the amount of fat. The milk from Alpines, for example, is about 4.8 percent butterfat; from La Manchas, about 3.9 percent. As a dairy farmer, you'll work like a French vintner, blending from different breeds to produce a balanced product.

And that's the goat tally. Go forth and herd. Or failing that, eat.

DECONSTRUCTED LASSI

YOU'LL END UP WITH FOUR FIRST-COURSE STARTERS FOR A MEAL.

Lassi *is a broad name for a range of yogurt drinks, enjoyed across Southeast Asia and into India. Some are savory with even saffron in the mix; others are quite sweet, laced with fruit purees. This version is my own whimsy—rather than whirred together in a blender, it's left in pieces, a first course on a plate, not in a glass. The simple concoction highlights elemental flavors and really gets everyone ready for the bigger flavors to come in the meal.*

2 cups (480 ml) regular or low-fat
   goat yogurt

¼ teaspoon ground cinnamon

¼ teaspoon salt

⅛ teaspoon ground cardamom

2 ripe mangoes

¼ cup (55 g) chopped unsalted,
   shelled pistachios or cashews

2 tablespoons honey

1. Mix the yogurt, cinnamon, salt, and cardamom in a small bowl. Cover and refrigerate for at least 4 hours or overnight.

2. Peeling and pitting a mango can be a chore. First off, you've got to get around the seed inside. It's fairly flat and shaped much like the fruit itself. The two fleshy, protruding sides of the fruit mound over the flat sides of the seed. Set the mango on your work surface on one of its thin sides. Cut straight down on each protruding side, slicing as close to the seed as possible and removing the mounding flesh with its skin. Score the flesh inside each half with a knife, making a checkerboard pattern without cutting through to the skin. The smaller you make the checkerboard, the smaller the dice you're creating. Now begin to bend the flesh back, as if you were starting to turn the thing inside out. The little cubes you made will pop up as you do so. Slice these off, as close to the skin as possible.

3. Divide the diced mangoes among four plates. Top each with ½ cup (120 ml) of the yogurt. Sprinkle 1 tablespoon of the chopped pistachios or cashews over each serving, then drizzle each with 1½ teaspoons of the honey.

CELERY ROOT RAITA

IT'LL MAKE ABOUT EIGHT SIDE-DISH SERVINGS.

This creamy but light salad is a cross between céleri-rave en rémou-lade *(celery root remoulade), a French sauce and Indian raita—a cross made possible because of the goat yogurt, which balances all those flavors beautifully. Serve this salad as a side to almost anything off the grill—especially goat chops (see page 20). Or offer it as a topper for hot dogs or sausages at your next barbecue, a new twist instead of sauerkraut.*

1 large celery root (a.k.a. celeriac), peeled

2 cups (480 ml) regular or low-fat goat yogurt

1 small cucumber, peeled, seeded, and finely diced

¼ cup (55 g) minced fresh mint

1 teaspoon ground cumin

½ teaspoon salt

Several dashes of hot red pepper sauce, such as Tabasco, or to taste

1. Bring a big pot of water to a boil over high heat.

2. The hardest part of this recipe is dealing with that gnarly celery root. After you peel it, you have to get it into fine threads or small matchsticks. You can do this in several ways:

☞ Use a Benriner, the Japanese kitchen tool that makes those long threads from daikon or carrots, usually wound into little nests onto sushi plates. Follow the manufacturer's instructions for selecting the right blade and turning the celery root into long threads. These should then be cut into manageable bits so they're not too irritating on a fork. (Nobody wants to slurp a raita.)

☞ Shred the peeled celery root using the large holes of a box grater or the large-holed shredding blade of a food processor.

☞ Cut the root into ⅛-inch (.3-cm) slices, then cut these into ⅛-inch-wide (.3-cm) matchsticks. Some of the matchsticks might be a little long for a forkful, so cut these in half.

3. Once you've got the celery root prepared, drop the bits into the pot of boiling water and blanch for 1 minute. Drain in a colander set in the sink and rinse with cool water, tossing all the time, until all the pieces are cool to the touch. Drain well again, then spread them out on paper towels and blot them dry. Place them in a serving bowl.

4. Add all the other ingredients. Stir well and serve, or chill for up to 8 hours, stirring again before serving.

CREAMY CARROT-DILL SOUP

**CONSIDER IT ENOUGH TO SERVE FOUR FOR A MAIN COURSE
WITH A SALAD, UP TO EIGHT FOR A FIRST COURSE.**

*Goat milk brightens this comforting soup, tilting it from a mere winter
warmer into a fresh, gorgeous bowl of big flavors. It's even better the
next day—although you may have to thin it out with a little extra broth
when reheating it over medium-low heat.*

3 tablespoons (45 g) **goat butter**

1 small **yellow onion**, chopped

3 tablespoons **all-purpose flour**

2 cups (480 ml) **reduced-sodium
chicken broth**

2 cups (480 ml) **regular or low-fat
goat milk**

1 pound (455 g) **carrots, peeled and
cut into thin rounds**

2 tablespoons minced fresh, stemmed,
dill fronds

1 tablespoon **Worcestershire sauce**

½ teaspoon freshly ground **black
pepper**

Salt (optional)

1. Melt the butter in a large saucepan over medium heat. Add the onion
   and cook, stirring often, until translucent and soft, about 5 minutes.

2. Sprinkle the flour over the onion and stir for 1 minute.

3. Whisk in a few dribbles of the broth, then more, and then the rest in a
   slow, steady stream, taking care to dissolve the flour into a paste before
   whisking constantly and efficiently to make sure there are no lumps.

4. Whisk in the milk (no need for caution here if the flour has been properly dissolved in the broth); then continue whisking over the heat until
   the mixture comes to a simmer and thickens a bit, probably a couple
   minutes.

5. Stir in the carrots, dill, Worcestershire sauce, and pepper. Once the soup
   returns to a simmer, cover the pan, reduce the heat to very low, and simmer slowly until the carrots are tender, stirring fairly often, about 40
   minutes.

6. Transfer the soup to a large blender, working in batches as necessary, so
   that the canister is never more than about half full. Cover the canister,
   but remove the lid's center plug. Doing so will help equalize the pressure
   under the lid so hot stuff doesn't spew all over the kitchen. However,
   also place a clean kitchen towel over the lid as extra insurance. Blend the
   soup to a smooth puree. Pour into a bowl if you're working in batches;
   but once it's all pureed, pour it back into the saucepan. Set over medium
   heat just to warm it through before serving. Worcestershire sauce is
   salty, but check the overall taste to make sure the soup is salty enough
   for your liking.

> **MORE GOATY GOODNESS**
>
> Serve the soup with goat
> cheese croutons floating in
> each bowl (see page 181).

CHILLED BLUEBERRY TZATZIKI SOUP

DEPENDS. MAYBE SIX SERVINGS AS A LUNCH WITH A SALAD;
A FEW MORE SERVINGS AS A FIRST COURSE FOR DINNER.

Bruce had a lot of fun morphing the classic Greek dip of cucumbers and yogurt into a fresh, summery soup. He added blueberries as a sweet accent against the goat yogurt—and then added a canned chipotle for some fire. It's all about balance on our culinary pentagon (see page 121).

2 medium cucumbers

2 cups (455 g) blueberries

1 cup (240 ml) regular or low-fat goat yogurt

2 tablespoons honey

2 tablespoons lemon juice

1 teaspoon minced fresh oregano leaves

½ teaspoon salt

2 medium garlic cloves, minced

1 canned chipotle chile in adobo sauce, seeded and chopped (see page 59)

1. Peel the cucumbers, then cut them in half lengthwise. Use a small spoon to scrape out the seeds; discard them. Chop the cucumbers into chunks and put them in a food processor fitted with the chopping blade or in a large blender.

2. Add all the other ingredients. (Make sure you get that last ingredient right: one canned chipotle in adobo sauce, not a whole can of them.) Process or blend until the soup is fairly smooth, if a little chunky, just for a bit of texture.

3. Serve at once at room temperature—or store in the fridge in a sealed container (even the blender's canister) for up to 5 days. In this case, the soup tastes best when it's only slightly chilled, just a tad below room temperature, so let it sit out on the counter for 20 minutes before serving.

GARLIC AND PARSNIP FLANS

YOU'LL END UP WITH SIX INDIVIDUAL FLANS.

These flans are rich and savory, a great way to forgo the potatoes or rice with dinner but still have a sophisticated side dish that complements bolder flavors—like those in the Shoulder Roast (page 27).

4 large parsnips, peeled and cut into ½-inch (1.2-cm) slices	2 large egg yolks, at room temperature
6 medium garlic cloves, peeled	½ teaspoon salt
1 cup (240 ml) regular goat milk (do not use low-fat)	½ teaspoon freshly ground black pepper
Goat butter for greasing the ramekins	Boiling water

1. Put the parsnips and garlic in a medium saucepan, pour in the milk, and bring to a simmer over medium heat. Cover, reduce the heat to very low, and simmer slowly until the parsnips are tender when poked with a fork, about 30 minutes. Set the pan aside off the heat and cool, still covered, for 30 minutes.

2. Meanwhile, get the rack into the center of the oven and preheat that oven to 350°F (175°C). Lightly butter six ⅓-cup (75-ml), oven-safe ramekins, making sure to get the fat down into the angle between the bottom and the sides. Set these in a large baking dish or a roasting pan.

3. Pour the contents of the saucepan into a large food processor fitted with the chopping blade or into a large blender. Pulse or blend a bit to get the parsnips and garlic mushed. Add the yolks, salt, and pepper. Process until smooth.

4. Pour the contents of the food processor into the prepared ramekins, dividing the mixture evenly among them. It's a tad difficult to pour from a processor bowl, so you might want to scrape the mixture into a pitcher and pour from there.

5. Set the baking dish or the roasting pan with the ramekins on the oven rack, then pour boiling water into the dish or pan until the water level comes about halfway up the ramekins.

6. Bake until set, until a knife inserted into one of the flans comes out clean, 35 to 40 minutes. Remove the ramekins from their water bath (remember that the water is hot!) and set them on a wire rack to cool for 5 minutes. Run a thin knife around the inside edges of the ramekins to loosen the flans, then turn the custards upside down onto serving plates.

CORN PUDDING

IT SHOULD FEED ABOUT EIGHT AS A SIDE DISH. WON'T, BUT SHOULD.

I grew up on this stuff, but without goat milk. Which was a shame, because the chiles and spices overrode the other flavors. Unbalanced, for sure. So goat milk and cheese to the rescue!

6 husked corn ears, any silks removed

6 tablespoons (90 g) goat butter, plus more for greasing the dish

6 medium shallots, minced

2 jalapeño chiles, stemmed, seeded, and minced

½ teaspoon cumin seeds

5 large eggs, at room temperature, whisked in a medium bowl until smooth

2 cups (480 ml) regular or low-fat goat milk

½ cup (115 g) finely ground yellow cornmeal

8 ounces (225 g) fresh chèvre or soft goat cheese

3 tablespoons minced fresh basil leaves

2 ounces (55 g) grated hard goat cheese, such as goat Gruyère or goat Gouda, or a crottin you've aged yourself (see page 199)

1. Prepare a grill for high-heat (about 550°F [288°C]) cooking—that is, either preheat a gas grill to high heat or build a high-heat, red-hot-but-well-ashed coal bed in a charcoal grill. Alternatively, heat a grill pan over medium-high heat.

2. Set the corn ears on the grill grate directly over the heat source—or in the grill pan. Grill until charred a bit on all sides, turning with tongs once in a while, perhaps 2 to 3 minutes.

3. Set the corn on a cutting board. Position the rack in the center of the oven and preheat the oven to 375°F (190°C). Butter the inside of a 9-inch (23-cm) square baking dish, a 2-quart (2-L) round soufflé dish, or a 2-quart (2-L) au gratin pan.

4. Cut one end off the corn cobs so they'll stand up straight on the cutting board, then run a paring knife down the ears, slicing off the kernels. Put the grilled kernels in a large bowl.

5. Melt the butter in a large saucepan set over medium-low heat. Add the shallots and jalapeños; cook, stirring occasionally, until the shallots soften and begin to turn golden, about 5 minutes. Stir in the cumin seeds; cook for 15 seconds or so. Then scrape the contents of the pan into the bowl with the corn kernels.

6. Stir in the eggs, milk, cornmeal, fresh chèvre, and basil until fairly smooth. Pour this mixture into the prepared baking dish; sprinkle the grated hard cheese over the top.

7. Bake the pudding until set and even browning a little across the top, perhaps 40 to 45 minutes. Cool on a wire rack for 5 minutes and serve.

FRIED CHICKEN

HOW MANY PEOPLE DO EIGHT TO TEN PIECES OF FRIED CHICKEN
SERVE? THREE NORMAL PEOPLE, SIX PEOPLE BEING GOOD, OR
A HUNDRED AND TWENTY THOUSAND SUPERMODELS?

Marinating chicken in yogurt is an old-fashioned technique, hailing from the days when a barnyard fowl's skin was pretty tough. It's not really necessary these days—except as a boost to flavor. And who can argue with how goat yogurt adds a pop to this comfort-food classic?

One 4-pound (one 1.8-kg) **chicken,
any giblets removed, cut into 8 to
10 pieces**

1 cup (240 ml) **regular or low-fat goat
yogurt**

1½ cups (185 g) **all-purpose flour**

1 tablespoon **mild paprika**

2 teaspoons **salt, plus more to taste**

2 teaspoons **freshly ground black
pepper**

½ teaspoon **freshly grated nutmeg**

About 4 cups (960 ml) **peanut oil**

1. Place the chicken pieces in a large glass baking dish, stainless steel bowl, or other nonreactive container. Add the yogurt and stir well. Refrigerate for 2 to 4 hours, stirring occasionally.

   Do not let the chicken sit in the yogurt for any longer. It can turn the chicken skin from tough to tender and then back to tough again. Plus, there are issues with bacterial growth. Be safe, not sorry.

2. Put the flour, paprika, salt, pepper, and nutmeg in a big bag, like an unused paper supermarket bag. Seal it and shake it well to distribute the spices throughout the flour.

3. Pour enough peanut oil into a large, high-sided sauté pan to bring the oil to a depth of about 2 inches (5 cm). Clip a deep-frying thermometer to the inside of the pan and warm the oil over medium heat until the temperature registers 350°F (175°C).

4. Add the chicken pieces with any yogurt still adhering to them to the bag with the flour mixture. Seal again and shake well to coat the chicken. You may need to hit the bag on the bottom a couple of times to bounce all the pieces into new positions, to coat them thoroughly.

5. Remove the chicken pieces from the bag and place as many as will fit without crowding in the hot oil. (Leave the remainder of the pieces in the bag.) Fry until golden brown on both sides, turning once or twice, about 10 minutes for the wings and legs, 15 minutes for the thighs, and up to 20 minutes for the breasts. You'll need to adjust the burner's temperature so that the oil temperature remains constant. And resist turning the pieces too quickly. You want a dark crust. Is there another reason why you're frying chicken?

6. Set a double layer of paper towels under a wire cooling rack, then use tongs to transfer the chicken pieces to that rack. (The paper towels will catch any drips.) Sprinkle a little salt over the pieces while they're still hot. Then go ahead and fry more pieces, if you need to. Throw out any remaining yogurt marinade and the excess flour mixture in the bag.

GO ALL OUT! GO ALL OUT! GO ALL OUT! GO ALL OUT! GO ALL OUT!

Fried chicken needs a well-stocked salad with a creamy dressing. Try this one, based on rouille, the thickener used in bouillabaisse. First, toast ⅓ cup (76 g) chopped hazelnuts in a dry skillet over medium-low heat until lightly browned and aromatic, about 4 minutes. Pour the hazelnut pieces into the bowl of a food processor, let cool for 10 minutes, then add 2 bottled roasted red peppers, 2 chopped garlic cloves, 3 tablespoons olive oil, 1½ tablespoons white wine vinegar, ½ teaspoon sugar, ½ teaspoon salt, and ½ teaspoon freshly ground black pepper. Whir this up into a dressing. Pour it on a mixed salad of peeled, seeded, and chopped cucumbers, thinly sliced celery, pitted and halved cherries, sliced radishes, torn-up romaine leaves, and a little bit of chopped basil or tarragon leaves.

TANDOORI GAME HENS

HERE'S THE MATH: TWO BIRDS = FOUR SERVINGS.
FEEL FREE TO MULTIPLY AT WILL.

LESS TO DO

Admittedly, step 2 is a pain. If you don't want to do your own butchering and skinning, ask the guy at your supermarket to do it for you.

MORE GOATY GOODNESS

This technique of the spice rub and yogurt marinade will also work with goat rib chops (see page 22). To match the marinade, plan on a similar weight of chops (about 3 pounds' [1.4 kg] worth).

Was there ever a country like India, so well versed in what to do with goat in all its forms? Here, the yogurt does good service against the cayenne and lemon juice. A tandoor oven is a super-hot-fire cave that flash-roasts meats. Since most of us don't have one of these fancy gizmos at home, a grill will do—or even a broiler. Serve this flavorful dish with Celery Root Raita (page 135) as well as bottled chutney and cooked basmati rice.

2 tablespoons lemon juice

1 teaspoon cayenne pepper

1 teaspoon salt

Two 1½- to 1¾-pound (two 680- to 800-g) **game hens**

⅓ **cup** (75 ml) **regular or low-fat goat milk**

⅓ **cup** (75 ml) **regular or low-fat goat yogurt**

1 tablespoon minced peeled fresh ginger

3 medium garlic cloves, minced or put through a garlic press

1 teaspoon ground cumin

½ teaspoon ground turmeric

¼ teaspoon ground cinnamon

¼ teaspoon ground cloves

1. Mix the lemon juice, cayenne, and salt in a small bowl until a wet paste.

2. Split the game hens in half lengthwise. Here's how: Set them, breast side up, on a cutting board. Look inside the large chamber and see where the backbone runs. Insert a sharp chef's knife and cut down on both sides of the spine, thereby removing it in each bird. Now open the birds out on the counter with the skin side facing you. If you press down a bit, you may hear the breastbone crack. Cut right down the center length of each bird, dividing it in half. Now that the birds lie in two halves, peel off the skin, cutting it in places with a knife to help it come free, particularly around the wings and the legs.

3. Rub the cayenne paste into the meat of the split game hens. Set them in a baking dish or roasting pan and refrigerate, uncovered, for 30 minutes.

4. Meanwhile, whisk the milk, yogurt, ginger, garlic, cumin, turmeric, cinnamon, and cloves in a medium bowl. Set this aside at room temperature until the hens have marinated in their spice rub for the full 30 minutes.

5. Pour the milk mixture over the hens. Cover loosely with plastic wrap and refrigerate for at least 2 hours but no more than 4 hours, turning the hens once so that everything sits in the marinade.

6. Fire up the grill. Heat a gas grill to high heat (about 550°F [288°C]) or build a high-heat, well-ashed-if-still-red-hot coal bed in a charcoal grill. Alternatively—in winter, perhaps?—heat up the broiler with the rack 4 to 6 inches (10 to 15 cm) from the heat source.

7. Remove the chicken from the marinade with bits of the mixture still adhering to each hen. Grill directly over the heat until cooked through, until an instant-read meat thermometer inserted into the meat without touching bone registers 165°F (74°C), 14 to 16 minutes, turning once. Or broil the hens on a lipped baking sheet for about the same amount of time, to the same internal temperature, turning once, about 16 minutes. Cool for 5 minutes before serving.

GOAT BUTTER 101

1. It's almost pure white (unless someone has dared to add fake coloring). That's because a grazing goat has already converted all the carotene she's consumed from roughage into vitamin A. A cow's digestion is less efficient on this count—and thus the butterfat has a yellow tinge from residual carotene.

2. Goat butter is a pain to make because the smaller fat globules do not easily separate from the milk, which must be set out at room temperature overnight and perhaps put through an industrial centrifugal separator.

3. Goat butter has a vaguely fresh-chèvre taste, a little more acidic, but also more floral, and certainly more umami. Try it on bagels with strawberry jam, a substitute for cream cheese.

4. Goat butter has a fairly low melting point, almost precisely at human body temperature. Although home-churned cow butter has a melting point around this same temperature, the cultured stuff and some of the tightly packed, low-moisture cow butters at the supermarket melt around 100°F (38°C), even up to 104°F (40°C). (Solid vegetable shortening, by contrast, melts around 110°F [43°C].)

5. In terms of cooking, if you're going to sauté or panfry with goat butter, watch the heat closely, dropping it if the butter begins to brown too much.

6. In terms of baking, goat and cow butter are interchangeable—except with the note about the more pronounced flavor in goat butter (and perhaps the additional salt if you normally use unsalted cow butter).

7. The best way to experience goat butter for the first time is to spread it on crustless white-bread sandwiches layered with thinly sliced radishes and a sprinkle of crunchy salt. Cut the sandwiches into triangular wedges. And don't forget the white gloves.

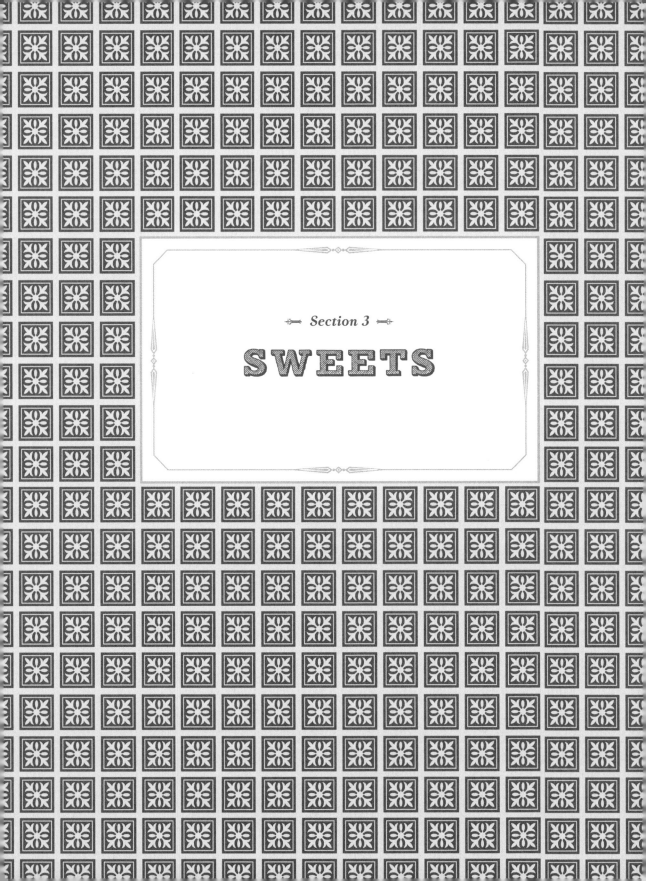

Section 3

SWEETS

WE'D COME TO the Pachecos' dairy and Achadinha Cheese Company in Sonoma County, California, on a brilliant morning, the thunderstorms of the night before a distant dream. Jim and Donna herd their goats near enough to the coast that the golden hills begin to stack up on each other, crumpled cloth. The Pachecos' is a family business that has stood the test, started back in the mid-fifties and still running in these tough times.

As we pulled up the long driveway to the house and buildings clustered on a topknot, we were met first by some friendly farm dogs—who quickly showed us to Donna, a bright force on her own, still full of optimism about the business. We stood outside in the morning breeze, did the usual farmish introductions (which devolve into questions of families) and then went off to see the girls: eighteen hundred goats, living dormitory style in open barns. Soon, we were surrounded by contented, curious ruminants, chewing, head-butting, trying to get our attention, and trying to get the top position on little bits of log or even in the food trough.

That goaty smell? I barely noticed it. In fact, I felt comforted by it. It was simply *farm*. Not industrial farm. Not the nightmare of pigs in coffin-shaped pens, unable to move even when giving birth. Not the horror story of thousands of chickens stacked so deep, they peck each other to death. No, this was just a goat farm, the biggest we'd see, but still not a factory in any way.

It had to be big. The Pachecos supply milk to some pretty important yogurt and cheese producers. They also make some pretty fine Italian-style, olive-oil-washed cheeses on their own.

As we talked, the goats filed out the back of the barns, a few at a time, udders full. Most dairies have to coax the animals into the milking parlor with food. But these goats went into the line about twenty at a time with nary a bribe, waiting patiently outside the milking parlor. Well, patiently for goats.

"You want to watch the milking?" Donna said, her eyes beaming.

If you've ever been on a dairy farm, you know that's not a simple invitation. It involves sanitizing your shoes, putting on plastic caps, cleaning just about everything on you. We were undeterred.

Suited up and in the parlor, we watched a group of about twenty goats climb the steps to the milking stand. They turned and faced the wall, almost on cue: a perfect chorus line, their butts toward us, front feet up a step.

Out of the blue, Donna turned to Bruce and asked, rather innocently, if he wanted to have a go at milking.

Another complicated invitation. This time, he shot me a look. *What have you gotten me into?*

Sure, I've milked before. I have relatives who are farmers. I could even tell you about the time I ended up shoulder deep in a cow, learning how to inseminate it. But that's for another day. This was Bruce's time. And his first with a mammary of any sort. I motioned him on.

I swear he giggled. Like a schoolboy.

Goats have two udders; cows, four. Because goats are not as meaty as cows, the udders pop right out the back of their legs, particularly when they put their front legs up on a step. There's not a lot intervening between you and those udders.

Donna washed a pair with iodine, then stepped back. "Go ahead. Just take ahold."

He did—like he holds a knitting needle, between two fingers.

"Whole hand," Donna said. "Around the udder."

He giggled again, then sort of shook himself and bore down on the task. He wrapped his hand around the udder and squeezed.

Nothing happened.

"That's everyone's first time," Donna said.

"I thought I was going to hurt her," he said.

"She's been around the block."

She didn't look it. Her brown hair was shiny and beautiful, almost combed. But I swear she did turn around and throw him a look. *Are we getting on with this or what?*

So he squeezed and pulled, running the tension through his fingers and down the udder.

A thin wire of milk shot across the parlor.

"My God," he said, stepping back.

"You'll get the hang of it." Donna laughed.

Somehow, I doubted it.

CAJETA

YOU'LL END UP WITH 1 CUP (250 ML), WHICH YOU CAN
DRIBBLE ONTO ICE CREAM, WAFFLES, BROWNIES, OR POUND CAKE—
OR SCRAPE OFF A SPOON AT MIDNIGHT WHEN YOU CAN'T SLEEP.

There may be no more iconic goat milk sweet than cajeta *(Spanish, kah-HAY-tah), a creamy, silky caramel that's long-cooked to a thick sauce, then stored in the fridge for months, only to be rewarmed until pourable when needed. (Often.)*

4 cups (960 ml) **regular goat milk (do not use low-fat)**

⅛ teaspoon baking soda stirred until smooth in 2 teaspoons water

1 cup (200 g) **sugar**

1. Bring the milk to a low simmer in a large saucepan over medium heat.

2. Pour in the soda mixture, which will cause the milk to rise in the pan. Stir it down, then stir in the sugar.

3. After bringing the mixture back to a full boil, reduce the heat a bit. (To medium? Medium-low? It depends on your stove and how much heat it puts out.) Cook at a very low boil, stirring occasionally, for 1 hour.

4. Now the hard part. Clip a candy thermometer to the inside of the pan and continue cooking, *stirring constantly*, until the internal temperature registers 236°F (113°C) (that is, soft-ball stage) and the *cajeta* is thick and golden, about 30 minutes, maybe longer, depending on the day's humidity and the residual fat content of the milk. Cool the hot *cajeta* for about 10 minutes in the pan, then pour it into a heat-safe glass jar or glass container of some sort, perhaps a canning jar. Cover and store in the refrigerator for up to 2 months. Reheat it in dribs and drabs in a bowl in the microwave, or set the whole storage jar in a warm water bath in a medium saucepan over low heat for a few minutes, until the *cajeta* is again spoonable.

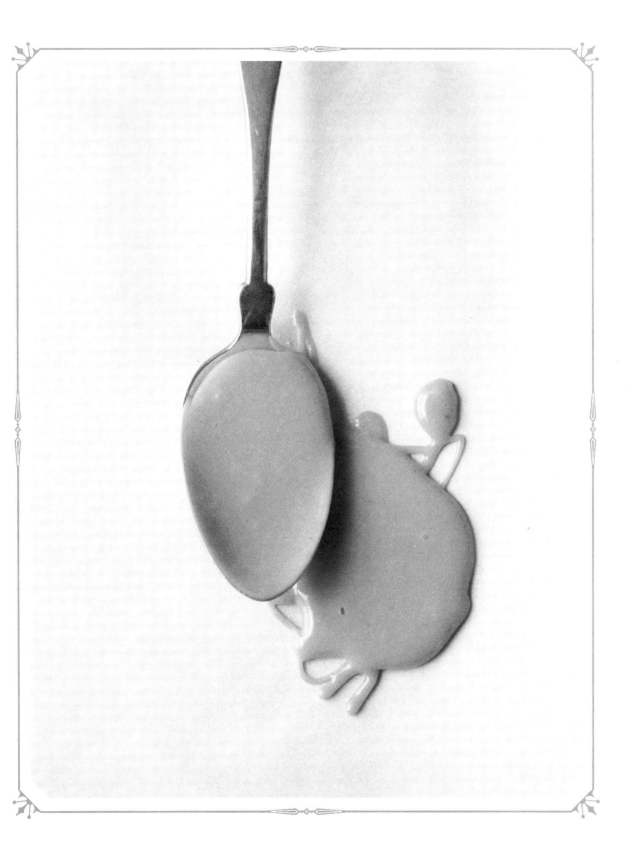

GOAT MILK FUDGE

TWELVE SERVINGS OR SO.

This is honest-to-goodness candy making, so you'll need a candy thermometer and a good eye for detail to pull off this cross between chocolate and goat milk—all of which makes a perfect fudge: decadent, a little tart, very adult. The kids will probably want something sweeter. Good for them. More for you.

3 cups (600 g) sugar

1½ cups (360 ml) regular goat milk (do not use low-fat)

4 ounces (115 g) unsweetened chocolate, chopped

¼ cup (60 ml) light corn syrup

¼ teaspoon salt

⅛ teaspoon cream of tartar

2 tablespoons goat butter, plus extra for buttering the loaf pan

1 tablespoon vanilla extract

1. Whisk the sugar, milk, chocolate, corn syrup, salt, and cream of tartar in a large saucepan set over medium-low heat until barely bubbling.

2. Clip a candy thermometer to the inside of the pan, adjust the heat so that the mixture simmers slowly, and continue heating without stirring until the temperature registers 236°F (113°C) (soft-ball stage).

3. Remove the pan from the heat and dollop the butter on top. It will melt, forming a protective barrier over the hot fudge in the pan. Keep the candy thermometer clipped to the pan's inside and cool on a wire rack until the fudge's temperature underneath the butter is 110°F (43°C), a couple of hours, maybe several, depending on the day's temperature and humidity. Busy yourself by buttering the inside of a 5 x 9-inch (12 x 23-cm) loaf pan.

4. Remove the candy thermometer from the fudge. With an electric mixer at medium speed, beat the top layer of butter and the vanilla into the chocolate mixture until the mixture loses its sheen, 1 to 3 minutes. However, timing is very hard. There are many factors at play. You're looking for it to lose any shine—and that's not long at all. It's better to underbeat it and have the fudge a little soft and gooey than to overbeat it and have it crystallized and grainy. People practice for years with fudge.

5. Pour and scrape the fudge into the prepared loaf pan. Let stand at room temperature until set, about 4 hours. After that, cover the pan and store at room temperature for up to 5 days. Cut it right out of the pan, taking out slices, then cutting these into smaller bits. If the fudge has been underbeaten a tad, you can set the loaf pan in the fridge to firm the whole thing up—but you won't have that same, velvety texture. That said, you'll still have fudge; so how bad can that be?

CHOCOLATE PUDDING

YOU CAN WHIP UP ABOUT SIX SERVINGS, PROVIDED EVERYONE REMAINS RATIONAL.

Here's our second, out-of-the-ballpark combo of chocolate and goat milk—a duo that makes an incredibly elegant pudding, rich and intense. Again, because of the increased flavors in the milk, we need more chocolate. Lots more. From three sources: cocoa powder, white chocolate, and unsweetened chocolate.

3 cups (720 ml) regular or low-fat
   goat milk

⅓ cup (65 g) sugar

6 tablespoons unsweetened cocoa
   powder, preferably Dutch-processed

⅓ cup (40 g) all-purpose flour

2½ ounces (70 g) white chocolate,
   chopped

1 ounce (30 g) unsweetened chocolate, chopped

3 large egg yolks, at room temperature, whisked until creamy in a big
   bowl

¼ teaspoon almond extract

¼ teaspoon salt

1. Whisk the milk, sugar, cocoa powder, flour, white chocolate, and unsweetened chocolate in a large saucepan set over medium heat until thick and bubbling, about 5 minutes.

   Flour in chocolate pudding? Indeed. With this much added fat coming from the chocolates, flour helps protect the mixture, particularly keeping the egg yolks from scrambling as they come in contact with the hot fat bits.

2. Whisk about half the hot chocolate mixture into the egg yolks until smooth, then whisk this combined mixture back into the remaining chocolate mixture in the pan.

3. Reduce the heat to low. If you're working on an electric stove, the burner's temperature may not drop quickly enough, so put the saucepan over a burner just now turned to low. Bring the chocolate mixture to a very low simmer, just a few bubbles; then reduce the heat even further. Cook for 1 minute, whisking constantly.

4. Remove the pan from the heat. Whisk in the almond extract and salt. Pour into 6 individual ramekins or 1 larger serving bowl. If you're at all concerned about lumps, strain the mixture through a fine-mesh sieve. Refrigerate for at least 1 hour, then cover and keep refrigerated for up to 3 days.

MORE TO KNOW

Dutch-processed cocoa powder includes an alkali that improves the cocoa's ability to dissolve in liquids. Without that chemical addition, some of the cocoa solids can prove resistant to liquefying. That said, if you only have so-called natural cocoa powder, it'll work just fine in this recipe—you'll just have to whisk more aggressively over the heat to get it to dissolve.

HONEY GOAT MILK GELATO

THE RECIPE YIELDS 4 CUPS (1 L). THAT'S ENOUGH FOR
SIX PEOPLE AFTER DINNER, FOUR PEOPLE ON THE DECK,
OR ONE PERSON THE NIGHT AFTER A BREAKUP.

Gelato is Italian ice cream, except there's often no cream. Traditionally, it's made with whole milk and lots of eggs (although some gelateria in Italy now add cream to satisfy the tastes of tourists). In the case of goat milk, there's a little less dairy fat than in Italian whole-cow-milk production (although there is more than in American cow milk production). Bruce's answer to all this? A little goat butter in the mix for that classic smooth, rich finish. Ever wanted to butter your ice cream? Oh, come on, you know you have.

3 cups (720 ml) **regular goat milk**

1 tablespoon **goat butter**

1 **vanilla bean,** split in half lengthwise

7 large **egg yolks,** at room temperature

½ cup (100 g) **plus 2 tablespoons sugar**

¼ teaspoon **salt**

1. Heat the goat milk, butter, and split vanilla bean in a large saucepan set over medium heat until bubbles start to fizz around the pan's inner edges and whiffs of steam rise off the milk. Cover and set aside at room temperature for 1 hour.

2. Remove the vanilla bean halves. Lay them, cut side up, on a work surface and run a small knife along the bean, gathering up the seeds. Scrape these back into the milk mixture, then set the pan over low heat. Do not let the mixture boil, or the taste will become too much like canned evaporated milk. Instead, just keep it warm during the next step.

3. Beat the egg yolks, sugar, and salt in a big bowl with an electric mixer at medium speed until creamy, thick, pale yellow, and even fluffy, about 8 minutes, scraping down the inside of the bowl once in a while to make sure all the sugar is getting beaten with the eggs.

4. Remove the saucepan from the heat. Beat about half the warm goat milk mixture into the egg mixture until smooth, then beat this combined mixture back into the remaining warm goat milk mixture.

5. Return the saucepan to the stove and reduce the heat to very low. On an electric stove, use a different burner, just now set to low. Cook, stirring constantly—do not leave it alone—until the custard is somewhat thickened, almost like melted ice cream or nearly set pudding. It should coat the back of a wooden spoon in such a way that when you run your finger through the coating, the line you make is permanent, the mixture not flowing back in place, perhaps 4 to 5 minutes.

6. Strain the hot custard through a fine-mesh sieve and into a pitcher or other container. Cover and refrigerate for at least 4 hours or (preferably) overnight.

7. Prepare an ice cream maker according to the manufacturer's instructions. For the creamiest gelato, put the dasher, lid, and any other pieces in the freezer for 15 minutes before using them. The colder they are, the less air you'll beat into the mixture—and so the creamier the gelato.

8. Pour in the custard and freeze according to the manufacturer's instructions until thick, creamy, and scoopable yet still soft. Scrape the gelato into a bowl or a clean container—if you can wait—and set it on the floor of your freezer to firm up. However, the gelato tastes best when it's a little melty, so remove from the freezer for 10 minutes or so before scooping it up.

RASPBERRY FROZEN YOGURT

ONCE AGAIN, YOU'LL MAKE 4 CUPS.

You'll need to strain the yogurt to get it thick enough to make a creamy frozen dessert. For instructions on how to strain the yogurt, see More to Know. If you end up with more strained yogurt than you need for this recipe, you'll have a treat for breakfast the next day: a creamy, rich, thick yogurt, sort of like Greek-style yogurt.

12 ounces (340 g) fresh raspberries

3 tablespoons raspberry-flavored liqueur, such as framboise

1 cup (240 ml) regular or low-fat goat milk

2 large eggs, at room temperature

¾ cup (170 g) sugar

¼ teaspoon salt

½ teaspoon cornstarch or potato starch

1 cup (240 ml) strained whole goat yogurt

2 teaspoons vanilla extract

MORE TO KNOW

To strain yogurt, line a colander with cheesecloth or a big coffee filter. Pour in the yogurt—about double the amount you'll need when strained—and set the full strainer over a bowl to catch the drips. Refrigerate overnight or up to 24 hours. The resulting yogurt will certainly be thicker, less like a slightly soured milk, the way goat yogurt sometimes can be.

1. Put the raspberries and the raspberry liqueur in a large blender or a food processor fitted with the chopping blade. Blend or process until pureed.

2. Strain the puree through a fine-mesh sieve into a bowl to remove any seeds. You should end up with about 1 cup (240 ml) raspberry puree.

3. Heat the milk in a large saucepan set over medium-low heat until little bubbles fizz around the pan's inner edges.

4. Meanwhile, beat the eggs, sugar, and salt in a large bowl with an electric mixer at medium-high speed until light, fluffy, and thick, about 5 minutes. Beat in the cornstarch.

5. Remove the saucepan from the heat. Beat half the hot milk into the egg mixture until smooth, then beat this combined mixture back into the remaining hot milk in the pan until smooth.

6. Set the pan back over the heat, now reduced to low. If you're working on an electric stove, use a burner just now turned on to low. Cook, stirring constantly, until the mixture thickens and can coat the back of a wooden spoon (see step 5, page 152, for a fuller explanation), about 4 minutes.

7. Strain this mixture through a fine-mesh sieve into a large bowl to remove any bits of inadvertently scrambled egg. Stir in the raspberry puree as well as the strained yogurt and the vanilla, all until smooth. Set the bowl in the fridge and chill for at least 4 hours or overnight. (Cover it if you're chilling it for more than 4 hours.)

8. Freeze the raspberry yogurt mixture in an ice cream machine according to the manufacturer's instructions. Serve right from the machine or scoop the frozen yogurt into a large bowl, cover, and store in the freezer for up to 2 weeks.

The Greenest Lawn Ever

Nanna dropped by on Thursday afternoons, along with the rest of the girls. They came once I decided we were going to be green *and* goaty. That is, after I hired a goat lawn-mowing service.

We live in a very rural part of New England. We have an acre cleared. I thought goats were our answer.

Mostly because I don't mow. I have to draw the line somewhere. When we first bought the house, I drove to the local store that sold well pumps, generators, and other curiosities of country life.

I climbed up on a riding mower and felt instantly backlit by klieg lights. Like Liberace on a rugby team.

I pictured me in a cap. One with a logo. And a cup holder nearby. I got down, walked out, and called a guy down the road from us.

"How much to mow?"

"Forty bucks," he said. "Cash."

Done. And easy. Until I decided to let him go to try this goat mowing thing.

Lest you think I was nuts, the lawn-mowing goatherd had a full schedule. "You're about the last I can take on," he said. "How about Thursdays?"

"Wow, a prime spot."

"Most people want earlier in the week."

I didn't hear the warning. I wanted a nice lawn. I wanted to reduce my carbon footprint. And I wanted to be a little morally superior. It should be easy to connect those things up.

The first Thursday, I was agog. There was a herd of goats across our lawn.

And then in our flower beds. I saw a stalk of purple echinacea go down. I ran outside. "They can't eat that!"

The goatherd gave me that blank New England stare. "What? The weeds?"

"I planted those!"

He harrumphed, got off his truck, and headed over to the offending goat, which was already chomping another stalk. "Out of there," he said. Not very forcefully, might I add.

"I'm serious," I said, a little panicked.

"How much am I charging you?"

"Twenty. You said this is food for your goats."

He looked back down at the echinacea. "Uh-huh."

He did manage to get the goat out of the flower beds. Mostly because he let his dog out of his truck. The lawn soon morphed into a green carpet studded with reddish goats and wiped with a blur of border collie. In minutes, the does were rounded into a nice pack, chewing down the broadleaf.

I could see what Bill Niman meant. They tended the ground, careful to take everything down without pawing up the roots. They weren't as heavy as cows. Or the occasional moose that uses our apple trees as an all-you-can-eat buffet.

I went back inside and found Bruce testing recipes. I was beaming, full of my own self-importance.

A while later, the goats were rounded back up and in the truck. I saw it head down our quarter-mile driveway, disappearing among the trees.

I went outside, so proud. And that's when I noticed it. The goat poop everywhere. And we had friends coming in twenty-four hours.

I got a shovel and started tossing the pellets into the woods. An hour later, my resolve was less pristine. I came in and Bruce handed me a scotch.

I figured I just had to get used to it. And then came the next week. And more downed echinacea. And more border collie. And more poop. And more friends on their way.

And then another week.

"There sure is a lot to pick up after they leave," I said to my goatherd.

"That's why people like to start earlier in the week."

Another week and I gave up, threw in the towel, called my forty-dollar lawn guy, who had suddenly become my fifty-dollar lawn guy.

Well, at least my do-gooder resolve knows another of its boundaries.

CHOCOLATE PANNA COTTA

IT YIELDS SIX SERVINGS.

Books are collaborative efforts. Yes, there are two of us here; but there's also a bevy of recipe-testers. Dale Brown is one of the latter, a go-to crackerjack in the kitchen. She's worked on half the books we've written, taking the recipes after I've set them into print and testing to see if she gets the same results we do. We visited her in California not too long ago and she served this delicious make-ahead chocolate panna cotta *(Italian, pah-NAH coh-TAH—that is, baked cream). Bruce instantly came home and tried her recipe with goat milk, to which he also added strained goat yogurt to provide some body, where cream did the duty in Dale's cowier version.*

1¾ cups (420 ml) regular goat milk (do not use low-fat), divided

2 teaspoons unflavored gelatin (that is, less than one ¼-ounce [10-g] packet)

⅔ cup (150 g) sugar

3 ounces (85 g) semisweet chocolate (about 55% cocoa solids), chopped

3 tablespoons unsweetened cocoa powder, preferably Dutch-processed

Goat butter, for greasing the ramekins

1½ cups (360 ml) strained regular goat yogurt (do not use low-fat; see page 154)

1 teaspoon vanilla extract

¼ teaspoon salt

1. Pour ½ cup (120 ml) of the milk into a bowl, then sprinkle the gelatin over the top. Set aside for 30 minutes at room temperature.

2. Heat the remaining 1¼ cups (300 ml) milk, the sugar, chocolate, and cocoa powder in a large saucepan set over medium heat, whisking all the while, until smooth and steaming.

3. Remove the pan from the heat and whisk in the milk-gelatin mixture until smooth. Cool at room temperature for 30 minutes. Meanwhile, lightly butter the insides of six 1-cup (240-ml) ramekins.

4. Whisk the strained yogurt, vanilla, and salt into the goat-milk mixture until smooth. Pour this into the prepared ramekins, about ¾ cup (180 ml) in each. Refrigerate for at least 4 hours or until set—or store in the fridge for up to 3 days, covering the ramekins with plastic wrap after 4 hours. To unmold, fill a bowl with hot tap water, then dip each ramekin about halfway into the hot water for a couple of seconds. Run a thin knife around the inside of the ramekin and then invert over a serving plate to let the panna cotta plop out, shaking the ramekin a bit as necessary to get the thing to come unstuck.

SPICED FLAN

Here, a caramel-lined loaf pan is filled with a rich goat-milk custard, baked, and chilled, before being turned out onto a platter so that the sauce runs all over the top. You must plan ahead with this dish because it must sit in the fridge at least overnight. In the end, the goat milk works wonders with the honey—this is a natural combination that you might also want to implement in your honey cake or quick bread recipes.

2 cups (500 ml) regular or low-fat goat milk

One 4-inch (one 10-cm) cinnamon stick

1 vanilla bean, split in half lengthwise

Several tiny black seeds from a green cardamom pod, perhaps 4 to 6, crushed with the side of a knife

2 cups (400 g) sugar, divided

¼ cup (60 ml) honey

¼ cup (60 ml) water

4 large eggs plus 4 large egg yolks, at room temperature, whisked in a bowl until smooth

Boiling water

1. Heat the milk, cinnamon stick, vanilla bean, and cardamom seeds in a large pot over medium heat until little bubbles rim the inside of the pot. Cover and set aside at room temperature for 1 hour.

2. Meanwhile, combine 1 cup (200 g) of the sugar, the honey, and the ¼ cup (60 ml) water in a skillet; stir over medium heat until the sugar melts.

3. Continue cooking, stirring occasionally, until the mixture turns golden brown—and is ridiculously hot. Pour it into a 5 x 9-inch (13 x 23-cm) heat-safe glass loaf pan, tilting the pan this way and that to get an even coating on the bottom.

4. Get the rack into the center of the oven, which you're going to heat to 300°F (150°C).

5. Fish the cinnamon stick and vanilla bean out of the pot. If you want a more intense vanilla taste, you can scrape the little seeds from the insides of the vanilla bean halves and put the seeds back into the milk. Otherwise, discard the cinnamon stick and the vanilla bean halves.

6. Whisk the beaten eggs and egg yolks into the milk mixture, then whisk in the remaining 1 cup (200 g) sugar until smooth. Pour this mixture into the caramel-lined loaf pan.

7. Set the loaf pan in a deep baking dish or a roasting pan on the oven rack. Pour boiling water into the baking dish until it comes about halfway up the level of the custard inside the loaf pan.

8. Bake for 1½ hours. Carefully remove the loaf pan from the water bath and let cool on a wire rack to room temperature. Then cover and refrigerate at least overnight or up to 2 days.

9. To serve, run a thin knife around the inside of the loaf pan, loosening up the flan inside. Turn the pan upside down onto a lipped serving platter and let the flan loaf plop out. Allow any melted and runny caramel sauce to drizzle out of the pan and all over the flan. Cut the flan into slices to serve, like cutting a loaf of bread, but also scooping up some of the caramel sauce for each slice.

GOAT CRÈME BRÛLÉE

IT'LL GIVE YOU FOUR SERVINGS.

If you want to get fancy, call it Crème Brûlée au Lait de Chèvre. *In other words, fired-up cream with goat milk. But it doesn't matter what you call it—no one will be listening. They'll be eating. Because these little desserts are the real deal: a creamy, silky custard on top of which a layer of sugar gets melted and caramelized, then hardens again so that you have to crack through it to get to the custard. And as if that's not enough, the custard under there includes a double goat hit, because it's made not only with goat milk but also with chèvre (or soft goat cheese).*

2 cups (480 ml) **regular or low-fat goat milk**

4 large **egg yolks, at room temperature**

10 tablespoons (145 g) **sugar, divided**

3 ounces (85 g) **fresh chèvre or soft goat cheese**

Boiling water

1. Set the rack in the oven's center and get the oven heated up to 325°F (165°C).

2. Whir up the milk, egg yolks, 6 tablespoons (85 g) of the sugar, and the fresh chèvre in a large blender or a food processor fitted with the chopping blade until the sugar and cheese are dissolved in the smooth mixture. Divide the mixture among four ¾-cup (180-ml) oven-safe ramekins. Cover each tightly with aluminum foil.

3. Place a deep baking dish or a roasting pan on the oven rack; then set the filled, covered ramekins in the dish or the pan, making sure they do not touch. Pour boiling water into the baking dish or pan until it comes about halfway up the ramekins' sides.

4. Bake for 55 minutes, or until set. Of course, the custards are covered—so you'll have to take a peek to see how they're doing. They shouldn't jiggle when set. But remember that the attendant water and the ramekins themselves are quite hot.

5. Very carefully transfer the baking dish or the roasting pan with the water and all the ramekins to a wire rack and cool for 20 minutes. Then transfer the covered ramekins to the fridge and chill for at least 6 hours or up to 3 days.

6. Uncover the ramekins and sprinkle the remaining 4 tablespoons sugar over them, 1 tablespoon on each. Now melt the sugar. You've got a couple of ways to do this:

☞ Set the rack so that the ramekins will be about 5 inches (12 cm) from the broiler's heat source. Fire up the broiler. Set the ramekins on a baking sheet, then place them so they're directly under the hot broiler element. Leave them there until the sugar melts, turns brown, and coats the top of each, 2 to 4 minutes, depending on how strong your broiler element is. But remember this: The pottery is going to be subjected to intense heat. Delicate ceramic ramekins may crack.

☞ Use a kitchen blowtorch to melt the sugar, pointing the flame directly at the top of each custard with its sugar coating and moving the flame in all directions until the sugar melts, bubbles, and browns.

In either case, cool the custards for 5 minutes to let the sugar get hard, then serve at once, the tops to be cracked open with a spoon to get to the light velvety custard underneath.

GOAT MILK RICE PUDDING

IT SHOULD SERVE EIGHT—BUT, BOY, IS THAT BEING OPTIMISTIC!

After years of trying it different ways, Bruce has settled on a formula for rice pudding that involves medium-grained arborio rice, the same rice used to make risotto. It gives the pudding a little more body than long-grained varietals. Don't use a risotto recipe to cook the rice, abrading its starch into a thickening broth to create that fabulous dish. Instead, cook the rice according to the package instructions, as you would any rice. It'll then go into this goaty version of Bruce's favorite dessert—with fresh chèvre in the mix for good measure.

Goat butter, for greasing the baking dish

2 cups (455 g) cooked arborio rice

4 cups (960 ml) regular or low-fat goat milk

3 large eggs plus 3 large egg yolks, at room temperature

½ cup (100 g) sugar

2 tablespoons vanilla extract

½ teaspoon salt

¼ teaspoon freshly grated nutmeg

4 ounces (115 g) fresh chèvre or soft goat cheese

1. Set the rack in the center of the oven and heat the oven up to 350°F (175°C). Butter the inside of a 10-inch (25-cm), round baking dish with a little fat on a wadded-up paper towel.

2. Whisk everything together in a big bowl until smooth and creamy. Pour the mixture into the prepared dish.

3. Bake until set when jiggled, about 45 minutes. Cool the pan on a wire rack for 10 minutes before dishing up the pudding. Or cool to room temperature, then cover and refrigerate for up to 3 days.

 GO ALL OUT! GO ALL OUT! GO ALL OUT! GO ALL OUT! GO ALL OUT!

You can stir some dried fruit into the mix: apricots, raisins, pitted dates, even Chinese jujubes. Just make sure the fruit itself is diced into small bits. Otherwise, the whole dried fruit will plump and become a super-hot, mouth-burning bomb in the pudding as it bakes.

GOAT YOGURT PIE

ONE 9-INCH (ONE 23-CM) PIE.

This is a goat yogurt take on a Southern favorite: buttermilk pie. Bruce's crust calls for lard—because it's so good—but feel free to use solid vegetable shortening if you really don't want to go the distance. The small amount of lemon juice in the crust keeps the flour's glutens from elongating into breadishness, thereby keeping the crust crisp and flaky.

For the crust:

1 cup (125 g) all-purpose flour, plus more for dusting

1 teaspoon sugar

¼ teaspoon salt

4 tablespoons cool unsalted goat butter, cut into pieces

2 tablespoons solid vegetable shortening or lard

3 tablespoons very cold water, even ice water, plus more as needed

½ teaspoon lemon juice

For the filling:

1½ cups (340 g) sugar

6 tablespoons (85 g) goat butter

3 large eggs, at room temperature

1 cup (240 ml) thick, but not necessarily fully strained, goat yogurt (see page 154)

2 tablespoons all-purpose flour

2 tablespoons lemon juice

1 tablespoon finely grated lemon zest

1 tablespoon vanilla extract

MORE TO KNOW

Again, because of protein and fat molecule differentials, some goat yogurts are thicker than others, most pretty thin. For this recipe, you want 1 cup (250 ml) of goat yogurt that's about the consistency of cultured buttermilk. If yours is very thick, thin it out with some goat milk until it's the right consistency. If yours is very thin, strain it a bit (see page 154)—but don't let the yogurt get too thick.

LESS TO DO

You can make the crust in a food processor fitted with the chopping blade. Pulse the dry ingredients a couple of times, then add both fats and pulse until the mixture resembles coarse sand. With the blade running, pour in the water and lemon juice until a soft dough forms, adding a little more water if the thing won't cohere. Scrape it out and continue with the recipe from step 4.

1. Position the rack in the center of the oven and heat the oven to 350°F (175°C).

2. To make the crust, use a fork to stir 1 cup (25 g) flour, 1 teaspoon sugar, and the salt in a large bowl. Add the 4 tablespoons (55 g) goat butter bits and the shortening or lard. Use the tines of the fork or a pastry cutter to push the fat through the flour, constantly repositioning the tines so that the fat keeps getting worked into the mixture, until it all resembles coarse cornmeal.

3. Add the water and ½ teaspoon lemon juice; stir with a fork until a soft dough forms, adding a little more water in ½-teaspoon increments until a soft, pliable dough forms. The dough shouldn't be too wet or it will stick. However, it should be wet enough that it coheres.

4. Sprinkle a clean, dry work surface with a few drops of water, then set a large piece of wax paper on top of it. Set the dough in the middle of the wax paper and flatten it with your palm until it is a thick disk. Lay a second piece of wax paper on top of the dough and roll the dough with a rolling pin until it's a circle about 11 inches (28 cm) in diameter.

5. Peel off the top sheet of wax paper, then pick up the bottom sheet with the dough still adhering to it. Turn this upside down into a 9-inch (23-cm) pie plate. Position it directly in the center, then peel off the wax paper, pressing the dough into place to form the crust. Fold the dough at

the rim so that it stands up a bit and is thick, then crimp the edges of the dough for a scalloped, decorative look. You can get the job done a couple of ways:

☞ Take one hand and make a *U* out of your thumb and forefinger. Set this *U* inside the pie plate at the rim, right on the crust. Position the forefinger of your other hand on the outside of the pie plate so that that finger will fit right in the *U*. Now push your hands together, the one finger in the *U*, so that the crust makes a crimped indentation. Repeat this procedure all the way around the rim of the crust.

☞ Push the crust into a crimped edge using the tines of a fork.

In any case, lay a clean kitchen towel over the crust while you prepare the filling.

6. To make the filling, beat 1½ cups (340 g) sugar and 6 tablespoons (85 g) goat butter in a large bowl with an electric mixer at medium speed until creamy, smooth, and pale yellow, no obvious graininess of the sugar left, about 4 minutes.

7. Beat in the eggs one at a time, making sure each is well incorporated before adding the next. Beat in the goat yogurt until smooth, then beat in the flour until fully dissolved, about 1 minute. Scrape down the inside of the bowl and beat in 2 tablespoons lemon juice, the lemon zest, and vanilla.

8. Pour this mixture into the prepared crust. (You removed the towel first, right?) Then bake until the filling is puffed and golden brown, 50 to 55 minutes. The center should be set when jiggled, not firm—still movable for sure, but not liquid, either. Transfer the pie to a wire rack and cool to room temperature, about 2 hours, before slicing and serving.

Bruce and I are old enough to have watched goat cheese morph from a gag-me no-no in the *Mad Men* sixties to the full-on cliché it is today: crumbled into salads, deep-fried into balls, melted into casseroles.

It's hard to remember how revolutionary that first beet-and-goat-cheese salad was.

Let's face it. It wasn't the cheese. It was the goat. That's what pushed the envelope for most of us.

There are few records documenting the historical provenance of goat cheese versus all the other types of cheese; but given that goats were most likely one of the first animals domesticated in human settlements, right along with dogs, we can make an educated guess that goat cheese has been around for quite a while.

After all, making cheese from the milk of all the right sort of ruminants—cows, sheep, water buffalos, yaks, camels, and (yes) goats—has been part of human culture for millennia. Remnants of cheese have been found encrusted on pottery shards in Egyptian tombs dating from the Bronze Age, about 2300 B.C.E.

But no matter how far back cheese making goes, no matter how much the French morphed it from a homespun craft to a fine art starting in the eighteenth century, goat was the hurdle for many of us in North America. Back when we started deep-frying our first rounds, sometime in the shoulder-pad eighties, much of what passed for chèvre wasn't (shall we say?) of sterling quality. It was sour and obstreperous, a dull thud.

Back then, I was in graduate school in Madison, Wisconsin, home to the nation's finest farmers' market, ringing the state capitol. It was an event to make any Calvinist proud: obscenely decent (not a shred of trash outside a bin) and in order (everyone walked counterclockwise).

That said, the eighties hadn't quite made it to the upper Midwest. Madison was still home to the flannel set, exemplified by one group of women farmers who caught my attention every week. Not because one of them had a groomed mustache.

Mostly because they waited with blank faces in a perfectly straight line behind a small table offering little tubs of goat cheese, a thing I'd never tasted.

One Saturday, fortified by caffeine, I decided to give it a go. I didn't know what to expect: a violent Virginia Woolf explosion of fury and goat (*We need a table of one's own!*) or simply an overdose of patchouli.

Surprisingly, I got smiles and nods. "Would you like to try a taste?" one asked me, her prairie skirt billowing in the breeze. She proffered a little, flat wooden spoon, like we used to use for ice cream tastes, a mound of stark white cheese atop its bulb.

Seduced by unexpected friendliness, I muttered the expected bit of Scandinavian gratitude ("Yah, sure, OK") and scraped the cheese off the spoon by running it through my teeth.

She leaned over the table, my culinary instructor. "Now push it against the roof of your mouth."

I couldn't. It was bitter and defiant. Here was the outrage I'd expected. In cheese. I squinted.

"Oh, that's it," she said. "You like it, don't you?"

I didn't know how to tell her these were not tears of joy. There was no refinement, no overtones, no shades of flavor. Instead, it was just stinky and acidic, rough and rustic. We may have been on the cusp of something, but it sure didn't seem like it.

Truth be told, some people are still on that cusp. They have a similar aversion to goat cheese, mostly because they've gone only for the primitive, gritty stuff, tossed willy-nilly into big salads at the forced-fun chain restaurants.

Their distaste may well be biological. Cheese making is a trying, exacting passion, related chemically to winemaking and chocolate making. All are exercises in spoiling edible food. The process is controlled, yes; but what results is nonetheless partially decomposed, or rotted, or fetid, or whatever word you want to use. It's no wonder then that the Symbolist poet Lèon-Paul Fargue once wrote that Camembert *fleure les pieds du bon Dieu*, smells like the feet of God—partly because it's so divine, but mostly because it's so stinky.

Our aversion to spoilage keeps us safe, healthy, and even alive. But it also puts a line down in our behavior: *Don't go there.*

It's a really good thing we love to cross lines. Cheese—along with wine and chocolate—offers us a safe, tantalizing, vaguely erotic way to overcome a biological limit.

We're not carrion fowl. The spoiled bits we relish are crafted in heavily controlled environments. How controlled? Let's look at the primary components of goat milk to understand how goat cheese moves from rustic to sublime.

1. Lactose. It's the only carb in the mix, a bond between two relatively simpler sugars, glucose and galactose. Goat milk is slightly—but only slightly—lower in lactose than cow milk (about 4.1 percent of the various milk solids, as opposed to about 4.8 percent). Although snapped-apart lactose is a major nutrient (mammal brains run on glucose), its primary purpose in the milk is twofold: pleasure and preservation.

As to pleasure, lactose is sweet. Therefore, we go for it early and often. It makes baby-candy.

But that natural sweet we crave can be a problem. Lactose on its own will cause any attempts at making cheese to falter for two reasons: (1) Lactose impedes structural development, and (2) it provides fodder for bad bugs that can make the cheese sour or even inedible. So to craft controlled spoilage, lactose itself must be controlled.

Fortunately, it is by nature—from almost the moment the milk is produced. It comes with bacteria in tow that instantly begin to break it down and turn it into lactic acid. Thus, the milk quickly becomes too acidic for many bad bugs.

Which is probably why we got to drinking milk in the first place millennia ago: It's a high-nutrition, glucose-rich food that our ancestors could keep on the hut's shelf for a few days—or that we can keep in the fridge for a few weeks.

We keep it because we crave it. And we crave it because of the sugars, which are really just an excuse to get us to ingest . . .

2. The fat. Although the individual fat molecules are small in goat milk, these globules are still the largest bits in the mix.

Making cheese is all about building a structure that will hold these tasty globules in place. They can *clump* together—some fat may skim the rim of high-quality, high-fat goat yogurt, for example—but they cannot build a lasting, cohesive structure on their own. Both whipped cream and butter of all animal varieties are notoriously unstable at room temperature: Whipped cream can break, the water oozing out of suspension; and butter becomes spreadable, even runny, hardly a good candidate for cheese. Goat cream makes an even less stable whipped cream than cow cream, what with the smaller molecules—among other things.

That said, the fat is the main reason we as infants drink milk. We may want milk for the glucose, but we need it for the fat—which is the major source of the milk's vitamins. The fat-soluble vitamins A, D, E, and K ride on the globules' backs, as it were. Fat is also the primary ingredient our bodies use to build both nervous system tissue and the walls of every single cell in us.

Still, goat cheese is not about nutrition. A good cheese maker knows that he or she really needs all that luscious fat to carry forward . . .

3. The flavor compounds. These are intensified on the palate by the fat, but they're originally brought into the milk by whatever the herd has been eating: wildflowers, thistles, hay, grass, etc. Better feed (not just dried silage, but living plants) results in better milk, which results in better cheese.

These bits and remnants of botanical flavors give the goat cheese its primary characteristics (along with the introduced bacterial cultures—which we'll get to down the line). Since goats have a more varied diet than cows, any cheese made from goat milk will by necessity have a wider array of flavor compounds remaining in the curds, which are made from . . .

4. The casein. You've probably made a very rudimentary cheese without even knowing it: the skin on chocolate pudding. Chocolate is slightly acidic—and therefore causes the casein to coagulate into a thin, soft layer on top of pudding.

In a sense, casein is the very essence of cheese. The four types of protein molecules we call *casein* are all made up of loose, wiggly protein strands roped together by a barrette of calcium molecules. (Thus, casein is the primary source of milk's calcium.)

But here's the rub: Casein can't form any sort of structure on its own because all four varieties are negatively charged. They're naturally sticky—all those wiggly protein strands would love to knot together—but they cannot get near each other, just like the negative ends of two magnets cannot come in contact.

That's why milk will not coagulate in the presence of heat. In fact, it's the only edible protein source that won't. Think about it: Meat proteins coagulate in a hot oven. Throw a rib roast in there, and the proteins begin to line up, build structures, and the meat turns from raw to rare to (blech) medium-rare. Same with eggs: A frying pan, a little heat, and voilà, scrambled eggs.

Not milk. You can boil it almost to nothing and it will not coagulate. Yet getting the proteins to do so is the main problem when you're making cheese. Or to put it in ridiculously scientific lingo, you have to morph the casein into neutrally charged particles that can stick together, not pull apart. Once you do that, you've got curds—the casein sticky, coagulating around the fat and flavor compounds, which are now trapped inside almost by accident.

Casein is actually one of two protein structures in milk. The other is . . .

5. The whey. A.k.a. every other protein that's not a calcium-corseted casein.

Whey is a reference to both the proteins beyond casein and the watery mess left over when the curds fall out of suspension. Little Miss Muffet didn't sit on her tuffet just eating her curds and whey. She sat there eating her curds and whey and the water the whey is suspended in.

Curiously, the whey *will* coagulate in the presence of heat. It can't when you boil milk because it lives in the same house as the don't-touch-me casein. However, remove the casein (you do so when it becomes curds), and the whey will act like every other protein structure, coagulating as the water boils off. This is essentially how you make ricotta, a whey cheese.

All that said, the whey bits of protein are smaller than casein. Some whey proteins are only a single protein chain long. So they easily slip out of the milk and through any structure the casein is building because they're dissolved in milk's major component, which is . . .

6. Water. And here's how making cheese is just about like every other form of cooking and baking. Shove a roast in the oven, and you're dehydrating the meat, even if you want it rare. Put some muffin batter in a tin, and you're dehydrating it a bit so that the escaping steam creates tiny air pockets in the tightening batter, thus getting it to rise to that puffy, dry, crunchy top.

So it is with cheese making. From the get-go, you're pulling water out of the milk—all the way to the last stages: aging it for years, the cheese continuing to dehydrate, concentrating the flavors, building firmer structures, creating a more intense experience from those coagulated curds.

Think back to that rudimentary cheese called *pudding skin.* Yes, some of the casein clumps in the presence of the slightly acidic chocolate. But the skin will form only if you don't cover the pudding. Stick a piece of plastic wrap right on top of the pudding, and it won't form a skin because there's too much water, the casein not dehydrating enough to form any structure.

OK, before we get further into the specifics of the cheese-making craft, let's start by putting into practice what we just learned, making our own simple goat cheese that forms the rich elegance of this classic dish from India.

SAAG PANEER

FOUR WILL DOWN IT IN NO TIME.

To know more about making cheese, try this vegetarian dish (the name means something like "green-leaf cheese"). You'll make a rudimentary cheese from goat milk to create a stove-top casserole with spinach and a simple curry blend. Try this some weekend for a fun, creative project.

8 cups (2 L) whole goat milk (do not use low-fat)

¼ cup plus 3 tablespoons (105 ml) lemon juice, divided

1 teaspoon cumin seeds

1 teaspoon caraway seeds

1 teaspoon fennel seeds

1 teaspoon red pepper flakes

4 tablespoons (55 g) clarified goat butter (see page 81)

2 medium yellow onions, chopped

3 medium garlic cloves, minced

2 teaspoons minced, peeled fresh ginger

2 pounds (910 g) fresh spinach, any woody stems removed, the leaves washed (but not dried), then chopped (and thus still wet)

1 cup (240 ml) reduced-sodium vegetable broth

½ cup (120 ml) regular or low-fat goat yogurt

½ teaspoon salt

1. Pour the milk into a medium saucepan and bring it to a low simmer over medium-high heat (thereby continuing the process of breaking down the lactose into lactic acid; see page 169).

2. The second the milk starts to rise in the pan, stir in the ¼ cup (60 ml) lemon juice. Take the saucepan off the heat and set it aside for 15 minutes. At this point, you're curdling the milk, shifting the charge on some of that casein from negative to neutral because of the presence of the acid. We'll get to more specifics on the why and how in a bit. For now, suffice it to say that the mixture won't set like cheese but will begin to form simple curds. If in doubt, give it another 5 minutes.

3. When the curds have separated from the watery whey (in other words, when you have clumps of cheesy, milky solids in a cloudy liquid), line a large colander with kitchen-grade cheesecloth. Pour the curds and whey into the colander, catching the curds and letting the whey (and all that water) drain away. Strain in the sink for 1 hour.

4. Gather up the cheesecloth and gently squeeze the curds into a block or a mal-shaped mound. Work with even, delicate pressure so as not to break them up but to help them form into a solid mass, squeezing out a little of the excess moisture. Put the mound, still in its cheesecloth, in a cleaned sink, set a cutting board on top of it, and then weight it down with a 28-ounce (800-g) can of diced tomatoes or some such. Leave it be for 3 to 4 hours.

5. Meanwhile, make the curry powder by toasting the cumin seeds, car-away seeds, fennel seeds, and red pepper flakes in a dry skillet until lightly browned and very aromatic, about 2 minutes, tossing occasionally. Cool for 10 minutes or so, then grind in a spice grinder or a small coffee grinder to a fine powder.

If you've used a coffee grinder to make the simple curry powder, you'll need to clean it out to get rid of various spice oils. Fill it with raw white rice to a depth of about ½ inch (1.2 cm); whir that into a powder. Wipe out the rice powder with a dry paper towel and do that again, this time wiping down the inside of the grinder with a damp paper towel. You should now have removed most of the spice oils.

6. Remove the weight and the cutting board from on top of the cheese; unwrap the block. It should be somewhat firm, but not concrete. Use a sharp knife to cut it into 1-inch (2.5-cm) cubes.

7. Now you're ready to cook: Melt the butter in a high-sided sauté pan over medium heat. Add the onions and cook, stirring often, for about 3 minutes, or just until softened. Stir in the garlic, ginger, and the toasted spice powder; cook for 20 seconds or so.

8. Put the chopped spinach in the skillet, working in batches if you find there's too much to fit comfortably. Toss the spinach over the heat until it wilts enough that you can add more. Tongs work best here. Once all the spinach is in the skillet and wilted, pour in the broth and bring to a simmer. Cover, reduce the heat to low, and simmer for 5 minutes, tossing once in a while.

9. Stir in the yogurt, salt, and the remaining 3 tablespoons (45 ml) lemon juice. Cover and continue simmering slowly until the spinach is very soft, almost puree-able, and the sauce has thickened considerably, about 15 minutes.

10. Very gently stir in the homemade cheese cubes. Cover, reduce the heat even further, and cook for about 5 minutes, just until heated through.

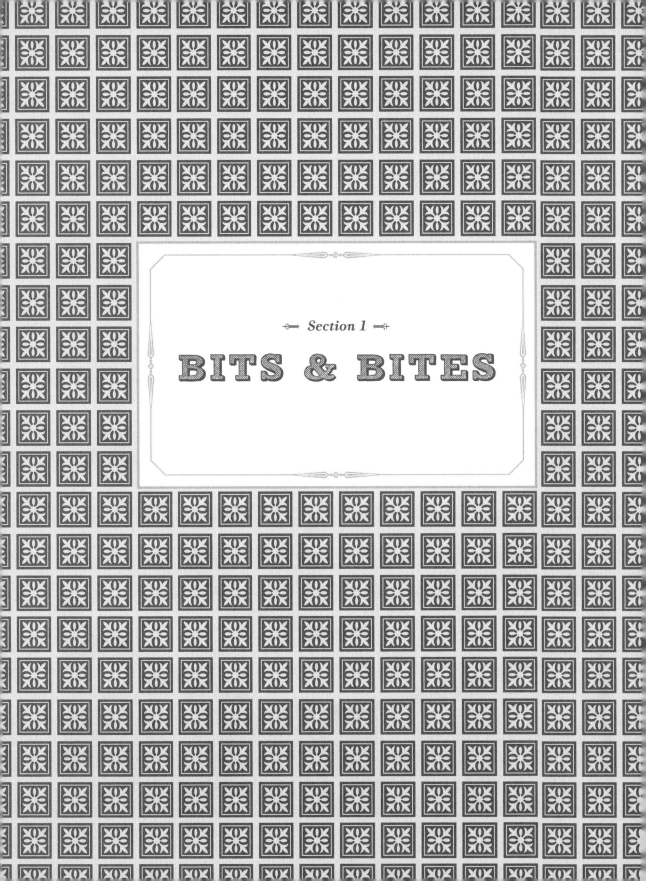

Section 1

BITS & BITES

MICHAEL POLLAN IS WRONG. He says that you shouldn't eat anything from a place where everyone is required to wear a surgical cap. You'd have to give up cheese. Everyone who makes it puts on the cap. And if not that, then at least a hairnet. No exceptions. It's part of the legal guidelines.

It's one of the many things we discovered one morning when we went back to Paul Trubey's Beltane Farm so Bruce could learn how to make cheese firsthand.

It was winter now: quieter, stiller, the ice thick in the driveway. Since Paul's goats had just about quit giving milk as the iron-cold New England dark settled around us, there was no need for staff. Except for Bruce. He had to wear the cap. And sterilize his shoes. And his hands. And put on the outerwear so that none of his ambient contaminants could get into the cheese.

"You, too," Paul said.

I stuttered that I was only along for the ride. And the tasting.

Some days, I could kill for an assistant. I got suited up and stepped inside what felt like a sauna on an otherwise bleak day.

Just as when we made the simple cheese for Saag Paneer (page 171), Paul also had to get the goat milk heated up. He opened the taps to run the milk from the milking parlor to a giant stainless steel cauldron in that cheese-making room.

Once the cauldron was full, he snapped on the gas flame, a thud resounding off the concrete floor. The milk had to be heated to 145°F (63°C), with an ambient air temperature in that stainless steel behemoth of 155°F (68°C)—then those temperatures had to be held for forty minutes. Just to make sure, a state-mandated monitoring device hung on a nearby wall.

Yes, via heat, Paul was continuing the process of turning lactose into lactic acid. But more importantly, he was pasteurizing the milk: heating it to and holding it at a temperature high enough to kill off any bad bugs. According to U.S. regulations, no one can make cheese from raw milk.

How can that be? you might ask. You've probably seen raw milk cheeses in the United States, labeled as such at high-end supermarkets or perhaps offered as a course after dinner at a fine restaurant. Parmigiano-Reggiano, Brie, and Gruyère are all raw milk cheeses.

There's a loophole in the law. If the cheese is made with raw, unpasteurized milk, it must be aged for at least sixty days—which is said to take care of the bad bugs in that high-salt, dehydrating process about the way heat takes care of them in the pasteurization process.

That said, raw milk is an ongoing debate among foodies. In Europe, some cheeses *cannot* be made with pasteurized milk: those three aged ones listed above, as well as Comté, Camembert, and Emmental; and then there are others that haven't been aged the necessary sixty days, but are nonetheless made with raw milk, and are thus illegal to import (or even make) in the United States.

Why are the Europeans so opposed to pasteurization, even though forgoing it knocks some of their cheeses out of the enormous U.S. market? Because as Bruce and Paul heated the goat milk, certain enzymes were rendered inactive and certain chemical compounds left over from the goats' foraging were destroyed, thus depriving the milk on two fronts of some of its flavor overtones.

After forty minutes, he shut off the gas. Now we had to wait for the milk to cool to almost 80°F. "Higher temperature will kill off the cultures," Paul said.

The cultures. That is, the main difference in a cheese maker's craft and our attempts to make a rudimentary cheese for Saag Paneer (page 171). We used lemon juice, a heavy hammer to get the casein to coagulate. Needless to say, artisanal cheese making needs a more refined instrument.

"You boys up for some chores?" Paul asked.

Bruce threw me a look.

Hey, you're the chef, I mouthed.

Without further ado, he and Paul went into the barn to clean out the milking cans. They tried to corral them, the gushing hot water making the cans rattle a bass-note thrum.

I looked up at the ice rimming the ceiling. Sometimes it's good to be the writer.

MARINATED GOAT FETA

YOU'LL END UP WITH ABOUT 1 POUND (450 G) OF
MARINATED CHEESE, GOOD FOR A PRE-DINNER STARTER, PLUS
SOME LEFT OVER FOR SNACKS IN THE DAYS AHEAD.

Goat feta has a deliciously silky texture and a sharp salty bite, a sure match to big herbs and spices.

1 pound (455 g) **goat feta cheese**

2 **fresh sage sprigs**

1 **fresh rosemary sprig**

3 medium **garlic cloves, peeled**

6 black **peppercorns**, just cracked open under the bottom of a small pot

First-cold-pressed olive oil

LESS TO DO

Skip the herbs—and even the garlic—by using an infused olive oil, sometimes available at high-end markets and specialty stores. Or check out the crazy-good smoked olive oils from The Smoked Olive in California. However, do keep the cracked black peppercorns as part of the mix: a little bite among the otherwise luxurious taste.

1. Drain the feta from its brine and pat it dry with paper towels. Cut it into 1-inch (2.5-cm) cubes.

2. Place these cubes and the herbs, garlic, and peppercorns in a 1-quart (960 ml) canning jar or decorative glass jar, layering the herbs and other flavorings among the chunks of cheese. It works best if the peppercorns get lodged under pieces of cheese; otherwise, they float.

3. Pour olive oil into the jar to drown the cheese and herbs. Set the jar in the fridge for at least 2 days or up to 2 weeks. To serve, transfer some of the chunks to a serving plate and pour a little bit of the herbed oil on and around them. And one note: Even when you've eaten all the cheese, the remaining oil is a wonderful condiment, aromatic and fresh. Strain it and drizzle it on steamed or grilled veggies.

Someone who sells cheese at your supermarket, farmers' market, or a gourmet store is called a *cheesemonger*. He or she is your best bet for up-to-the-minute information about what's fresh and eating well.

When speaking to him or her, remember that a ripened cheese has two parts: the *rind* (that is, the outer shell, sometimes soft, other times quite hard) and the *paste* (that is, the cheese inside, anything from brilliantly white and creamy to beige and crumbly).

Finally, pronouncing *chèvre* presents distinct problems for North Americans. Most of us simply say *shehv*. But in truth, there's a half-assed syllable off the back. Think of it this way: *shehv-ruh*. Now don't pronounce that last syllable. Instead, just start the *r* without completing the *uh*. Practice makes perfect.

BAKED GOAT BRIE

ONE BAKED WHEEL, ENOUGH FOR FOUR TO SIX WITH
GLASSES OF BUBBLY CHAMPAGNE ALONGSIDE.

You've probably never had this classic with goat Brie. It's undoubtedly a stronger taste—and so needs a stronger condiment, like chutney. Yes, you can use the standard, mango chutney (sometimes labeled Major Grey's), but why be pedestrian if you're working with goat? Scoop up this melty, gooey appetizer with baguette rounds or crunchy crackers.

¼ **cup plus 2 tablespoons** (85 g) **goat butter, melted**

8 sheets frozen phyllo dough, thawed according to the package instructions, then laid on a clean, scrupulously dry work surface under a sheet of plastic wrap and a clean kitchen towel to keep the sheets moist

One 6- to 8-ounce (170- to 225-g) **goat Brie wheel**

¼ **cup** (55 g) **chutney, particularly hot tomato chutney or a fruit chutney laced with ginger**

1. Position the rack in the center of the oven and preheat the oven to 400°F (205°C).

2. Brush a large baking sheet with a little of the melted butter. Place a phyllo sheet on the baking sheet, running basically the length of the sheet. Brush the phyllo sheet lightly with the melted butter. Set another sheet of phyllo on top of the first but at a 90-degree angle to it. Brush this sheet with the melted butter. And then keep going, laying the sheets on top of each other, each one at a 90-degree angle to the one below it, and brushing each with the melted butter. Take care to re-cover the unused sheets each time you take one off the pile so they stay moist and flexible.

3. Unwrap the goat Brie and set it in the dead center of the sheets, where they all overlap each other. Top the wheel with the chutney.

4. Slip each of your hands under the sheets and bring them up toward the center. Once the sheets are all gathered at the center, bring your hands together, as if you were starting to wring a chicken's neck (you can picture this, right?), making a little "throat" where the sheets meet. Squeeze this together and twist slightly, thereby making a narrow but sealed neck with a poof of flowery phyllo dough at the top.

5. Slip the tray into the oven and bake until the phyllo dough is golden brown and crunchy, about 30, maybe 40, minutes. Remove the tray from the oven and cool for 5 minutes before slipping a large spatula under the Brie bundle and transferring it to a serving plate. Serve by first cutting a wedge, just as you would a piece of cake. After that, everyone will gouge and slice to their heart's content.

CEDAR-PLANKED GOAT CHEESE

AN APPETIZER FOR SIX TO EIGHT WITH SOME COCKTAILS ON THE SIDE.

You'll need a small wheel (or a tomme; *see page 229) to make this grilled wonder. One warning: There won't be too many visual cues to know when the cheese has absorbed enough of the delicate cedar flavor from the plank. Prod it a bit—but be careful: It can run all over the grill. When done, serve it with sliced rounds of a baguette or crunchy crackers, the better to scoop up the runny cheese.*

1 cedar grilling plank

One 12- to 16-ounce (354- to 455-g) **goat wheel or** *tomme*

MORE TO KNOW

How do you know if you've gotten goat cheese that's beyond its prime?

1. It has a sharp odor, either like soap or (worse yet) like ammonia.

2. It begins to lose its shape, bulging, running, or sagging at various points on the wheel.

3. It becomes hard and dry.

1. Fill a big baking dish or a roasting pan with cool tap water and float the cedar plank in it for half an hour. Either weight the plank down with a small can so it's submerged or else turn it once during the soaking time.

2. Meanwhile, prepare the grill for high-heat, direct cooking. Either heat a gas grill to high heat (about 550°F [288°C]) with the lid closed or build a high-heat, red-hot, somewhat ashed coal bed in a charcoal grill. In either case, the heat source should be directly beneath the portion of the grill grate you intend to use.

3. Take the plank out of the water, unwrap the cheese, and set it directly on the wet plank. Without delay, set the wet plank directly over the heat and close the lid. Grill for about 15 minutes, or until the cheese is warmed through, slightly smoked, and definitely softer. The plank will get charred—and smoke quite a bit. Its bottom will look like a piece of charcoal. Do check it every once in a while to make sure it doesn't catch on fire. If it does, spritz it with water from a spray bottle.

4. Slip a thin metal spatula under the cheese and transfer the cheese to a serving platter. Cut into the cheese so it runs a bit.

GO ALL OUT! GO ALL OUT! GO ALL OUT! GO ALL OUT! GO ALL OUT!

The best cocktail for this dish is a well-balanced margarita. Fill a cocktail shaker with ice, then add 1½ ounces (that is, 3 tablespoons) each of tequila, Cointreau, and fresh lime juice. Also add ¼ teaspoon sugar, or a little more to taste—anything from up to 1½ teaspoons for a very sweet drink. Shake well, then strain into a glass with fresh ice cubes. Top with a splash—no more than ½ ounce (or 1 tablespoon)—of mescal, a smoky agave distillate.

SAVORY
SHORTBREAD ROUNDS

YOU'LL END UP WITH SIXTEEN SAVORY SHORTBREADS.

These are crunchy rounds, made with any variety of aged, firm goat cheese you choose, so long as you can grate it as you would Parmigiano-Reggiano. Once you make a log of the shortbread dough, you can keep it in your refrigerator for up to a week, slicing off rounds and baking as many as you want at a time.

MORE TO KNOW

In some recipes, we've "allowed" a substitute of some cow products: butter and/or milk, depending on if Bruce felt there was enough goaty flavor from just the cheese. The more goat, the better, in my book. But he felt we needed to make allowances.

¼ cup plus 2 tablespoons (85 g) **cool goat butter (or unsalted cow butter, if you must), cut into little bits**

4 ounces (115 g) **aged goat cheese, such as goat Gouda or goat Gruyère, grated through the small holes of a box grater or with a microplane**

¾ cup (80 g) **all-purpose flour**

½ teaspoon **dry mustard**

½ teaspoon **freshly ground black pepper**

¼ teaspoon **salt**

3 tablespoons **regular or low-fat goat milk (or cow milk, if you must)**

1. Place the butter bits, grated cheese, flour, dry mustard, pepper, and salt in a big bowl. Use a pastry cutter or a fork to mash the butter and cheese into the flour, continually wiping the tines, pressing it all against the sides and bottom of the bowl, and working it together until the mixture looks like coarse, wet sand. It will almost start mashing up into a dough but still be quite dry.

2. Stir in the milk with a fork to make a dough. Using your clean, dry hands, gather this dough into a ball, then form it into a log about 6 inches (15 cm) long, rolling it lightly against your work surface to help rid the log of any cracks. Wrap the log in plastic wrap and refrigerate for at least 2 hours or up to 1 week.

3. Position the rack in the center of the oven and preheat the oven to 375°F (190°C). Line a large baking sheet with a silicone baking mat or parchment paper.

4. When the oven's fully heated, unwrap the log and slice it into as many ¼-inch-thick (.6-cm) rounds as you choose. Set these on the prepared baking sheet and immediately get them into the oven while they're still cool. If you've got any of the log left, rewrap it in plastic wrap and pop it back into the fridge. Bake the rounds until golden and a little firm to the touch, about 20 minutes. Cool them on the baking sheet for 2 minutes, then transfer them to a wire rack to continue cooling. Serve warm or at room temperature.

RADISH AND GRAPE SALAD *with* GOAT CHEESE CROUTONS

IT'LL MAKE FOUR SERVINGS FOR LUNCH OR UP
TO EIGHT FOR A LIGHT FIRST COURSE.

*There's nothing better than a little melty goat cheese on crunchy crou-
tons, set atop fresh, springtime salad. If you really want the croutons
crunchy, toast the baguette rounds on one side under a preheated
broiler, cool them on a wire rack, then spread the goat cheese on their
"raw" sides and toast them a second time, cheese side up.*

1 medium carrot

10 red radishes, thinly sliced

1 cup (225 g) seedless red grapes,
halved

2 cups (455 g) baby arugula

Eight ½-inch-thick (eight 1.2-cm)
bread rounds, sliced from a thin
baguette

4 ounces (115 g) fresh chèvre or soft
goat cheese

3 tablespoons sherry or red wine
vinegar

2 teaspoons Dijon mustard

1 medium garlic clove, minced or even
put through a garlic press

½ teaspoon salt

½ teaspoon freshly ground black
pepper

½ cup (120 ml) olive oil

MORE TO KNOW

Arugula is a peppery green, a real
delight in a salad—but a bad, bitter
punch if the leaves get too large and
stemmy. Make sure you get the smallest leaves you can find. If the stems
appear woody or fibrous, cut them out
for a more appealing salad.

LESS TO DO

Use a bottled vinaigrette, especially
one made with balsamic vinegar. But
check the bottle to make sure it's not
laced with corn syrup, a too-sweet
addition to this fresh, light salad.

1. To make fancy-shmancy carrot curls, first fill a bowl with cold water
   and add a generous amount of ice cubes. Peel the carrot with a vegetable
   peeler, then continue making long, paper-thin strips along the length
   of the carrot, letting these fall into the ice water. If the strips are thin
   enough, they'll curl when they take a swim, somewhat like your toes in
   ice water.

2. Drain the carrot curls and put them in a big serving bowl. Add the radish
   slices, grape halves, and arugula leaves. Toss a bit to mix everything up.

3. Position the rack so that it's 4 to 6 inches (10 to 15 cm) from the broiler's
   heat source, then preheat the broiler. Lay the baguette rounds on a large
   baking sheet. Smear them with the soft goat cheese. Set the tray directly
   under the heat source and broil until the cheese has melted a bit and
   even turned a little light brown in places. Remove the baking tray from
   the oven and transfer the goat cheese croutons to a wire rack to cool
   while you make the dressing.

4. Whisk the vinegar, mustard, garlic, salt, and pepper in a medium bowl
   until the mustard has dissolved in the vinegar. Drizzle in the olive oil,
   whisking all the while, to make a thin but still creamy dressing.

5. Pour this dressing over the arugula mixture, then toss a bit. Spoon the
   salad onto serving plates and top each with 2 goat cheese croutons.

GOAT CHEESE QUESADILLAS

**TWO QUESADILLAS WILL FEED TWO FOR A LIGHT MEAL OR FOUR
TO SIX AT A COCKTAIL PARTY. DOUBLE OR TRIPLE AT WILL.**

*Goat Brie has a slightly soft, runny consistency, even meltier than cow
Brie. As such, it's the best thing for these easy quesadillas, sort of like
a small tortilla sandwich.*

2 large poblano chiles

Four 8-inch (four 20-cm) **flour tortillas**

3 ounces (85 g) **goat Brie, any rind
removed, the cheese softened to
room temperature**

¼ cup (55 ml) **bottled chutney or shallot marmalade**

MORE TO KNOW

If the Brie is very cold, the rind slices
off more easily, less of the gooey
cheese stuck to it. Stick the wheel in
the freezer for 30 minutes, then cut
off the rind.

1. Char the poblanos. There are several ways to get the job done:

☞ Set them on the grate over an open gas flame on your grill or stove,
turning once in a while with tongs, until blackened on all sides,
about 4 minutes.

☞ Or place them on a baking sheet and set them 4 to 6 inches (10 to 15
cm) from a preheated broiler, turning occasionally, until blackened
on all sides, about 5 minutes.

☞ Or place them over direct, high heat on a grill, turning once in a
while, until blackened on all sides, about 6 minutes.

In any case, once the chiles are charred, put them in a bowl and seal the
bowl with plastic wrap. Set aside for 15 minutes.

2. Peel back the plastic wrap, remove the chiles, and peel off the blackened
bits. You needn't get every speck, just most of the charred spots. Cut off
the stems, then slice the chiles open and remove the seeds and any inner
membranes. Finally, chop the flesh into long, thin strips.

3. Place all 4 tortillas on your work surface. Spread each with a quarter of
the goat cheese. Top 2 of them with 2 tablespoons of the chutney and the
chile strips. Top each with one of the other tortillas, cheese side down.

4. Heat a large skillet, preferably nonstick, over medium heat. Add 1 of the
tortilla sandwiches and dry-fry until the tortilla has browned in places
and is starting to turn crisp, about 3 minutes. Turn with a large spatula
and dry-fry for another 3 minutes. Transfer the quesadilla to a wire rack
and repeat with the other one. Once both are done, transfer them to a
cutting board and slice them into pie wedges to serve.

GOAT GOUGÈRES

MAKES TWENTY-FOUR CHEESE PUFFS.

These are traditional French puffs, little baked nothingnesses, best with cocktails before dinner. (May I suggest a Campari and soda?) Bruce twisted the recipe a bit with some chopped green olives, a little spike against the more assertive goat cheese, zippier than the Gruyère that's more common in gougères. *In any event, be ready: These puffs are best right out of the oven, while they're still hot and crunchy.*

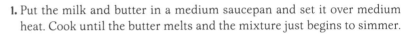

1 cup (240 ml) **regular or low-fat goat milk (or cow milk, if you must)**

8 tablespoons (115 g) **goat butter**

1 cup (125 g) **all-purpose flour**

1 teaspoon **salt**

4 large **eggs, at room temperature**

4 ounces (115 g) **fresh chèvre or soft goat cheese**

2 tablespoons **minced pitted green olives**

MORE TO KNOW

The eggs must be at room temperature for the dough to work. The proteins have to be elongated so that they can build structure in the batter. Cold eggs mean balled-up proteins, a bit like you in bed on a winter night. Leave the eggs out on your counter for 20 minutes before you use them—or immerse them in their shells in a bowl of warm (not hot!) tap water for 5 minutes.

MORE GOATY GOODNESS

Just before the little rounds go into the oven, sprinkle each with some finely grated hard, aged goat cheese.

1. Put the milk and butter in a medium saucepan and set it over medium heat. Cook until the butter melts and the mixture just begins to simmer.

2. Dump in the flour and salt. Stir until a dough forms, then reduce the heat to medium-low and continue cooking, stirring constantly, to dry the dough out, from 5 to 7 minutes. You'll know it's perfect when it leaves a dry, milky film around the inside of the saucepan. Once it's ready, scrape into the bowl of a stand mixer or a large bowl suitable for use with a portable electric mixer and cool on the counter for 15 minutes.

3. Position the rack in the center of the oven and preheat the oven to 375°F (190°C). Line a large baking sheet with parchment paper.

4. Beat the eggs into the dough one at a time, making sure each is fully incorporated before adding the next. Honestly, it's hard to overbeat the stuff. You want air, you want air, you want air. Once all the eggs have been added and the mixture is smooth and thick, beat in the chèvre and the green olives.

5. Scoop up rounded tablespoonfuls of the dough and drop these onto the prepared baking sheet, spacing them a couple inches apart. Slide the tray into the oven and bake until the rounds are puffed and golden, about 25 minutes. Cool for just a couple minutes on the tray before serving, still quite warm from the oven.

GOAT CHEESE MASHED POTATOES

CALL IT FOUR SERVINGS.

Not to brag too much on Bruce, but this may well be the best darn side dish. Ever. Especially alongside any of the grilled or roasted goat dishes in this book.

2 pounds (910 g) yellow-fleshed pota-toes, such as Yukon golds (about 4 large potatoes; no need to peel unless you really want to)

3 to 4 tablespoons (45 to 55 g) goat butter (or unsalted cow butter, if you must)

⅔ cup (165 ml) regular or low-fat goat milk (or cow milk, if you must)

1 very small leek (white and pale green parts only), halved length-wise, washed carefully for any grit in the inner chambers, then very thinly sliced

4 fresh sage leaves, minced

4 ounces (115 g) fresh chèvre or soft goat cheese, at room temperature

½ teaspoon salt

½ teaspoon freshly ground black pepper

1. Cook the potatoes until they're tender. You can do this in a couple of ways:

  ☞ In a vegetable steamer: Set up the contraption with about an inch (2.5 cm) or so of simmering water in the bottom part, then add the potatoes (in quarters if necessary), cover, and steam until tender when pierced with a fork, 20 to 30 minutes. Transfer the potatoes to a big bowl or the bowl of a stand mixer.

  ☞ In boiling water: Bring a large saucepan of water to a boil over high heat. Add the potatoes (leave them whole, so they don't get so water-logged), cover, and boil until tender when pierced with a fork, about 25 minutes. Drain the potatoes in a colander set in the sink, then transfer to a big bowl or the bowl of a stand mixer.

2. As the potatoes cook, place the butter, milk, leek, and sage in a medium saucepan set over medium-high heat. Bring to a low simmer, stirring once in a while. Then cover, reduce the heat to low, and simmer very slowly for 10 minutes.

3. Pour the hot milk mixture along with the leek and herbs over the pota-toes. Add the fresh chèvre, salt, and pepper. Mash with a potato masher or beat with an electric mixer at medium speed until smooth and creamy.

GOAT CHEESE, BLACK-EYED PEA, AND SWISS CHARD EMPANADAS

YOU'LL GET TWENTY EMPANADAS, EACH A SERVING. MAYBE.

OK, things are going to get a little complicated. Fortunately, this recipe is a real make-ahead—and in two different places. You can make the filling one day, save it for a couple of days in the fridge, prepare all the empanadas on a weekend day, and then freeze the baked little turnovers for months, until company drops by.

MORE TO KNOW

The goat milk needs to be cold so that it doesn't melt the cut-in butter, thereby making the dough too soft for rolling out.

For the filling:

2 tablespoons olive oil

3 medium garlic cloves, minced

½ teaspoon red pepper flakes

2 pounds (910 g) Swiss chard, stemmed, the leaves washed well and chopped (do not dry those leaves—they need to be sopping wet)

1 teaspoon ground cumin

½ teaspoon ground cinnamon

½ teaspoon salt

½ teaspoon freshly ground black pepper

1 cup (225 g) canned black-eyed peas, drained and rinsed

6 ounces (170 g) fresh chèvre or soft goat cheese, crumbled

For the dough:

3 cups (375 g) all-purpose flour, plus more for dusting your work surface

¼ cup (55 g) sugar

½ teaspoon baking powder

1 teaspoon salt, divided

8 tablespoons (115 g) cool goat butter (or 1 stick unsalted cow butter, if you must), cut into small cubes

¼ cup (60 ml) almond or vegetable oil

2 large eggs, divided

½ cup (120 ml) cold regular goat milk (do not use low-fat—or you can use whole cow milk, if you must)

2 tablespoons water

1. To start the filling, heat a large skillet over medium heat. Swirl in the olive oil, then add the garlic and red pepper flakes. Fry until the garlic is frizzled at the edges, about 1 minute.

2. Dump in the chopped, wet chard, which will splatter like mad. Stir or toss a bit until wilted; then stir in the cumin, cinnamon, ½ teaspoon salt, and pepper. Cover, reduce the heat to low, and cook until the chard is very soft, about 15 minutes, tossing occasionally.

3. Uncover the skillet and let any excess liquid boil away. The skillet needs to be dry when you're done. Cool the mixture for 30 minutes in the skillet, then stir in the black-eyed peas and the crumbled cheese. The filling can be made in advance; scrape it into a bowl, cover, and refrigerate for up to 2 days—but let it come back to room temperature before proceeding with the recipe.

4. To make the dough, mix the flour, sugar, baking powder, and ½ teaspoon salt in a small bowl. Add the butter and use a pastry cutter or a fork to work it into the flour mixture, pressing the fat through the tines repeatedly, working all around the bowl, until you've got a mixture that looks sort of like really coarse cornmeal.

5. Whisk the oil, one of the eggs, and the milk in a small bowl until pretty creamy; then pour this into the dry stuff and stir with a wooden spoon to form a dough. Divide the dough into 20 balls. Set them on a clean, dry part of your work surface and cover with a kitchen towel.

6. To make the empanadas, position the rack in the center of the oven and heat the oven up to 375°F (190°C). Whisk the remaining egg with the water in a small bowl until uniform and light. Set aside.

7. Dust another part of your work surface with a little flour, set a dough ball in the middle of it, and use a rolling pin to roll the dough into a circle about 4 inches (10 cm) in diameter, working the pin in various directions to get a circle without weird bumps in its circumference.

8. Place 2 tablespoons of the chard filling in the center of the circle, then fold the dough circle in half to create a half-moon-shaped empanada. Crimp the open edge closed by pressing the tines of a fork in it all the way around the curve. Brush the top side of the empanada with a little of the egg wash, then set the empanada, washed side up, on a large baking sheet.

9. Repeat steps 7 and 8 with the remaining balls of dough, making all 20 empanadas.

10. Bake the empanadas until golden brown, 30 to 35 minutes. Cool on the baking sheet for 10 minutes, then transfer to a wire rack to cool completely. Once baked and cooled, the empanadas can be stored in a sealed container at room temperature for 2 or 3 days—or frozen in zip-sealed plastic bags for up to 4 months (reheat them on a baking sheet in a preheated 350°F [175°C] oven for 10 minutes or so).

BRIWAT

YOU'LL END UP WITH SIXTEEN FRIED CHEESE ROLLS.

These are a traditional Syrian wonder, and a great appetizer for any party: crunchy fried goat cheese cigars that get dipped into honey. Wow. The real key here is the pepper: Aleppo, a dark red, musky but still fruity, cumin-scented, medium-heat pepper. Bruce has fallen so in love with the stuff that he's swapped out the black peppercorns in his everyday grinder for these little wonders.

9 ounces (255 g) fresh chèvre or soft goat cheese

½ cup (115 g) chopped, fresh cilantro leaves

2 teaspoons freshly ground Aleppo pepper

3 large egg yolks, divided

16 spring roll wrappers, thawed if necessary

Peanut oil, for frying

Honey, for dipping

MORE TO KNOW

While the Aleppo pepper is one key to this dish, another is the honey. Think about it: The tastes are pretty simple; each flavor is important. Go with a fragrant, floral, artisanal honey—like star thistle or eucalyptus. Or try one of the dark tree honeys, like chestnut, oak, or even the herbaceous pine.

1. Mix the fresh chèvre or soft goat cheese, cilantro, pepper, and one of the egg yolks in a bowl until creamy and smooth.

2. Whisk the 2 remaining egg yolks in a second bowl until creamy and light.

3. Put a spring roll wrapper on a dry, clean part of your counter so that it makes a diamond in front of you (one point facing you). Put 1 table-spoon of the goat cheese filling on it, situated a little toward you from the center, a little toward the "bottom" point.

4. Roll the bottom point over the filling. Then fold the points to the left and right over the filling. Brush the remaining "top" corner with a little of the beaten egg yolks and roll the spring roll over so that it sticks to this egg-washed corner. Press it a little to seal if you need to. One tip: Make sure you roll fairly tightly. Air pockets inside the packet will expand and can pop open as the thing is fried.

5. Repeat steps 3 and 4 with the remaining wrappers, filling, and egg wash.

6. Fill a sauté pan or a high-sided skillet with peanut oil to a depth of 1 inch (2.5 cm). Clip a deep-frying thermometer to the inside of the pan and heat the oil over medium heat until it reaches 325°F (165°C). Drop 4 to 6 briwat rolls into the hot oil—do not crowd the pan—and adjust the temperature so that the oil stays right around 325°F (165°C). Fry until golden, about 6 minutes, turning once. Transfer the rolls to a wire rack with paper towels underneath it to catch any grease drips. Continue fry-ing more. Once you've got them all done, set them on a serving platter with a bowl of honey on the side to dip them in one at a time. Pure bliss.

A MATCH MADE IN NORWAY

I ASK YOU, is everything in Norway cheery? Is that the way they thumb their noses at the more dour Swedes next door? Even the ubiquitous garden trolls seem a little manic.

No matter. By the end of our first day in Norway, we reasoned it all had to work in our favor. Some happy soul would help us find *gjetost* (*yay-TOAST*—or "goat cheese").

As I've said, not all cheese is made from casein (a.k.a. the curds). Some types come from the whey—like this one, made by boiling the goat whey with just a little extra milk and/or cream (sometimes from cows, sometimes strictly from goats), about as you would make *Cajeta* (page 148), boiling it until most of the water has been lost from the solution and the milk sugars have begun to caramelize. *Gjetost* is brown and creamy, absolutely stunning, with elegant caramelization and a sweet finish.

Why don't the caseins in the added milk and cream keep the mass from coagulating? First off, there are relatively few by volume. And they are partially denuded in the more acidic, strictly whey environment.

We figured a great place to start on our quest for *gjetost* was the elegant outdoor food market in Bergen. Perhaps there'd be an artisanal producer— although we were quickly sidetracked by the fish: rows of gorgeous specimens on ice.

As we strolled past one stall, the blonde behind the counter called out to offer us a taste of smoked whale. I wasn't to be deterred. (Back up, Disney.) I took the meaty chunks she handed over the ice. It was up there with the best smoked tenderloin I'd ever had. (Whales are mammals, after all.)

As I was gnawing away, Bruce asked her if anyone in the market sold *gjetost*.

Although almost everyone in Norway speaks impeccable English, she took two steps back like a Frenchman.

"*Yay* what?"

"*Gjetost*," he said. "Maybe my Norwegian isn't—"

"It isn't," she cut him off, that cheery disposition collapsing past Swedish severity and going straight to Finnish depression. "I have no idea what you're talking about."

How could she *not* know? She was Norwegian. Was she trying to torture us?

The woman next to her muttered something and she turned back to us. "Ah, *brunost*."

"No, *gjetost*," Bruce said. Like most New Yorkers, when faced with a head-on collision, he speeds up.

She turned positively Prussian. "You want *brunost*."

"Is that the same as *gjetost*?" Bruce asked.

"Over there." She pointed to a stall.

We followed her finger. An old woman sat behind a small glass case.

Bruce stalked off. But I couldn't be that rude. I turned back to say "thank you"—only to see that that big smile was back on her face for the next customer.

I hightailed it over to the stall just as Bruce plunged into it again. "*Gjetost?*" he asked.

"*Brunost*," the old woman said, handing over a package.

We looked at it, read it as we could, a phrase book in hand to make sure the label's English translation was on the money. Sure enough: the goat whey cheese itself. *Brunost*.

We'd been duped by marketing. Nobody in Scandinavia calls it *gjetost*. There is no *gjetost*. That's a name for Americans. In Norway, it's *brunost* (brown cheese). In Sweden, *mesost*. In Denmark, *myseost*. In Iceland, *mysuostor*. But never, ever *gjetost*.

Which isn't even a current Norwegian spelling. If you wanted to say *goat cheese* in Norwegian anytime after, oh, the Middle Ages, you wouldn't even spell it *gjetost*. You'd spell it *gietost*.

Ah, well. Score one for the international marketers. At least we'd found some of the best whey cheese in the world. And you can, too. Just don't call it *gjetost* in Norway. Because nothing is scarier than watching that practiced cheeriness slide off their faces.

GOAT CHEESE FONDUE

SIX WILL DOWN IT WITHOUT LOOKING BACK.

Although we'll give most of the fondue medals to the cows, a combination of goat Gouda and gjetost *garners the highest honors for the goat team. The two cheeses bring out the best in each other: soft, creamy, a little sharp, a little caramelized—in other words, a pot of melty marvelousness beyond compare. If you don't have a dedicated fondue pot, make the fondue in a saucepan, but return it to low heat every 5 minutes or so to make sure that the cheese mixture stays melted.*

1¾ cups (420 ml) sweet white wine, such as a muscat, Sancerre, or Riesling

4 fresh tarragon sprigs

1 medium garlic clove, smashed flat (but not into pieces) with the side of a heavy chef's knife or the bottom of a small saucepan

12 ounces (340 g) goat Gouda, finely grated through the large holes of a box grater

6 ounces (170 g) *gjetost*, finely grated through the large holes of a box grater

2 tablespoons all-purpose flour

Bread cubes, broccoli florets, or cauliflower florets, for dipping

GO ALL OUT! GO ALL OUT!

Once the fondue has been eaten down to almost nothing, there'll be crusty bits of cheese along the inner rim of the pot. Turn up the heat and add a little more wine, loosening up some of the bits by whisking frequently as the wine bubbles. Turn the flame to very low. Crack a large egg into a bowl, whisk it until yellow and uniform, then dump it into the fondue pot. Stir over the heat until the egg scrambles, picking up the cheesy bits as you go. Turn off the flame and smear these last bits with the scrambled egg on pieces of toasted bread.

1. Pour the wine into a stove-top-safe fondue pot. Drop in the tarragon and garlic. Bring to a simmer slowly over low heat. The moment the wine starts to bubble, cover the pot, take it off the heat, and let it stand for anywhere between 5 and 20 minutes to infuse the flavors.

2. Meanwhile, toss both kinds of grated cheese with the flour in a medium bowl until the flour is evenly distributed in the mixture, adhering to all the bits of cheese.

3. Remove the tarragon and garlic from the wine. Set the wine in its pot back over medium heat and bring to a low simmer, bubbles starting to form all around. Add a small handful of the floured cheeses. Whisk over the heat until the cheese melts—then add another small handful, whisking all the while as that melts, adding more afterward, and on and on, until all the cheese is in the pot, has indeed melted, and the concoction is bubbling slowly—the blub, blub, blub of the mud pots in Yellowstone. Bubble slowly for 2 minutes, whisking all the while.

4. Set the fondue pot on its base, adjusting the flame underneath until the fondue mixture is at a constant, low bubble while everyone digs in with their bread cubes or veggies on long-handled forks or fondue spears.

GRILLED GOAT CHEESE SANDWICHES ᴡɪᴛʜ PERSIMMONS AND HONEY MUSTARD

FOUR SANDWICHES.

Hands down, gjetost (or whatever it's called) makes the best grilled cheese sandwiches. That deep caramel taste melts into silky luxury, a real treat for dinner some night with a salad and a glass of Syrah. To get the cheese sliced thinly enough, (1) make sure it's cold, right out of the fridge, and (2) use a cheese plane, a spatula-shaped tool with a lip in the middle of the paddle, one you can pull across the cheese to make thin slices. Don't put much weight on the thing, or the slices will be too thick.

MORE TO KNOW

There are two types of persimmons: the orange Fuyu that can be eaten right away and the darker, squishier Hachiya, which must be ripened through a hard frost. Make sure you get the Fuyus, now common from California and sort of like a squat tomato with a sweet fragrance. If it's not winter and Fuyus are not in plentiful supply, consider substituting a sweet apple, like a Gala or a Fuji, peeled, cored, and sliced into paper-thin wedges.

LESS TO DO

Of course, you can make these sandwiches in a panini press, thereby taking away any need for a complicated device to weight down the sandwiches as they fry.

GO ALL OUT! GO ALL OUT!

To make your own honey mustard, whisk ¼ cup (60 ml) Dijon mustard, 1½ tablespoons honey, 1 tablespoon packed dark brown sugar, and 1½ teaspoons cider vinegar in a small bowl until smooth.

8 thick-cut bread slices, preferably a country-style sandwich loaf

8 teaspoons (40 ml) **honey mustard**

6 ounces (170 g) *gjetost*, **very thinly sliced, almost paper thin**

2 Fuyu persimmons, thinly sliced

3 tablespoons goat butter (or unsalted cow butter, if you must), divided

1. Spread the bread slices out on your work surface. Coat each slice with 1 teaspoon honey mustard.

2. Divide the cheese and persimmon slices among 4 of the bread slices, making sure the persimmon slices are sandwiched between slices of cheese on each. Top each of these slices with 1 of the other 4 bread slices, mustard side down.

3. Melt about 1½ tablespoons of the butter in a very large skillet set over medium heat. Place 2 of the sandwiches in the skillet, weight down the sandwiches, and fry until lightly browned, about 2 minutes.

   Weight them down? Indeed. Put a smaller frying pan inside the larger one so it sits on top of the sandwiches, then put a big can of tomatoes in the smaller frying pan, weighting it down onto the sandwiches.

   ☞ Or wrap 2 bricks in aluminum foil and set 1 on top of each sandwich.

   ☞ Or use the flat lid of another pan, pressing down gently but insistently the whole while.

4. Remove the weighting device, flip the sandwiches, weight them again, and continue frying until lightly browned, until the cheese has melted, another 2 minutes. Transfer these sandwiches to a cutting board, add the remaining 1½ tablespoons butter to the skillet, and fry the other 2 sandwiches the same way.

Lazy Lady

Years before we got to write this book, we got contracted by the Cooking Club of America to write a grilling book. And we lived in Manhattan. Were we to grill on our window air conditioner?

So we rented a house. In the Hamptons? Oh, no. We love tabbouleh. Vermont it was.

We found a cottage two miles from the Canadian border, in what's often called the *Northeast Kingdom*. Ours was a sweet place on a small river that poured down from Jay Peak.

We lived in a kind of grilling Eden: hunks and hanks of meat for days on end. But toward the end of the project, ninety recipes in thirty days, even I started to flag.

"Give me cheese," I said. (Swiss chard, apparently I know thee not.)

On a shopping trip down in Burlington, we raided the cheese counter at the Onion Street Co-op, the haunt for upland locavores. We couldn't resist one small round of goat cheese from a place named *Lazy Lady Farm*. It claimed to be made in a town two over from ours. It also had a phone number.

The cheese was pretty darn fine—it didn't make it back home—so I called the number.

The Lazy Lady turned out to be Laini Fondiller, an industrious, weather-beaten soul. She picked up the phone with a simple "What?"

I stammered something about writing a cookbook (as if that's a credential for much) and asked her if we could drop by to buy more cheese.

"You couldn't buy more at the store?"

"Sure. But why'd you list your phone number?"

"Frenchman who taught me how to make cheese talked me into it. He said people would trust the product. Think it wasn't pretentious."

"He was right."

"He also said no one would ever call."

But in for a penny, in for a pound, she gave us directions.

Which were once again none too helpful. What is it with people who work around goats? *Go until you can't anymore.* That's not a direction. That's an existential state.

She stared unblinkingly at the car as we drove up. "You found me," she said, none too pleased. Smears of mud highlighted her cheekbones. "Well, come on."

She led us to a dirt path down the hillside. She made her goat cheese in what can only be called *a hobbit hole*: a door directly into the side of a ravine. Above it, a plaque said *Blessed are the cheese makers*. A Monty Python reference!

Inside, the antechamber had bowls holding a nasty liquid chock-full of flies and other detritus. Through the next set of doors, we came into a dark room, an honest cave.

Bruce gasped. "Is it supposed to smell like that?"

"Doesn't smell like shit, does it?" she asked, chewing her lip.

"No."

"Then it's supposed to smell like that." She cut off hunks, handed them around. "I'm proud of that one. Came out nice."

It was runny, barely cohesive, and something like Époisses de Bourgogne, the fine French cheese known for its pungent aroma, like garbage in July: grassy, sweet. But somehow even creamier than that Gallic delight, mostly because of the goat milk. Hers barely held its shape as she knifed it at us.

"Holy shit," I said.

"You said it didn't smell like that."

"I mean the cheese."

"You boys like this kind of thing?" she asked. "Well, get some and get out of here. I got work to do. Goats don't milk themselves."

We picked out a large round, maybe 15 inches (38 cm) across, a soft cake of goat cheese. We hauled it through the doors, up the hill, and back to the car.

In some ways, Laini's cheese is the foundation under this book. It was a revelation: prickly, delicious, unctuous, smelling of flowers and the farm, well-rounded and bright without being cloying.

In some ways, that about sums up goat in all its forms.

Section 3

COMFORT FOOD

PAUL AND BRUCE HAD FINISHED their chores about the time the goat milk had cooled to the right temperature. They were now ready for step two: adding the rennet and cultures.

Having been outside the cheese-making room, we sanitized again, cleaned back up, snapped on the caps, and stepped back into the humidity.

Where things got trickier. Because this is a cheese maker's art. As with most artisanal products, there's a fine line between craft and art—a line that's continually crossed, even smudged.

It goes like this: On the craft side lie the rules, the temperature gauges, the state-mandated monitoring devices, the sterilized cans, and the chores. And on the art side? In some ways, the bending of those rules. Not their breaking—they are time-tested and this cheese making is a for-profit business, after all. Rather, the art morphs the tradition, gives it individuality. For someone who makes cheese, the art lies here—in the mixing of the cultures. And in the finishing step, as we'll see.

All that's a long way around to saying that Paul didn't want to give it away. New Englanders are not fools. He was happy to share his craft, more reticent when it came to his art. So he stepped to the fridge, got out his cultures, did some mixing with water pretty quickly, and poured the concoction into the stainless steel cauldron with the heated milk—all while avoiding my notepad.

Food writers are a curious lot. We traffic in the kindness of artisans. We walk into their studios (as it were) and ask them how they do what they do. Oddly, they comply—to a point, if they're smart. Still, the massive food corporations are far more cagey. Can you imagine some oil-square cheese conglomerate inviting us in for this kind of access?

I smiled. "What next?"

"More chores," he said.

Bruce seemed none too pleased. As a chef, he'd come for the art. But it doesn't happen without the craft.

"How long does this step take?" he asked.

"About an hour and a half," Paul replied.

Fortunately, we—or they—ran out of chores quickly. Paul had already done his milking. So he invited us up to the house for tea. We sat at the kitchen table in the late-morning light as the cats and dogs, ever companions on a farm, paced the floor. We talked about the business: ours and his, a linked camaraderie, food writers and food producers, a little wary of each other, mostly interdependent.

As we sipped our tea and talked about our work, a far more complex process was going on in the barn. As you may remember, the dominant protein in milk, casein, is negatively charged. It stays away from its own kin in the milk, like the negative ends of magnets.

When we added the lemon juice to the goat milk to make Saag Paneer (page 171), we did more than just change the charge on the casein. We unwound the calcium barrette holding the protein strands together, the very structure of casein itself. In other words, we made a rudimentary cheese by smashing the casein to bits. The little protein strands, once wound into gangly bunches by the calcium, were now on their own. Yes, many could glom together, but not in a really cohesive way. They clumped; they didn't build. Those curds we made wouldn't have stood the test of time, the most basic factor when making cheese. After all, cheese is preservation. We certainly couldn't have aged those curds. And besides, much of the flavor molecules, almost all the calcium, and even a lot of the fat had slipped off with the watery whey.

In the more complex art of making cheese, the rennet does what our lemon juice couldn't. It doesn't whack the casein into bits; instead, it gives each casein knot a haircut, specifically trimming away the negatively charged bits (the kappa-caseins), thereby rendering the casein largely intact, the calcium barrette still in place, but the whole structure chargeless. Now their gangly but shorn protein tentacles can stick together. It's like building with larger, modular pieces, rather than individual bricks. And as the casein builds its latticelike structures (rather than just a dumped pile of protein bricks), it traps many more fat globules and flavor compounds inside.

Rennet is an enzyme found in the fourth of the five stomachs of almost all ruminants: cows, deer, sheep, and even goats. It's what allows them to digest their mother's milk. Humans stumbled

on its cheese-making properties probably by accident. Sometime about three thousand years ago, someone plopped a bit of a calf's stomach in milk, probably to cook it, and the milk curdled. Eureka!

These days, most of the cheese made in the United States is made with so-called vegetable rennet, a chemical concoction made to resemble the original stomach enzyme. But there are still artisanal cheeses here and even more so in Europe made with the original stomach enzymes added to the milk.

But rennet only offers the structure. Much of the flavor in cheese comes from the other thing Paul added to the milk: the cultures. These are specific to each cheese maker and even to each cheese made. The cultures (a.k.a. bacteria and molds) thread through the forming curds, adding levels of taste and aroma not necessarily found in the milk. Some cultures enhance the flavors in whatever the goats have been eating; others—like the Roquefort or other penicillin molds used to make blue cheese—add a pop all their own.

By contrast, the cheese we made for Saag Paneer (page 171) was not cultured. It got its flavor strictly from the goat milk—and any complexity in the meal from the curry powder.

Done with our tea, we headed back to the barn—more sanitizing, more putting on the caps—to check the cauldron. It was as if the goat milk had solidified into a shiny white, wet plastic.

"Now what?" Bruce asked.

"We cut up the curds," Paul said.

It's usually done with a cheese harp, a long-handled angel-food-cake cutter, dragged through the cheese. But Paul, ever the frugal New Englander, doesn't mess with gadgets. He uses an old, sterilized, wooden-handled, long, quite intimidating knife.

He and Bruce ran the knife repeatedly through the curd, cutting it into smaller and smaller chunks, releasing more and more of its water (and the whey) with each slice. The cutting had to happen in all directions, even horizontally. The more slices, the more water (and whey) came out of the curds, leaving them floating in the opaque muck.

Paul and Bruce then gathered the curds together and hung them in sterilized cheesecloth bags over a stainless steel trough. Although so much whey had been left in the cauldron, more was already pouring out of those bags, running down the trough and into a big trash can at the end.

"Pig food," Paul said, pointing to it.

Like any good farmer, he won't feed it back to the goats. That's the best way to get disease looped into the herd: to feed the goats their own milk, as it were.

We were almost ready for step three in the cheese-making process, far more art than craft. We'll save that for our last section. For now, I'm hungry. Let's get to the recipes.

SPAGHETTI WITH OVEN-ROASTED TOMATOES, SHIITAKE MUSHROOMS, AND GRATED GOAT CHEESE

DINNER FOR TWO (DOUBLE IT FOR FOUR).

By slowly roasting the tomatoes in a low-heat oven, you assure they stay firm but, more importantly, intensely flavorful, concentrated and luscious. If you double this dish for more servings (and the amount here could easily serve four as a fancy first course), make sure you have quite a large skillet to hold it all for the final toss.

1 pint (455 g) grape or cherry tomatoes

2 tablespoons olive oil

2 medium garlic cloves, minced

½ teaspoon red pepper flakes

4 ounces (115 g) shiitake mushroom caps (do not use the stems), sliced

1 teaspoon packed fresh thyme leaves

¼ cup (60 ml) dry white wine or dry vermouth

2 tablespoons reduced-sodium vegetable broth

8 to 10 ounces (225 to 280 g) fresh spaghetti, cooked and drained according to the package instructions

2 ounces (55 g) hard, aged goat cheese, like a goat Gouda or even a goat crottin you've aged yourself (see More to Know)

1. Position the rack in the center of the oven and preheat the oven to 250°F (121°C). Cut the tomatoes in half (lengthwise if grape tomatoes) and set them on a large, lipped baking sheet. Place in the oven and roast until they begin to shrink and the skin shrivels a bit, about 2 hours. This step can be done in advance; use a metal spatula to get the tomatoes off the baking sheet and into a large container, then seal it and store at room temperature for up to a day.

2. Heat a large skillet set over medium heat. Swirl in the oil, then add the garlic and red pepper flakes. Cook for about 20 seconds, stirring constantly, just until aromatic. Add the sliced shiitake caps; continue stirring over the heat a couple of minutes. Once again, more flavors with goat. In this case, shiitake mushroom caps, rather than milder brown or white mushrooms.

3. Stir in the thyme, then pour in the wine or vermouth. As the liquid boils, scrape up any browned stuff on the skillet's bottom.

4. Pour in the broth; stir in the tomatoes (as well as any juice on their baking sheet or in the container where they've been stored). Toss well, add the pasta, toss again, and transfer to 2 dinner plates. Grate half the cheese over each.

MORE TO KNOW

Crottins (French, *croh-TANZ*) are round buttons of goat cheese, often an inch or two (2.5 or 5 cm) high. They have a somewhat sturdy, wrinkled, edible shell, pasty white from molds. Inside, the cheese is pure white, creamy and luscious, often with nutty or earthy overtones, like a fine Chardonnay.

When a crottin is aged, it darkens, turns brown, even black—and thus its name, which means something like "animal droppings." The flavors intensify and concentrate. There's further dehydration, after all—as well as the further blooming of the cultures and molds.

If you'd like to age a crottin, the better to grate it over pasta or shave it over salads, wrap it in plastic wrap or butcher paper, then put it in the humid, high-moisture hydrator of your refrigerator. Every week or so, turn it over, for four to six weeks. It will harden and may even darken as it ages, depending on the exact humidity inside your hydrator. In any event, it will soon enough be perfect to grate. If you wait. Because waiting is the game in almost every art.

PIZZA WITH GOAT CHEESE, SQUASH PUREE, CARAMELIZED ONION, AND PECANS

ONE PIZZA—CALL IT TWO SERVINGS, OR FOUR WITH A SALAD ON THE SIDE.

In truth, there's no standing on ceremony when it comes to the sauce smeared on a pie: tomato sauce, for sure; but also pesto, mustard, hoisin sauce, you name it. One of our favorites is squash puree. It offers a sweet, light flavor, a great foil against the rich chèvre and caramelized onion.

1 small acorn squash, halved and seeded

2 tablespoons goat butter (or cow butter, if you must), plus more for the baking sheet

1 large onion, halved, then sliced into paper-thin half-moons

One 1-pound (455 g) pizza dough (either packaged dough from the supermarket, thawed if necessary, or dough bought from a pizza parlor)

8 ounces (225 g) fresh chèvre or soft goat cheese

½ cup (115 g) chopped pecan halves or pieces

2 tablespoons *harissa* (see page 93; optional)

2 tablespoons finely grated goat Gruyère or other hard, aged goat cheese, even a crottin you've aged yourself (see page 199; optional)

LESS TO DO

Forget about baking the squash and search for squash puree in your supermarket's freezer case. Thaw before using; also set it in a fine-mesh colander in the sink for 10 minutes or so to drain off any excess moisture. Nobody likes a soggy pie.

1. Set the rack in the center of the oven; preheat the oven to 375°F (190°C).

2. Place the acorn squash, cut side down, on a large, lipped baking sheet or in a 9 x 13-inch (23 x 33-cm) baking dish. Bake until quite soft, collapsed a bit and almost mushy, 40 to 50 minutes. Cool just until you can handle it, about 15 minutes; then scrape out the soft inner flesh with a flatware spoon. You'll need about ¾ cup (180 ml) of this puree for the pie. The rest you can save to add to mashed potatoes or use as a spread in vegetable wraps.

3. While the squash cooks, melt the butter in a large skillet over low heat. Add the onion and cook very slowly, stirring once in a while, until it is golden, caramelized, and quite soft, 25 to 35 minutes. If you find the onion is browning in any way, lower the heat even further and stir more often.

4. Increase the oven's temperature to 400°F (205°C). Lightly butter an 11 x 17-inch (28 x 43-cm) baking tray (often called a half hotel sheet tray). It's best not to use a nonstick baking sheet, because you're going to cut the pizza right on it. Place the pizza dough on the sheet and dimple the dough with your fingers; then stretch it out by its edges, dimple it again, stretch it out again, and so on, until it just about covers the baking sheet. Will it perfectly cover the whole thing? No. But you can get it close enough.

If you like, you can also toss it into a round. To do so, first flatten the dough to a fat disk, then pick it up, hold the edge with one hand, insert your fist into the center, and begin turning the dough, stretching and pulling it with both hands into a circle about 13 inches in diameter. Set it on the baking sheet.

5. Spread the squash puree over the dough, then top with an even layer of the caramelized onion. Dot with the fresh chèvre, then sprinkle with the pecans. Finally, if you like, dot with the *harissa* and sprinkle with the grated cheese.

6. Bake until the cheese has melted and the crust is puffed and lightly browned, about 17 minutes. Check the pie a couple of times as it bakes. If you see big bubbles forming in the crust, pop them with a fork so that the crust remains even on the baking sheet. Cool on the baking sheet for 5 minutes, then cut into squares or irregular pieces to serve.

NOTES FROM THE CAVE

At the most basic level, there are two types of goat cheese: (1) fresh chèvre, a soft goat cheese, sometimes sold in supermarkets under a brand name like Montrachet or available from myriad cheese makers across North America; and (2) aged goat cheese, anywhere from bits that have been aged for several weeks and have developed a white, soft rind to the hard cheeses like goat Gouda and Gruyère—and the fantastic Capricious made by the Pachecos at Achadinha in California. Most of what you cook with is the fresh stuff, the creamy goat cheese, also often crumbled into salads in North America. The aged cheeses become increasingly precious, based on their cultures and molds. Yes, a few—like that goat Gouda—are fine for cooking; most of the others, like a runny Le Lingot du Quercy (see page 225), would be a rank waste in a dish and should be saved for enjoying on their own.

PIZZA WITH GOAT CHEESE, PEACHES, AND ALMOND-TARRAGON PESTO

YOU'LL END UP WITH ONE PIE.

Bruce has created a terrific pesto here, one that uses almonds (rather than pine nuts) and tarragon with the basil. You'll make about twice as much as you need for the pie. Either double the other ingredients and make two pizzas or save the remainder of the pesto in the fridge for a couple of days or in the freezer for a couple of months.

⅔ cup (150 g) **sliced almonds**

2 cups (455 g) **packed fresh basil leaves, any thick stems removed**

⅓ cup (75 ml) **almond oil, or olive oil for a stronger taste, plus more as needed**

⅓ cup (75 ml) **finely grated hard, aged goat cheese, such as a goat Gruyère or goat Gouda**

¼ cup (55 g) **packed fresh tarragon leaves**

2 tablespoons **water**

1 medium **garlic clove, quartered**

½ teaspoon **salt**

½ teaspoon **freshly ground black pepper**

One 1-pound (455 g) **pizza dough (either packaged dough from the supermarket, thawed if necessary, or dough bought from a pizza parlor)**

2 ripe **peaches, halved, pitted, and sliced into thin wedges**

4 ounces (115 g) **fresh chèvre or soft goat cheese**

LESS TO DO

Use a prebaked 12-inch (30.5-cm) pizza crust, but get one without added spices or flavorings. You'll need a different size baking sheet: A round crust won't work on a lipped rectangular baking sheet. If all else fails, you can set a prebaked crust right on your oven rack—but it takes a little dexterity (and a big spatula) to get it out of the oven and onto a serving platter or cooling rack.

1. Toast the sliced almonds in a dry skillet set over medium heat, stirring occasionally, until lightly browned and fragrant, about 4 minutes. Dump them into a food processor. Add the basil, almond oil, grated cheese, tarragon leaves, water, garlic, salt, and pepper. Process until a grainy pesto, scraping down the inside of the canister once or twice.

Don't have a food processor? You can do this operation by mincing the almonds, herbs, and garlic, then scraping them into a bowl and stirring in the oil, cheese, water, salt, and pepper.

2. Position the rack in the center of the oven; preheat the oven to 400°F (200°C). Lightly oil an 11 x 17-inch (28 x 43-cm) baking sheet. Set the dough on the sheet; as you did with the previous pie (see page 200), press and dimple the dough into a shape about the size of the baking sheet.

3. Spread half of the pesto on the pie, leaving a ½-inch (1.2-cm) border around the edges. Put the remainder of the pesto in a sealable container, pour a thin film of almond oil over it, and store, covered, in the fridge.

4. Arrange the peach slices in a decorative pattern over the pesto on the pie. Crumble the goat cheese evenly over the top.

5. Bake until the crust is golden, 17 to 20 minutes. If you notice any bubbles in the crust as it bakes, pop them with a fork. Cool on the baking sheet for a few minutes, then cut into pieces.

BAKED SPINACH-AND-GOAT-CHEESE DUMPLINGS

IT'S A MEAL FOR FOUR (UNLESS I'M THERE—THEN BACK OFF, BECAUSE THE WHOLE DISH IS MINE).

Bruce made these for lunch one day, and, I swear, I almost passed out. They're light dumplings, sort of like gnocchi, baked in a creamy white wine sauce. I was supposed to eat the accompanying salad. But who could waste calories on salad?

One 10-ounce (one 280-g) package frozen chopped spinach, thawed

8 ounces (225 g) fresh chèvre or soft goat cheese, at room temperature so that it's very creamy

4 ounces (115 g) hard, aged goat cheese, such as goat Gouda, finely grated and divided

3 large egg yolks

¾ cup (170 g) semolina flour, plus more for rolling the little dumplings (see More to Know)

1 tablespoon finely minced chives or the green part of a scallion

1 teaspoon salt

½ teaspoon finely grated lemon zest

½ teaspoon freshly ground black pepper

¼ teaspoon freshly grated nutmeg

1 tablespoon goat butter (or unsalted cow butter, if you must)

1 tablespoon all-purpose flour

1 cup (240 ml) regular or low-fat goat milk (or cow milk, if you must)

2 tablespoons dry white wine or dry vermouth

MORE TO KNOW

Semolina flour is a coarse meal made from hard durum wheat, long favored in Italian (and Canadian!) cooking. Do not substitute all-purpose flour—or even cornmeal (as often suggested in some recipes).

1. First, grab the frozen spinach in small handfuls and squeeze as hard as you can over the sink to get rid of as much excess moisture as you can. Put the bundles in a big bowl and use a fork to separate the spinach back out into bits and threads.

2. Whisk in the fresh chèvre or soft goat cheese, half the grated hard goat cheese, the egg yolks, semolina flour, chives, salt, lemon zest, black pepper, and nutmeg. You want a creamy but somewhat stiff mixture, because you're going to form it into balls.

3. Sprinkle a little more semolina flour onto a clean, dry work surface. Pick up a little bit of the spinach mixture, a little smaller than a golf ball. Roll this in the semolina flour to form an oblong ball, sort of like a football but without the pointed ends. Set aside and continue rolling more, adding more flour to your work surface as need be (but not too much, or the balls will turn gummy). You'll end up with about 24 dumplings.

4. Bring a large pot of water to a boil over high heat. Add 5 or 6 dumplings. Lower the heat so the water barely simmers. Poach for 10 minutes. Use a slotted spoon to transfer the dumplings from the pot to a 9 x 13-inch (23 x 33-cm) baking dish or an oblong roasting pan. Then add 5 or 6 more dumplings to the pot and repeat the poaching process again—and

again—until all the dumplings are done and in the baking dish or roasting pan. Why not just toss them all into the water at once? Because they'll crowd the pot and stick together. You want enough space so they can bounce around freely in the simmering water.

5. Position the rack in the center of the oven and preheat the oven to 375°F (190°C).

6. Melt the butter in a small saucepan set over medium-low heat. Whisk in the all-purpose flour. Whisk over the heat for 30 seconds. Then whisk in the milk in dribs and drabs, a little bit each time to form a paste—and then more at a time, although never more than a slow, steady drizzle. Once all the milk is in the pan, whisk in the wine, raise the heat to medium, and whisk until bubbling and slightly thickened, just a minute or so.

7. Pour this sauce over the dumpling balls in the baking dish or roasting pan. Sprinkle the remaining grated cheese over the dish. Bake until the sauce is bubbling and just beginning to brown, about 15 minutes. Cool in the pan for 5 minutes before serving.

GOAT CHEESE VARIETIES

Bonde de Gâtine (*bond-duh-gah-TEEN*). From the marshlands of Poitou in France, this small cylinder has a distinctly blue mold on its wrinkled skin. The creamy paste inside ripens over time, turning dried and coarsely textured, for a grainy finish in a creamy mask.

Brunet. Many Italian goat cheeses are quite dry, but this one, aged only a month, is quite creamy, if also a little cakey. A small, flat disk from the Piedmont region of northern Italy, it's salty but bright, the texture quite velvety.

Capricious. The Pacecos' Achadinha Cheese Company's aged goat cheese is a ridiculous indulgence, based on Caprino from Italy, a line of aged, olive–oil– washed cheeses that dry out, get gnarly, and develop an unbelievable earthiness. Capricious is the best of the bunch: pungent yet mellow, stinky yet sweet, a hearty cheese with a velvet touch.

FETA AND GREENS PIE

IT WILL FEED SIX.

This is a classic casserole: a phyllo-lined baking dish filled with a creamy Swiss chard and spinach mixture, laced with goat feta—which offers some nice umami points to the culinary pentagon (see page 121), shifting the mix a bit away from the overly sweet thing it so often becomes.

½ cup (120 ml) olive oil, divided

1 large yellow onion, chopped

2 to 4 medium garlic cloves, minced

8 ounces (225 g) fresh spinach, woody stems removed, the leaves washed and chopped, but not dried

8 ounces (225 g) Swiss chard, thick stems removed, the leaves washed and chopped, but not dried

8 ounces (225 g) goat feta, crumbled

1 large egg

1 large egg yolk

1 tablespoon minced fresh marjoram leaves

1 tablespoon minced fresh basil leaves

½ teaspoon finely grated lemon zest

½ teaspoon red pepper flakes

½ teaspoon freshly grated nutmeg

½ cup (115 g) pine nuts

8 sheets frozen phyllo dough, thawed according to the package instructions, then laid on a clean, scrupulously dry work surface under a sheet of plastic wrap and a clean kitchen towel to keep the sheets moist

1. Get the rack into the oven's center; heat the oven up to 350°F (175°C).

2. Set a large skillet over medium heat. Pour in 2 tablespoons of the olive oil, then toss in the onion. Cook, stirring often, for about 3 minutes, just until the onion begins to soften.

3. Plop in the minced garlic, stir a few times, then drop in all the chopped spinach and chard leaves with any water still adhering to them. Toss and stir over the heat until the leaves steam and wilt, about 4 minutes. Tongs are best for this task. Also, stir often to make sure no liquid remains before you move on to the next step.

4. Scrape the contents of the skillet into a large food processor fitted with the chopping blade. Add the crumbled feta, egg, egg yolk, marjoram, basil, lemon zest, red pepper flakes, and nutmeg. Process, scraping down the inside of the canister once, until pretty smooth. Then add the pine nuts and pulse a few times until they're a grainy mixture in the filling. Set aside.

5. Brush a 9-inch (23-cm) square baking dish with some of the remaining olive oil. Set a sheet of phyllo inside it and press it into place, letting it overlap the sides as it will. Brush the phyllo sheet with the olive oil. Set another in the baking dish, at a 90-degree angle to the first. Brush it with the olive oil—and then continue with the sheets, turning them this way

and that, never the same way twice, and brushing each with the olive oil, the sides all overlapping every which way out of the dish.

6. Scrape the spinach, chard, and feta filling into the baking dish and smooth it out into an even layer. Fold all the phyllo ends over the filling, leaving a little hole in the center uncovered. Crimp and smooth them into a decorative edge.

7. Bake until the phyllo has browned and the filling is set, about 40 minutes. Cool for 5 minutes on a wire rack before cutting into squares to serve.

NOTES FROM THE CAVE

If you're thinking of storing fine goat cheese at home, forget about it. You should consume aged cheese pretty soon after buying it.

However, you may want to try aging your own crottins (see page 199). Or you might not be able to eat a hunk fast enough. If so, store it in the cheese drawer or butter compartment of your fridge, wrapped and sealed in a double thickness of butcher paper or unwrapped from its plastic-wrap mummification and rewrapped in two sheets of butcher paper.

When goat cheese is stored too long, it gets a boggy bottom, a layer of thick goo that has fallen out of suspension as the cheese has sat around. Yes, some cheeses goo by nature—but you should see this happening uniformly across the cheese, or even just at the center, never just along the bottom. You can try to solve the boggy bottom syndrome by turning the cheese on its head, letting the moisture drift back through the round or slice. However, the best laid plans . . . You should consider consuming the boggy bottom cheese the day after you turn it upside down.

Redwood Hill Farm

There's a foolish idealism that has descended on the discussion of real food in the United States. Writers make proclamations like mad: Food shouldn't be this, shouldn't be that. One of the most common rules is that food shouldn't come from a factory.

Anyone who thinks that doesn't know Redwood Hill Farm in California. Not all mechanization is bad. I dare say neither Bruce nor I intend to sprout our own wheat anytime soon. Or eat only cheese we make at home.

Don't bother Redwood Hill's wiry and quick Sharon Bice with any of that foolishness. She knows the truth. Or, as she put it to us, "the numbers."

"You can't win without the numbers," she said. "And you've got to square those with what you know is right."

In other words, mechanization is neither good nor bad. The product is what counts.

"Dad moved the family up here to Sonoma County from L.A.," she told us. "He was in 4-H. He wanted his kids to do the same. So we come by it naturally. And we're not losing that."

We'd already taken a spin through Redwood Hill's enormous facilities—the rooms with the feta lined up in huge blocks on stainless steel tables, the vats to hold the milk to be cultured, waiting to start the journey into one of the nation's largest line of goat milk products.

Frankly, the whole place took us by surprise. And knocked any snobbery senseless. Yes, there was an economy of scale and efficiency. No cheese-making facility we visited was ever this large. But we were also enamored with the goat cheese that was the end result, especially the two-month-aged crottins, little buttons of goaty goodness that can be eaten on their own, creamy and delightful; or aged further into grating buttons, perfect for salads and baked potatoes.

"Do you have any consistency problems?" I asked as I sucked on a small bit of the briny, sharp feta.

"Not so much anymore."

Bruce and I were shocked. After all, the lack of consistency was the cheese maker's refrain in our research.

Sharon must have sensed our hesitation. "Because more people are getting into the goat dairy business," she said, "we have so many producers to choose from."

Undoubtedly the goat dairy business is thriving because of facilities like this one. That rustic vision, the one of a small farm and a few stainless steel cans of milk, is sure diverting. Paul Trubey nobly carries it on. But it's also important to realize that millions of people need feeding in this country alone. And if producers can learn to hold both goals in their minds—local and large—we might have at least some answers to the problems currently strafing the food scene.

The Bices haven't lost their roots. We left the plant and took a drive out to their own dairy, set deeper into the hills.

We came across hundreds of goats, chewing, eating, head-butting. And we came across their old-fashioned milking parlor, much like Paul's: a small affair, just a dozen stanchions or so.

Does Redwood Hill buy goat milk from elsewhere? Of course. But when I asked various Bices why they maintained the goat dairy, I kept getting the same reply: "We don't want to lose this."

Without a doubt, that's the model for the new generation, one without the silliness of the current locavore movement: a business that looks to tomorrow while holding on to the past. By holding on to the goat dairy, Redwood Hill keeps their business close to what's important. By expanding to fit an ever-growing population, they're bringing their products to a wider audience, thereby continuing to support both their own dairy and the dairies of many more careful farmers in Sonoma County and beyond.

GOAT CHEESE *and* BLACK BEAN ENCHILADAS

MAKES SIX ENCHILADAS. WHAT IS THAT, A MEAL FOR SIX YAN-
KEES, THREE CONFEDERATES, OR TWO TEXANS?

Growing up in Dallas, around the corner from Saint Minks and All Cadillacs, I didn't even know about enchiladas like these. And so I preferred tacos, because of the crunch. But I've since learned that enchiladas are so much more than soggy tortillas, mystery meat, and gloppy sauce. They're comfort food—especially when made with goat cheese.

8 dried New Mexico red chiles, stemmed, seeded, and torn into bits (see page 59)

4 dried guajillo chiles, stemmed, seeded, and torn into bits (see page 59)

1 medium yellow onion, chopped

4 medium garlic cloves, minced

1 tablespoon minced fresh marjoram leaves

½ teaspoon ground cinnamon

½ teaspoon ground cumin

3½ cups (840 ml) reduced-sodium vegetable broth

1 canned chipotle chile in adobo sauce, seeded and chopped

2 cups (455 g) diced tomatoes

1 cup (225 g) canned black beans, drained and rinsed

2 teaspoons minced fresh oregano leaves

½ teaspoon salt

½ teaspoon freshly grated nutmeg

Six 8-inch (six 20-cm) flour tortillas

9 ounces (255 g) fresh chèvre or soft goat cheese

8 ounces (225 g) finely grated hard, aged goat Gruyère or goat Gouda

1. Toast the chile bits in a dry saucepan over medium heat, stirring often, until aromatic and lightly browned, about 3 minutes.

2. Add the onion, garlic, marjoram, cinnamon, and cumin. Continue to cook in the dry pan for 1 minute, stirring all the while.

3. Pour in the broth and add the canned chipotle. Cover the pan and bring the mixture to a simmer, stirring occasionally. Reduce the heat to low and simmer very slowly for 20 minutes.

4. Pour and scrape the contents of the saucepan into a large blender. Remove the topknot or button from the lid and place a clean kitchen towel over it. If you leave the lid sealed, the hot contents will spew out, the pressure inside too great. Better then to cover that hole with a breathable kitchen towel! Blend until smooth, scraping down the inside of the canister as necessary. Pour into a large bowl.

You can make this enchilada sauce in advance, storing it in a covered bowl in the refrigerator for up to 3 days. Let it return to room temperature on the counter before proceeding with the recipe.

5. Position the rack in the center of the oven and crank up the oven to 350°F (175°C). Pour a half cup or so of the enchilada sauce into a 9 x 13-inch (23 x 33-cm) baking pan. Mix the tomatoes, beans, oregano, salt, and nutmeg in a bowl.

6. Dip one of the tortillas into the remaining sauce in its bowl, then set it on a cutting board. Fill it with about ½ cup (120 ml) of the tomato mixture; crumble 1½ ounces (40 g) fresh chèvre or soft goat cheese over the tomato filling. Roll the enchilada up and put it in the baking dish seam side down. Continue making more with the remaining tortillas, tomato filling, and soft goat cheese.

7. Pour the remainder of the enchilada sauce over the rolled, stuffed tortillas in the dish. Sprinkle the grated cheese over the top.

8. Bake until bubbling and hot, about 50 minutes. Cool for at least 5 minutes before dishing up the enchiladas one by one.

Caprino di Vino. This may be the best of American whimsy, a semi-firm goat cheese ripened in Maine blueberry wine, the brainchild of Caitlin Hunter, an irrepressible force and perhaps one of the best pioneers among the agri-entrepreneurs today.

Chabichou du Poitou (*shah-bee-SHOE-dwew-pwa-TOO*). *Chabichou* is from the Arabic word for goat: *chebli*. This is French chèvre tradition at its best, a cheese originating from the time the Moors overran Europe. The rind is pale yellow with white wrinkles; the cheese inside, creamy, silky. Chabichou is actually another of *bondes* from France (*bonde* being French for "plug," meaning "in the shape of the plug on a wine barrel"). Chabichou de Poitou is more rustic, less refined, all in all simpler than the blue-tinged Bonde de Gâtine (see page 206).

Le Chèvre Noir. A goat cheese from Fromagerie Tournevent in Quebec, this creamy but dry cheese is sealed in black wax to preserve its moisture. Imagine the consistency of Cheddar, combined with the soft sweetness of butter, plus the slightly acid finish of goat cheese. It needs a red. My guess: a Cab Franc.

GOAT CHEESE, CRAB, AND TORTILLA CASSEROLE

CONSIDER IT DINNER FOR EIGHT.

This isn't a casserole of enchiladas; rather, it's a layered casserole, best for company, one of those hearty things you can make earlier in the day, then bake off at the last minute. Offer a vinegary side salad with diced mango among the greens.

1 tablespoon olive oil, plus more for greasing the baking dish

1 medium yellow onion, chopped

3 medium garlic cloves, minced

12 medium tomatillos, any papery hulls removed, the flesh chopped (about 3 cups [680 g])

¼ cup (60 ml) tequila or reduced-sodium vegetable broth

2 cups (480 ml) regular or low-fat goat yogurt

1 cup (225 g) chopped fresh cilantro leaves

3 poblano chiles, charred, peeled, seeded, and chopped (see page 182 for an explanation of how to accomplish this)

Eighteen 8-inch (eighteen 20-cm) corn tortillas

11 ounces (310 g) fresh chèvre or soft goat cheese

1 pound (455 g) lump crabmeat, picked over for shell and cartilage

4 ounces (115 g) hard, aged goat cheese, like a goat Gruyère or even a crottin you've aged yourself (see page 199), grated through the small holes of a box grater or with a microplane

1. After setting the rack into the center of the oven, preheat the oven to 350°F (175°C). Lightly oil a 9 x 13-inch (23 x 33-cm) baking dish by dabbing a little olive oil on a crumpled paper towel, then running the paper towel all around the inside of the dish, making sure to get into the corners and the edges where the bottom meets the sides.

2. Heat a large skillet over medium heat. Swirl in 1 tablespoon olive oil, then add the onion. Cook, stirring often, until translucent, about 3 minutes. Stir in the garlic and continue cooking for 30 seconds.

3. Dump in the chopped tomatillos. Stir well, then continue cooking, stirring once in a while, until the tomatillos begin to break down, perhaps up to 10 minutes, depending on how firm they were. Pour in the tequila or broth; then cover the skillet, reduce the heat to medium-low, and cook, stirring once in a while, until the whole thing has a salsa verde consistency, about 5 minutes. Cool for 10 minutes before stirring in the yogurt, cilantro, and chopped poblanos.

4. Spread each tortilla with an even layer of some of the goat cheese on one side only. It'll take about 1½ tablespoons cheese per tortilla.

5. Lay 6 of the tortillas in the prepared baking dish, cheese side up. Some may overlap. Spoon and spread a third of the tomatillo sauce over these tortillas, then sprinkle half the crab over the top.

Make another layer: six more cheese-coated tortillas, half the remaining tomatillo sauce, and the rest of the crab. This time, look for any spots where there may not have been great tortilla coverage in the bottom layer, now covering those spots with a bit of tortilla.

Finally, make one more layer of cheese-side-up tortillas, then spoon and spread the rest of the tomatillo sauce over the top. Top the whole thing with the grated cheese.

6. Cover the casserole: You don't want to put foil directly onto the acidy sauce, so first put a piece of parchment paper over the baking dish, then seal a piece of foil on top of that. Bake for 30 minutes. Remove the covering, then continue baking until the top is lightly browned and the casserole is bubbling, particularly around the edges, 15 to 20 minutes. Remove the baking dish from the oven and cool on a wire rack for 5 to 10 minutes before cutting it into gooey squares to serve.

GOAT CHEESE VARIETIES

Chevrotin des Aravis (*shehv-roh-TAN-day-zah-rah-VEE*). Not a smooth chèvre, this gorgeous, slightly runny goat cheese from the French border near Lake Geneva has a hard, washed, pink-hued rind covered in talc-like mold. Inside, the paste is firm (with a few holes), yet has a spreadable-like-cream-cheese part at the center. It's a fine dessert cheese: brisk, young, flavorful, a little floral, and velvety.

Crottin de Chavignol (*kroh-TAN-duh-shah-vee-NYOL*). This button of goat cheese from the Loire Valley may well be the one French goat cheese so many American makers strive to copy. It can be soft to hard, depending on whether the crottin has been aged. As the cheese ages, it changes in consistency, starting with the ever-whitening, even bluing rind and moving toward the center, the flavors becoming more intense, nuttier, but yet more mellow.

GOAT CHEESE 🐐 PUMPKIN RAVIOLI WITH SAGE BUTTER

YOU'LL MAKE EIGHT FIRST-COURSE OR FOUR MAIN-COURSE SERVINGS.

Here's the real deal: ravioli from scratch, roasted pumpkin, goat cheese, the whole thing. Is it a recipe for every day? Hardly. Bruce and I call ones like this marvel nonni recipes *(or* grand-mère recipes *or* abuela recipes *or* bubbie recipes, *depending on the ethnic tint). But, boy, does the work pay off!*

1 small pumpkin, halved through the stem, the stem removed, as well as any seeds and their fibrous membranes

¼ cup (55 g) fresh chèvre or soft goat cheese

1 large egg yolk

1 teaspoon packed fresh thyme leaves, or ½ teaspoon dried thyme

¾ teaspoons salt, divided

¼ teaspoon freshly grated nutmeg

1½ cups (340 ml) all-purpose flour, plus more as needed

½ cup (115 g) semolina flour

3 large eggs, at room temperature

2 tablespoons olive oil

4 cups (960 ml) sweet white wine, such as a Riesling or a Sancerre

1 tablespoon minced fresh sage leaves

6 tablespoons (85 g) goat butter (or cow butter, if you must)

LESS TO DO

First, you don't have to roast a pumpkin. Use canned pumpkin puree, the kind often used at Thanksgiving for pies. Just don't use sweetened pumpkin pie filling; simply buy the solid-pack, canned pumpkin.

Second, you don't have to make the pasta. Many Italian supermarkets and even high-end grocery stores sell big pasta sheets. You can use these for the ravioli, filling them as directed in the recipe.

1. Position the rack in the center of the oven and preheat the oven to 400°F (205°C). Set the pumpkin, cut side down, on a large, lipped baking sheet and roast until quite soft to the touch, about 1 hour. Cool for 10 minutes or so, then scrape out the inner flesh. You should have about 1¼ cups (300 ml) pumpkin puree.

2. Place the pumpkin puree in a large bowl; whisk in the chèvre, egg yolk, thyme, ½ teaspoon salt, and the nutmeg until smooth. The filling for the ravioli can be made in advance; store this mixture, covered, in the refrigerator for up to 2 days.

3. To make the pasta, mix both kinds of flour and the salt in a large bowl. Make a well in the center of the flour mixture, mounding it up the sides of the bowl. Crack the eggs into that well and add the olive oil. Whisk the eggs and oil with a fork in that well until creamy and uniform, getting as little of the floury walls into the mixture as possible. Once the egg mixture is creamy, start picking up more and more of the flour, adding it as you whisk with the fork, making sure the flour dissolves each time before adding a little more. There'll come a point in which it's hard to mix in any more. At this point, clean and dry your hands and get them in the bowl, working in the remaining flour.

4. Once the whole thing is a pasta dough, divide it into 8 balls and set them aside under a clean kitchen towel for 10 minutes at room temperature. Now run 1 dough ball through a pasta machine, adding a little extra

flour if it sticks; knead it several times through the largest setting, folding it back on itself each time before you run it through and adding a little flour if it sticks in any way. Then continue running the sheet through the rollers, decreasing the setting on the machine as the manufacturer instructs, until you get a thin, long pasta sheet.

Dust your work surface with flour, set the sheet on the flour, cover with another clean kitchen towel, and continue making more until all 8 balls have been rolled out and lie under towels.

5. To start the sauce, bring the wine to a boil in a medium saucepan over high heat. Continue boiling until the wine has been reduced all the way down to ¼ cup (60 ml). Add the sage leaves and set aside off the heat.

6. Uncover 1 pasta sheet, scoop up the filling in 1-tablespoon increments, and place it down the center of the sheet, spacing these little mounds 2 inches apart. You'll probably get about 8 on the sheet. Dampen your fingers with tap water and wet the entire perimeter of the sheet. Top with a second pasta sheet, covering the little mounds. Press the edges together all the way around to seal—pick them up and press them together so they really seal. Cut between the rounds to make the ravioli, preferably with a scalloped pasta cutter. Repeat this step 3 more times to use all the pasta sheets.

7. Bring a large pot of water to a simmer over high heat. Meanwhile, set the wine and sage in its saucepan over very low heat. Do not let it boil any more—just keep it warm.

8. Drop all the ravioli in the big pot of water and cook until they float, about 3 minutes. Don't let the water boil—just simmer slowly. Remove with a slotted spoon and drain fully on paper towels. Then transfer them to serving plates.

9. For the final step in the sauce, whisk the butter 1 tablespoon at a time into the warm wine. Once all the butter has been whisked in, whisk in the remaining ¼ teaspoon salt and spoon this sauce over the ravioli on the plates.

GOAT CHEESE LASAGNA WITH MUSHROOMS, SPINACH, AND TARRAGON

YOU'LL END UP WITH A 9 X 13-INCH (23 X 33-CM) BAKING PAN OF LASAGNA.

What is it about spinach that pairs so well with goat cheese? Probably the earthy, bitter, but slightly sweet, bite, a great balance. There's no denying this dish is a crowd-pleaser—as well as a button-buster.

10 tablespoons (1 stick plus 2 table-spoons [145 g]) goat butter—or unsalted cow butter, if you must), divided

1½ pounds (680 g) cremini or white button mushrooms, thinly sliced

One 10-ounce (one 280-g) package frozen chopped spinach, thawed and squeezed of excess moisture (see page 205 for specific directions on how to do this)

2 tablespoons minced fresh tarragon leaves

½ teaspoon ground allspice

1 large yellow onion, minced (*not* chopped)

6 tablespoons (40 g) all-purpose flour

2 cups (480 ml) reduced-sodium veg-etable broth

2 cups (480 ml) regular or low-fat goat milk (or cow milk, if you must)

1 cup (240 ml) dry white wine or dry vermouth

1 pound (455 g) fresh chèvre or soft goat cheese

12 dried lasagna noodles, cooked and drained according to the package instructions

LESS TO DO

You can skip cooking the lasagna noodles and use no-bake lasagna noodles, a modern miracle. If so, use nine of them in all, three per layer. These you set the short way in the dish with some space between (because they swell in the sauce as they bake).

1. Set the rack in the oven's center. Heat the oven up to 400°F (205°C).

2. Melt the 2 tablespoons butter in a large skillet set over medium heat. Add the mushrooms and cook, stirring often, until they give off their liquid and it reduces to a thick glaze, about 6 minutes. Stir in the spinach, tarragon, and ground allspice. Stir over the heat for 1 minute, then set the skillet aside.

3. Melt the remaining 8 tablespoons (115 g) butter in a large saucepan over low heat. Add the onion even before the butter has fully melted. Cook very slowly, stirring once in a while, until the onion turns incredibly soft and golden. If it is minced finely enough, the onion should almost melt into a sauce. If you see that it is turning brown at all, reduce the heat further and stir more often. It should take about 20 minutes to get the onion right.

4. Whisk the flour into the onion; continue whisking over the heat for 1 minute. Then whisk in the broth in small bits, just a drizzle or two at a time—but work quickly and efficiently to get a thin paste. Once the flour has started to form one, start whisking in more broth in a slow, steady stream.

5. Whisk in the milk and cook, whisking constantly, until bubbling and somewhat thickened, 5 to 7 minutes. Pour in the wine and cook for another 2 minutes, whisking all the while. Now to take it over the top: Crumble in the chèvre and whisk until melted. Set the pan off the heat.

6. Spread ½ cup (120 ml) of the cheesy velouté in the bottom of a 9 x 13-inch (23 x 33-cm) baking dish. Add a layer of 4 noodles to the dish. Spread a third of the remaining velouté over these noodles, then top that with half the mushroom-spinach mixture, spreading it out into an even layer. Add another layer with 4 more of the noodles, another half of the remaining velouté, and the rest of the mushroom-spinach mixture. Finally, add the final layer of 4 noodles, then spread those with the rest of the cheesy velouté.

7. Bake until bubbling and lightly browned at the edges, about 40 minutes. Cool for 5 to 10 minutes before cutting into meltingly gooey squares to serve.

GOAT CHEESE VARIETIES

Garrotxa (*gah-ROHTCH-ah*). The modern foodie craze brought this Spanish goat cheese back from the edge of extinction a few years ago. It's a dry cheese, quite nutty; it often comes in large, 2-pound (900-g) wheels. Although Garrotxa pairs wonderfully with runny or creamy cheeses on a dessert plate, you can even consider this a sturdy comer, great shaved into a salad or on top of steamed vegetables.

Harbourne Blue. From South Devon, England, this is a micro-batch goat cheese, one of the new breed of artisanal cheeses springing up by agri-entrepreneurs across Great Britain. It's sweet, sort of like Gorgonzola, with the consistency of fudge and lots of balancing earthiness.

Harvest Cheese from Hillman Farm. A stunning aged goat cheese from western Massachusetts, these small-batch runs sell out year after year, mostly because of the nutty mellowness and the mushroomy accents, all found under the gnarly rind.

NO-HOLDS-BARRED
MAC AND CRAB AND GOAT CHEESE

IT WILL SERVE EIGHT IF EVERYONE WANTS TO LIVE INTO THEIR SEVENTIES, FEWER IF NO ONE CARES.

There's really nothing to write about a casserole with three kinds of goat cheese and a rich cream sauce to hold the noodles together. Oh, except that Bruce tossed in broccoli, probably out of guilt. Actually, it's an inspired addition: a little green among the creamy marvelousness. He also baked the thing in a 9 x 13-inch (23 x 33-cm) baking dish, rather than the more usual round dish, so that there could be more crunchy topping across the whole casserole (the part I pick off and eat first).

1 pound (455 g) dried ziti or rigatoni

4 cups (910 g) broccoli florets (large ones cut in half)

4 tablespoons (55 g) goat butter (or unsalted cow butter, if you must), plus more for greasing the baking dish

1 small leek (white and pale green parts only), halved lengthwise, washed carefully for any grit in the inner chambers, then very thinly sliced into half-moon bits

1 small red bell pepper, stemmed, seeded, and diced

¼ cup (30 g) all-purpose flour

3 cups (720 ml) regular or low-fat goat milk (or cow milk, if you must)

½ cup (120 ml) dry white wine or dry vermouth

12 ounces (340 g) fresh chèvre or soft goat cheese, crumbled into little bits

5 ounces (140 g) goat Brie, rind removed, cut into little bits

3 ounces (85 g) hard, aged goat cheese, like a goat Gouda, grated through the large holes of a box grater

1 pound (455 g) lump crabmeat, picked over for shell and cartilage

1 tablespoon Dijon mustard

2 teaspoons fresh stemmed thyme leaves

1 teaspoon minced fresh marjoram leaves, or 2 teaspoons dried marjoram

1 teaspoon salt

½ teaspoon freshly ground black pepper

1. Bring a large pot of water to a boil over high heat. Add the dried pasta and cook until still a little crunchy at the center, perhaps 6 minutes, maybe a little longer. The pasta will cook longer in the casserole to come, so it needs to be undercooked at this point. Fish it out with a slotted spoon and put it in a colander. Set this in the sink and run cool water over it to stop the cooking. Dump it into a large bowl.

2. Make sure that pot of water is still boiling at high heat. Add the broccoli florets and blanch for 2 minutes. Drain them in that same colander and again run cool tap water over them to stop the cooking. When they're cool to the touch, drain well, then add them to the bowl with the pasta.

3. Position the rack in the center of the oven and preheat the oven to 375°F (190°C). Lightly grease a 9 x 13-inch (23 x 33-cm) baking dish with a little bit of butter on a piece of wadded up paper towel.

4. Melt the butter in a large saucepan over medium heat. Add the leek and bell pepper; cook, stirring often, until slightly softened, about 3 minutes.

5. Sprinkle the flour over everything, then stir over the heat for about 30 seconds to get rid of any raw flour taste. Now whisk—do not stir—in the milk, slowly at first, a little at a time, to make sure the flour begins to dissolve. Once it does, you can add the milk more quickly, but always in a slow, steady stream, whisking all the while. Continue to whisk over the heat until bubbling and thickened, about 3 minutes.

6. Whisk in the wine or vermouth, then drop the whisk, pick up a spoon, and stir in all 3 kinds of cheese. Continue stirring just until melted, about 1 minute. Stir in the crab, mustard, thyme, marjoram, salt, and pepper. Remove the pan from the heat and stir in the cooked pasta and blanched broccoli florets.

7. Pour all of this mixture into the prepared baking dish. Place it in the oven and bake until the top has browned somewhat and the casserole is bubbling along the hot rim, about 35 minutes. Cool on a wire rack out of the oven for 5 minutes before scooping up into bowls to serve.

GOAT CHEESE VARIETIES

Humboldt Fog from Cypress Grove. Creamy and intense, a sort of fog for the tongue, this goat cheese is reminiscent of the weather in its birthplace in northern California: gentle but still complexly bright, mellow without being a wallflower, moist and irrepressible. A line of vegetable ash through its center skews the pH away from the acidic and more to the alkaline (or sweet). Under no circumstances should this cheese be eaten cold from the fridge. It needs time to develop. Take it out before a dinner party so it's ready several hours later.

Ibores (*ee-BORE-ays*). This goat cheese is from the Extremadura region of Spain, the same place that gives us *jamón ibérico*. The cheese ranges from soft to semi-firm, depending on how long it's been aged. It's got small holes throughout; the sweetness is balanced by a little spinachy bitterness. The rinds are washed with either olive oil or paprika—or sometimes both.

Section 4

LITTLE NOTHINGS

IN THE EARLY NINETIES, I took my parents to Paris, their first trip.

But I made a mistake. Not the whole France vs. America thing. Instead, I'd crossed a barrier. Unbeknownst to me, I'd morphed from a backpack-toting college kid to a full-fledged, thirty-something tourist. I bought maps and packed deodorant.

Our first night in town, I took them to one of my old haunts, a down-and-dirty Lebanese-French place, hidden in the warren of twisty streets on the Left Bank. My mother's heels clacked against the cobblestones. It wasn't a good sign.

The restaurant was so old-school, it didn't have menus. Or even a chalkboard. The waiter recited the night's offerings with a Middle Eastern clack, French with thick gutturals. I suggested the lamb to my parents. Mostly because I couldn't miss *d'agneau* in the spitfire but heavily accented list.

It was a marginal dinner—at best. I may have been well into my academic career, but I was already cooking my way through glossy food magazines every month. I knew the sauces were gelatinous with cornstarch. I could tell the difference between mutton and lamb.

When it came time for dessert, our menu-less waiter again rattled off a list. I heard *chèvre*. I suggested it all around.

My mother knew better. She crossed her arms and asked for a coffee.

But my father and I were game. We got bowls of soupy goat cheese, honey on the side.

One bite, and we asked for the check. It was horrid: a distinctly ammonia smell. Maybe it had gone off. I just wanted out.

The rest of the trip went fine. The next two decades, not so much. I never heard the end of it. "Does that have goat cheese in it?" my father asked whenever I brought something to the table, whenever anybody—except my mother, who knew better—brought something to the table.

Until Bruce brought the Chèvre Truffles (see page 222) to the table.

"Do those have goat cheese in them?"

For once, we could give it a resounding *yes*.

My mother and I couldn't give it much more. We were moaning in delight.

My father was glum. "I don't want any of that," he kept saying, although no one was listening. Kept saying it although we were already talking about something else. Kept saying it even after we cleared out and went into the kitchen.

When I glanced back into the dining room, to my utter shock, I saw him take a truffle and bite into it. A delicate nibble. But a bite, nonetheless.

He looked up and our eyes locked.

"Good?" I asked.

He thought about it. Gave it that trapped Michael Scott look. And grinned, knowing he was out of luck. Do you know how many years it takes to work up a good refrain?

CHÈVRE TRUFFLES

YOU'LL MAKE ABOUT EIGHTEEN TRUFFLES. WHO KNOWS HOW MANY WILL MAKE IT OUT OF THE KITCHEN?

Truffles are traditionally made with ganache, a chocolate and cream mixture. In this case, it's a chocolate and chèvre mixture, a bit of goaty indulgence, sweetened with maple syrup, then rolled into balls and coated in tempered chocolate, all before being sprinkled with a few grains of coarse salt. No wonder my father had to get a new refrain.

MORE TO KNOW

Maple syrup is sold in various grades: usually three (A, B, and C, or 1, 2, and 3), with the first grade often divided into various subcategories (Grade A Light Amber, or Grade 1 Dark Amber, for example). As a match to goat cheese, choose the darkest grade from the first category—or even the second category altogether (B or 2). The higher grades are fine for pancakes, but their delicate flavors would be lost among the bold tastes of the cheese.

1 pound plus 6 ounces (625 g) bitter-sweet chocolate (between 70% and 85% cocoa solids), chopped

6 ounces (170 g) fresh chèvre or soft goat cheese

2 tablespoons maple syrup

1 tablespoon coarse salt, such as coarse sea salt or kosher salt

1. To make the goat cheese ganache, first melt 6 ounces (170 g) chopped chocolate. You can do this in several ways:

☞ Bring about an inch (2.5 cm) of water to a boil in the bottom of a double boiler, then set the top half of the double boiler in place, add the chocolate, drop the heat to low so the water simmers slowly, and stir until about two-thirds of the chocolate has melted. Remove the top half of the double boiler from over the simmering water and stir off the heat until all the chocolate has melted.

☞ If you don't have a double boiler, do this same operation, but use a medium saucepan and a heat-safe bowl that fits securely in the pan without its bottom touching the simmering water. In this case, make sure no steam can escape from between the pan and the bowl. Any steam that condenses into the chocolate can cause it to seize—that is, turn into little, hard threads with the chocolate liqueur having fallen out of suspension. If this happens, you can remove the bowl from the heat and stir in a tablespoon or two of heavy cream to try to get the whole thing to re-emulsify. It may not and then you'll have to start over. Good luck.

☞ Or you can melt the chocolate in the microwave. Put it in a microwave-safe bowl and heat on high in 6-second increments, stirring after each. Once about half the chocolate has melted, remove the bowl and continue stirring at room temperature until it has all melted.

In any case, cool the melted chocolate for 5 minutes at room temperature.

2. Crumble the fresh chèvre or soft goat cheese into the lukewarm chocolate, pour in the maple syrup, and stir until smooth. Set the bowl in the refrigerator and chill until the mixture is firm enough to form into balls, about 5 minutes.

3. Now the second batch of melting chocolate, the remaining pound—except this time, the whole operation has to be more precise because the chocolate has to be tempered to get the lovely shine of hardened chocolate on the truffles. Melt that remaining pound in any way you choose above, but use a chocolate thermometer to make sure the melting chocolate never gets above 130°F (54°C), no matter what. (If you're using a microwave, you'll have to put the thermometer in and out of the chocolate as the bowl keeps coming out of the oven.) If the temperature goes above that mark, the chocolate will lose its sheen. So you may have to melt it partially; let it cool a bit, stirring all the while; then continue melting more in whichever fashion you choose. Tedious, to be sure. Once about half of the chocolate has melted, continue stirring away from the heat until it's all melted. Put the chocolate thermometer back in the mixture and wait until its temperature falls to about 105°F (41°C). When you drizzle a little chocolate off the tines of a fork and back into the mixture, those drizzled bits should hold their shape on top for a moment or two before melting into the batch.

4. Line a large baking sheet with wax paper. Roll the chilled goat cheese ganache into 1-inch balls. You'll probably get about 18 from the batch. Stick a toothpick or thin, pointy bamboo skewer into one ball; then dip it into the chocolate, rolling it gently from side to side to coat. Lift it up to let some of the excess chocolate dribble back into the bowl or pan. Transfer the truffle to the prepared baking sheet and sprinkle a grain or two of coarse salt over it while the chocolate is still melty. Then continue to make more in the same way. You'll know that you're coating them too heavily if the chocolate puddles around their bottoms. It's a little bit of trial and error at first, but soon enough you'll be a whiz. If you really want to go over the top, you can skip the jury-rigged toothpicks or skewers and buy chocolate dipping rings and forks that allow you to hold the truffles up out of the tempered chocolate to let some of it run off before you transfer them to the prepared baking sheet.

5. Set the baking sheet with the dipped truffles in the refrigerator and chill until firm, about 30 minutes. After that, you can put them in a smaller container between sheets of wax paper and store them in the fridge for up to 1 week. However, let them come back to room temperature, setting them out on the counter for 15 to 20 minutes before serving.

LESS TO DO

Do you have to temper the chocolate so obsessively in step 3? Well, probably not. You might still get the proper sheen and texture if you just melt half of the chocolate in a double boiler or the alternate saucepan-and-bowl contraption, then stir away from the heat until the chocolate has completely melted—and keep stirring until it develops a beautiful, shiny sheen. It won't be perfect but it will also work. However, in no case should you melt the chocolate in the microwave without a chocolate thermometer at the ready. The chocolate can very easily overheat at the sides of the bowl, thereby bubbling, singeing, and turning bitter.

CHOCOLATE-DIPPED GOAT CHEESE BALLS

YOU'LL END UP WITH ABOUT TWENTY-FOUR.

Maybe you want something simpler than the chèvre ganache delights on page 222. Here you go! There's no chocolate in the filling of these simple, goaty candies, so you'll need to freeze the little cheese balls first to make sure they hold their shape without the melted chocolate's adhesive properties.

10 ounces (280 g) **fresh chèvre or soft goat cheese, at room temperature**

¼ cup (55 g) **sugar**

2 teaspoons **vanilla extract**

¼ teaspoon **salt**

1 pound (455 g) **bittersweet chocolate (but a little sweeter than the chocolate in the Chèvre Truffles recipe on page 222, between 60% and 65% cocoa solids)**

1. Stir the fresh chèvre, sugar, vanilla, and salt in a large bowl until creamy. Use a rounded teaspoon or a very small ice cream scoop to make about 24 balls. Place these on a sheet tray and set them in the freezer for 2 hours.

2. Meanwhile, temper the chocolate. See step 3 on page 223 for exact instructions.

3. Line a large baking sheet with wax paper. Following the instructions on page 223 for using toothpicks, skewers, or more complicated professional tools, dip the frozen balls one by one into the tempered chocolate, setting them on the prepared baking sheet. Once done, store the baking sheet in the refrigerator for at least 2 hours to let the cheese inside thaw completely. After that, you can take the balls off the baking sheet and store them between sheets of wax paper in a sealable plastic container. They should last about a week—although I promise they won't. For the best taste, let them sit out on the counter for 15 to 20 minutes to come closer to room temperature before eating. (As if anyone other than Job has such patience.)

Le Lingot du Quercy (*luh-leen-GOAH-dwew-kvehr-SEE*). It's like a little brick from southwestern France, with a white, striped rind and a ridiculously runny, fruity, floral cheese inside. It is perhaps a goat version of the renowned stinky Époisses de Bourgogne. It should be served strictly at room temperature so the flavors pop at first bite, then linger in the nose.

GOAT CHEESE VARIETIES

GOAT CHEESE RUGELACH

THERE'LL BE ABOUT THIRTY-SIX, PERHAPS TWO PER
SERVING, MAYBE THREE (OR FOUR).

Here's the classic New York deli pastry, reinvented with goat cheese in the dough, rather than the usual cream cheese. When Bruce was testing this recipe, I inadvertently told my mother about them one day. She made me promise to put a bag in the freezer, in anticipation of their visit months away. From then on, every time she called, she asked if the bag was still there. Sheesh, it's tough raising parents.

8 ounces (225 g) fresh chèvre or soft goat cheese

8 tablespoons (1 stick (115 g)) cool goat butter (or unsalted cow butter, if you must), cut into chunks

1⅔ cups (205 g) all-purpose flour, plus more for dusting

¼ teaspoon salt

¾ cup (170 g) raspberry jam

1 cup (225 g) sliced almonds

1½ teaspoons ground cinnamon

1. Beat the goat cheese and the butter in a large bowl with an electric mixer at medium speed until fluffy and light, almost like beaten cream cheese, 4 to 5 minutes.

2. Pour in the flour and salt; continue mixing at low speed until a soft dough forms. Scrape down the inside of the bowl, mix a few seconds more just to make sure everything is incorporated and the flour has all dissolved, then divide this mixture into thirds and form them into three balls. Put 1 of the balls on a large sheet of wax paper, on your work surface. Spread it into a circle about 1 inch (2.5 cm) thick. Fold the wax paper around it and put it in the refrigerator. Repeat with the other 2 balls. Chill them for at least 3 hours or up to 3 days.

3. Position the rack in the center of the oven and preheat the oven to 350°F (175°C). Line a large baking sheet with parchment paper or a silicone baking mat.

4. Dust a clean, dry work surface with flour, then place 1 of the chilled dough rounds on it. Roll into a 12-inch (30.5-cm) circle. Do it slowly and carefully, repositioning the rolling pin after each pass so that the circle is as even as you can make it.

5. Spread the circle with ¼ cup (55 g) of the raspberry jam; sprinkle ⅓ cup (76 g) of the sliced almonds and ½ teaspoon of the cinnamon over the top.

6. Cut the circle into 12 pie-piece wedges, like long, narrowing triangles. The best way to do this is to make 2 perpendicular cuts, 1 toward you

and 1 parallel to where you're standing. The circle is now in 4 quadrants. Cut each of these quadrants into 3 long, thin pie-wedge triangles. Separate the triangles from one another other a bit and then roll each of them up, starting at the pointy tip and rolling toward the curved back. Some of the jam will ooze out a little or just be exposed at the edges. Set the rugelach on the prepared baking sheet, spacing them about 1 inch apart.

7. Repeat steps 4 through 6 with the other 2 dough circles, re-dusting your work surface with flour each time and making sure there are no little bits of dough anywhere that can cause subsequent circles to stick. In fact, you can bake off 1 batch of *rugelach* and save the other 2 circles in the fridge for other times in the days ahead.

8. Once you've got all you want on the baking sheet, bake the *rugelach* until golden brown, about 30 minutes. Cool on the baking sheet for a couple of minutes before transferring to a wire rack and continuing to cool to room temperature, about 1 hour. Seal them up in a plastic bag and store them at room temperature for up to 3 days or in the freezer for God knows how long, until your mother comes to visit.

GOAT CHEESE VARIETIES

Mothais sur Feuille (*moh-TAY-soor-fuh-EE*). This is one of the most delicate goat cheeses, a bumpy mold-white round aged on a chestnut leaf, which holds in some of the moisture, keeping the white cheese soft and creamy. It's subtle—don't pair it with a blue or a runny, stinky cheese—but the firm texture yields the gentle flavors if you let a small piece dissolve on your tongue as you press it against your hard palate.

Majorero (*mah-hoh-RAY-roh*). From the Canary Islands, this Spanish goat cheese is aged, dense, salty, a little sour, even a little drying in the mouth (flavors and textures brought on because the goats have to eat lichen off rocks on these hot, volcanic islands). It's rubbed in lard before aging to give it a soft, sweet, umami-laced rind.

Monte Enebro. This Spanish goat cheese from west of Madrid is sold in flattened tubular logs. It's not for the faint of heart. The rind is a brown-and-white mottle, bloomed blue in spots. The paste inside is dense, intense, goaty, sour, and aggressive.

BIGGER SOMETHINGS

BACK AT PAUL TRUBY'S CHEESE SCHOOL, after Bruce hung a few bags of curds to drain, Paul had others ready to go, about half the size of the ones he and Bruce had just made. Paul snapped down a couple, set them on another table, and undid the cheesecloth to reveal a creamy mound of fresh goat cheese. He then handed Bruce a box of kosher salt.

And so begins the last step of the process of making goat cheese—which is divided into two parts based on the cultures previously added to the milk. On this day, Paul and Bruce were making fresh chèvre, a soft cheese, often sold in tubes or tubs. There's not much more to it than kneading in some salt and packaging the stuff. Bruce's day at cheese school had just about come to a close.

Why the salt? Twofold. One, taste, of course. But it also stops some bad bacterial activity. Consider cheese making sort of like curing a ham: You're trying to pull the water activity down far enough that bad bugs die of thirst. That's why hams can hang in open barns in Spain for up to five years, whereas a fresh piece of pork in your refrigerator might spoil in a number of days. Salt is also why some cheeses, cultured in certain ways, can be put through an intense ripening process—or *affinage* (French, *ah-fee-NAHJ*, meaning something along the lines of "the finishing"). If a cheese maker morphs craft into art with the cultures he or she chooses for the milk, there's a second time when art trumps craft: in the *affinage*.

In the course of researching this book, we saw a lot of cheese caves, places where goaty wheels, *tommes*, pyramids, and logs were aged for days, months, or years; some left alone, others washed with brines or oils so that surface molds could bloom, could begin to interact with the cheese just underneath, could develop that white outer coating, that brown beige wrinkling, or (in extreme cases) that craggy, gravelly look.

The first thing I learned in our tours is that a cheese cave is not a cave. Only one cheese maker we visited had anything even slightly resembling a cave (see page 195). The word *cave* is probably a holdover from some *ancien régime*, from the days when cheeses were in fact put in caves to absorb ambient molds.

These days, most caves are temperature- and humidity-controlled rooms with racks (sometimes wood, sometimes metal) stacked deep with the molded forms of curdled cultured milk. Controlled spoilage, in other words.

"Step back" was the refrain we heard most often. A cheese cave is a pristine place, a petri dish of spores. Molds develop, bloom, stick around, adhering to the cheese, developing trace flavors, creating the set, texture, and taste.

Most artisanal goat cheese makers are very particular during this step. Anything can set the cheese off, cause it to go bad, mostly because (1) goat milk has that notoriously thin consistency, which can cause the cheese to fail during *affinage*, and (2) the cave with all its molds and spores is a cheese maker's treasure chest. Ruin it, and someone might have to wash it out and start again. That's like asking a whiskey maker to throw out his or her barrels.

When a cheese finally emerges from the cave, it's ready to go. Most aged cheeses lead James Dean lives: brilliant and short. To be ridiculously simplistic, they are still rotting. Yes, in a controlled way. But ongoing, nonetheless. Cheeses come out of the cave at their gorgeous point, the cheese maker satisfied with the product. The cheese needs to be sold. Almost instantly. And eaten. Almost instantly.

The only exceptions are the rock-hard, aged cheeses, the ones that have become dry enough to be crumbly. These have a little more stable shelf life.

GOAT CHEESE BROWNIES

IT DEPENDS ON HOW YOU CUT THEM OUT OF THE PAN,
BUT PLAN ON TWENTY-FOUR BROWNIES.

Even if I failed to convince the television cameras on our failed pilot that we'd forgotten to include the brownies in a cookbook, there's no gainsaying brownies are the best American dessert—and now even more so with goat cheese in the mix. In this case, the chèvre takes the place of some—mind you, some—of the butter.

MORE TO KNOW

In order to trap air and build structure in a batter, butter must be cool, not room temperature. Near room temperature or above, the fat begins to spread out, unable to hold up even its own weight. If you don't believe me, go out to a pool on a cruise ship and look at what's going on in the deck chairs. You'll see what I mean.

10 tablespoons (145 g) cool goat butter (or cow butter, if you must), cut into small bits, plus a little extra for greasing the baking dish

2 cups (250 g) all-purpose flour, plus more for the baking dish

4 ounces (115 g) dark or bittersweet chocolate (between 60% and 72% cocoa solids), chopped

4 ounces (115 g) unsweetened chocolate (sometimes called baking chocolate), chopped

½ teaspoon baking powder

½ teaspoon salt

8 ounces (225 g) fresh chèvre or soft goat cheese

1¾ cups (425 g) sugar

1 large egg, at room temperature

4 large egg yolks, at room temperature

1 tablespoon vanilla extract

1. Make sure the rack is in the center of the oven and get the oven heated up to 350°F (177°C). Take a little butter on a wadded-up paper towel or piece of wax paper and run it around the inside of a 9 x 13-inch (23 x 33-cm) baking dish, coating the whole thing, particularly the corners and edges. You can also use the butter wrapper for this job because it often has butter still adhering to its inside.

2. Put a little flour in the baking dish and turn it this way and that to make sure the flour covers the bottom and sides, knocking it against the counter to get the flour off sticky spots and moving easily across the dish. (You'll also be able to see if you've got any spots without a slick of butter—you can fix these at this point.) Tap the baking dish on one edge against the counter to get all the flour down in one corner, then dump out the excess flour.

3. Melt all the chocolate. You can do this in one of several ways:

   ☞ Set a double boiler with about an inch (2.5 cm) of water in the bottom part over medium heat. Bring the water to a simmer, add both kinds of chocolate to the top part, and reduce the heat to low so the water simmers slowly; stir until about two-thirds of the chocolate has melted. Turn off the heat, remove the top part of the double boiler from the bottom pan, and continue stirring on the counter until the chocolate has fully melted.

☞ Do a similar operation with a jury-rigged double boiler: a medium saucepan and a mixing bowl that fits securely in it without touching the water bubbling beneath. Be careful when you remove the bowl—escaping steam can cause nasty burns.

☞ Put both kinds of chocolate in a big bowl and microwave on high in 6- or 7-second increments, stirring after each, until the chocolate is about two-thirds melted. Then take the bowl out of the microwave and continue stirring on the counter until all the chocolate has melted.

4. Mix 2 cups (455 g) flour, the baking powder, and salt in a bowl with a fork to make sure the baking powder and salt are evenly distributed throughout the flour.

5. Beat the butter, chèvre, and sugar in a separate bowl with an electric mixer at medium speed until creamy and light, maybe up to 5 minutes. You can barely overbeat the thing at this stage. You want it light and airy, the sugar mostly dissolved.

6. Beat in all the melted chocolate, scrape down the inside of the bowl, and beat in the whole egg until fully incorporated. Then beat in the egg yolks one at a time (or close enough if you've already got them together in one small bowl—the real point is to make sure the eggs get fully mixed into the batter). Finally, beat in the vanilla.

7. Stop the beaters, scrape them down, and remove them. Add the flour mixture and fold it in with a rubber spatula or a wooden spoon, turning it over in the batter just until there are no more bits of undissolved flour. You *can* overbeat—and even overstir—the mixture at this point, getting that gluten too gooey and stretchy. Once there's no more white flour in the mix, scrape and spread the batter into the prepared baking dish.

8. Bake until set, until a toothpick or cake tester inserted into the center of the brownie comes out with a few moist crumbs attached, about 25 minutes. The more crumbs, the fudgier the thing will be. But no wet batter on the toothpick, please. Cool the brownies in the baking dish on a wire rack for at least 10 minutes before cutting into squares. These can be stored between sheets of wax paper in a sealable plastic container for up to 5 days at room temperature or up to 4 months in the freezer.

CHOCOLATE CHIP GOAT CHEESE BLONDIES

AGAIN, ABOUT TWENTY-FOUR BLONDIES.

Blondies are all about the chocolate chips. Better quality makes better blondies. Don't cheap out. And for heaven's sake, don't use milk chocolate chips. They don't provide enough contrast to the goat cheese.

- 8 tablespoons (115 g) **cool goat butter (or unsalted cow butter, if you must), cut into small bits, plus a little more for greasing the baking dish**
- 2 cups (250 g) **all-purpose flour, plus more for the baking dish**
- 1 teaspoon **baking powder**
- ½ teaspoon **salt**
- 8 ounces (225 g) **fresh chèvre or soft goat cheese**

- 1 cup (225 g) **granulated sugar**
- 1 cup (225 g) **packed dark brown sugar**
- 2 large **eggs, at room temperature**
- 1 large **egg yolk, at room temperature**
- 1 tablespoon **vanilla extract**
- 1½ cups (340 g) **dark chocolate chips**

MORE TO KNOW

The blondies here bake longer than the brownies on page 230 because the brownies (1) are fudgier (and thus a little underdone) and (2) have more fat, thanks to all the chocolate and the additional butter.

1. Get the rack in the center of the oven before heating the oven up to 350°F (175°C). Dab a little butter on a wadded-up paper towel or piece of wax paper and grease the inside of a 9 x 13-inch (23 x 33-cm) baking dish. Add a little flour, tap it around the dish to make sure the dish is fully coated, and then tap out any excess.

2. Whisk the all-purpose flour, baking powder, and salt in a bowl.

3. Beat the butter, chèvre or soft goat cheese, granulated sugar, and brown sugar in a big bowl with an electric mixer at medium speed until creamy, light, and even fluffy, about 6 minutes, maybe more.

4. Beat in the whole eggs one at a time, making sure the first is fully incorporated before adding the second. Then beat in the egg yolk and vanilla until smooth.

5. Remove the beaters, scrape any batter adhering to them back into the bowl, and add all the flour mixture. Fold it in with a rubber spatula or wooden spoon, using arching motions to make sure the flour gets fully dissolved without stretching out the gluten. Fold in the chocolate chips. Then scrape and spread the batter into the prepared baking dish.

6. Bake until lightly browned and set, until a toothpick or cake tester inserted into the center of the cake comes out with a few moist crumbs attached, about 45 minutes. Cool in the baking dish on a wire rack for 10 minutes before cutting into squares. These should be cooled to room temperature before being stored in a sealable plastic container between sheets of wax paper at room temperature for up to 3 days or in the freezer for up to 4 months.

GOAT CHEESE SHEET CAKE WITH MAPLE-GOAT CHEESE FROSTING

AT A CHURCH POTLUCK, IT'LL PROBABLY SERVE ABOUT THIRTY EPIS-
COPALIANS, TWENTY PRESBYTERIANS, OR TEN BAPTISTS.

*Sheet cakes rule the roost at Southern suppers: a big, thin layer of cake
made in a lipped 11 x 17-inch (28 x 44-cm) baking tray and then iced
in situ. Honestly, the point is just to have enough cake (and no more!)
to hold the big glop of frosting in place—here, with lots of goat cheese,
of course.*

For the cake:

32 tablespoons (4 sticks or 1 pound [450 g]) cool goat butter (or unsalted cow butter, if you must), cut into small bits, plus a little extra for greasing the baking sheet

3½ cups (795 g) cake flour

1 teaspoon baking powder

½ teaspoon salt

1 cup (225 g) granulated sugar

1 cup (225 g) packed light brown sugar

10 large eggs, at room temperature

1 tablespoon vanilla extract

For the frosting:

12 ounces (340 g) pecan halves or pieces, chopped

10 ounces (280 g) fresh chèvre or soft goat cheese

6 tablespoons (85 g) goat butter (or unsalted cow butter, if you must)

6 tablespoons (85 g) maple syrup (see page 222)

1 teaspoon vanilla extract

6 to 7 cups (1.4 to 1.6 kg) confectioners' sugar

1. Position the rack in the center of the oven; preheat the oven to 350°F (175°C). Lightly butter a lipped 11 x 17-inch (28 x 43-cm) baking sheet (sometimes called a half hotel sheet tray). Make sure you get the butter into the seams and corners.

2. Whisk the cake flour, baking powder, and salt in a bowl, making sure the latter 2 ingredients are evenly distributed in the flour.

3. Beat the 32 tablespoons or 1 pound (450 g) butter and both kinds of sugar in a bowl with an electric mixer at medium speed until creamy and light, about 7 minutes, maybe longer. Don't shortchange this step— really beat the butter until it's well incorporated and the sugar has almost fully dissolved.

4. Beat in the eggs two at a time, making sure each addition is fully incorporated and creamy before adding the next. Beat in 1 tablespoon vanilla. (Oh, go ahead—be completely decadent and add a dribble more. What can it hurt?)

5. Turn off the beaters, remove them from the batter, and scrape any bat-

ter adhering to them back into the bowl. Fold in the flour mixture, just until there are no undissolved bits of flour. Scrape and spread this batter evenly into the prepared baking sheet.

6. Bake until lightly browned, until a toothpick or cake tester inserted into the center of the cake comes out with a few moist crumbs attached, 25 to 30 minutes. Transfer the cake in the baking sheet to a wire rack and cool fully to room temperature, about 1 hour.

7. To make the frosting, first dry-toast the chopped pecans in a skillet over medium-low heat until lightly browned and fragrant, about 5 minutes, stirring often. Pour the pecans onto a plate and cool to room temperature, about 15 minutes.

8. Beat the goat cheese and 6 tablespoons (85 g) butter in a bowl with an electric mixer at medium speed until creamy and smooth, about 3 minutes.

9. Beat in the maple syrup and 1 teaspoon vanilla. Turn off the beaters, add 3 cups (300 g) of the confectioners' sugar, and beat at low speed for a minute or so, then at medium speed until fully incorporated and creamy. Begin adding the rest of the confectioners' sugar in ¼-cup (55 g) increments, beating in each addition until smooth, until you get a spreadable, thick frosting. There's no real telling how much sugar it will take because of ambient humidity and moisture in the butter and cheese. You'll have to play with it a bit to get it right. But be careful: Too much sugar, and the thing can turn liquid.

10. Spread the frosting over the cooled cake in the baking sheet, then sprinkle the toasted pecans over the top. Gently press the nuts in place, just so they'll stick. The cake can stay at room temperature, lightly covered with a clean kitchen towel or plastic wrap, for up to 2 days—although it's much better the day it's baked.

GOAT CHEESE CHEESECAKE

ONE CHEESECAKE. DEPENDS ON HOW DEPRESSED YOU ARE TO
KNOW HOW MANY SERVINGS YOU'LL GET OUT OF IT.
(DON'T EVER MAKE A CHEESECAKE THE DAY AFTER A BREAK-UP.)

Goat butter (or unsalted cow butter, if you must), for greasing the pan

1 cup (200 g) plus 2 tablespoons sugar, divided

¾ cup (175 ml) sliced almonds

6 large eggs, at room temperature, separated

1 pound 6 ounces (625 g) fresh chèvre or soft goat cheese

3 tablespoons all-purpose flour

3 tablespoons lemon juice

1 teaspoon finely grated lemon zest

1 tablespoon vanilla extract

Boiling water

1. Set the rack in the center of the oven and heat the oven up to 325°F (165°C). Put a little butter on a crumpled paper towel and grease the inside of a 9-inch (23-cm) springform pan, taking special care to get into the seam where the sides meet the bottom.

2. Grind 2 tablespoons sugar and the nuts in a food processor or a large spice grinder until a fine powder. Pour this mixture into the springform pan, then tilt and tip it this way and that to coat the bottom and the sides thoroughly. You'll be able to see if you've missed any spots with butter and fix them now. With whatever sugar-and-nut mixture is left in the pan, shake it a bit so that this excess coats the bottom evenly.

3. Beat 6 egg yolks with ¾ cup (150 g) sugar in a large bowl, using an electric mixer at medium speed. Keep beating until the mixture changes color to a pale yellow and is quite creamy, perhaps 5 minutes. Beat in the goat cheese until creamy.

4. Clean and dry the beaters. In a separate, scrupulously clean and dry bowl, beat the egg whites with the mixer at high speed until soft, droopy peaks can be formed when the beaters are turned off and dipped back into the whites.

5. Beat in the remaining ¼ cup (50 g) sugar, adding it in small increments so that the sugar dissolves into the beaten egg whites.

6. Using a rubber spatula, fold the beaten egg whites into the egg yolk mixture, using wide arcs so that you retain as much air from the egg whites in the batter as possible. Also fold in the flour, lemon juice, lemon zest, and vanilla. Pour and scrape this mixture into the prepared springform pan, doing so gently so as not to disturb the almond crust coating the inside.

MORE TO KNOW

Many traditional cheesecake recipes don't include flour. In fact, its addition is anathema to some aficionados. However, this cake has a different fat structure, thanks largely to the goat cheese. In essence, the fat strands are of differing lengths and need a little help building a good structure. Thus, the flour. Don't freak out. Just go with it.

7. Set the springform pan in a large baking dish or roasting pan and fill the dish with boiling water until it comes about halfway up the outside of the springform pan. Gently put this whole kit and caboodle in the oven and bake until puffed and set, about 50 minutes. The center of the cheesecake should still jiggle slightly like a custard.

8. Turn the oven off, open the oven door, and cool the cake where it is in the water bath in the oven for 30 minutes.

9. Remove the springform pan with the cake from the baking dish and cool to room temperature on a wire rack. Refrigerate until you're ready to serve it, at least 2 hours—then unsnap the sides of the springform pan to release the cake. If you're really brave, you can run a thin knife under the cake to remove it from the bottom of the springform pan, then transfer it to a cake plate with a big, flat, wide spatula. But, honestly, is anyone going to complain that it's still sitting on the pan's bottom?

GOAT CHEESE VARIETIES

O'Banon. If we had to pick just one cheese from Judy Schad's Capriole dairy in Greenville, Indiana, it would be this, best exemplifying her whimsy and craft: a fresh chèvre, wrapped in chestnut leaves that have first been soaked in bourbon, then aged for a month. The leaves (and liquor) brown the cheese a bit, giving it a nutty, elegant finish.

Osage Orange. If we had to pick one goat cheese to represent old-fashioned American-style cheese, the sort we grew up with, it would be this four- to six- month-aged Muenster-style cheese from Missouri's Goatsbeard Farm. It's creamy and firm, a good slicer, delicious on its own but fine in sandwiches or even as grilled cheese.

Persillé de Tignes (*pair-see-LAY-duh-TEE-nyuh*). Perhaps the best of the French *tommes* (*tohm*; that is, cylindrical wheels from the Alpine region abutting Switzerland), this creamy goat cheese is marvelously white inside, perhaps a hint of its clean, bracing flavor. The rough, beige rind is laced with blue-cheese bacteria, which slowly permeate the paste as it ages, rendering it increasingly assertive, like steroids for a ballet dancer.

DUKKA CHEESECAKE

MAKES ABOUT SIXTEEN SERVINGS.

Dukka *is an Egyptian spice mixture, often used as a dip for flat-breads—first into olive oil, then into this heady, fragrant blend. Bruce has long loved it and so decided to develop a cheesecake that takes advantage of its unusual, full, rich, even a little savory, nose.*

⅔ (150 g) cup hazelnuts

¼ cup (55 g) white sesame seeds

2 tablespoons packed dark brown sugar

1 teaspoon coriander seeds

¼ teaspoon cumin seeds

½ teaspoon ground cardamom

¼ teaspoon salt

¼ teaspoon freshly ground black pepper

4 tablespoons (½ stick [55 g]) goat butter (or unsalted cow butter, if you must), melted and cooled just a bit until it's still liquid, just not hot

6 sheets frozen phyllo, thawed according to the package instructions, then laid on a clean, scrupulously dry work surface under a sheet of plastic wrap and a clean kitchen towel to keep the sheets moist

1½ pounds (680 g) fresh chèvre or soft goat cheese

¾ cup (180 ml) honey

3 large eggs, at room temperature

3 tablespoons all-purpose flour (see page 235)

1 tablespoon vanilla extract

¼ teaspoon salt

1. Position the rack in the center of the oven and preheat the oven to 325°F (165°C). Put the hazelnuts on a large, lipped baking sheet and bake until aromatic and lightly browned, stirring occasionally, about 8 minutes. Remove them from the oven and dump them onto a clean kitchen towel. Cool for 5 minutes, but maintain the oven's temperature.

2. Meanwhile, toast the sesame seeds in a dry skillet over low heat, stirring occasionally, until lightly browned and fragrant, about 4 minutes. Dump these into a food processor fitted with the chopping blade.

3. Wrap the hazelnuts in the towel and rub them together, thereby taking off their papery skins with friction against both the towel and one another. You needn't get off every speck of skin—just most of it. Dump the hazelnuts into the food processor.

4. Add the brown sugar to the food processor along with the coriander seeds, cumin seeds, ground cardamom, salt, and pepper. Process until the consistency of coarse sand.

5. Brush the inside of a 9-inch (23-cm) springform pan with some of the melted butter. Lay a phyllo sheet in the pan, pressing it into place so that it goes up the sides and even overlaps a bit. (Keep the other phyllo sheets covered as you work with them one by one.) Brush this first sheet with the melted butter—then add a second sheet in a different direction, pressing it into place and brushing it with the butter as well. Continue

on with the rest of the sheets, positioning them this way and that, never the same way twice, all pressed into place and brushed with the melted butter, lapping over the rim of the pan every which way but covering the bottom and sides completely.

6. Beat the goat cheese and honey in a bowl with an electric mixer at medium speed until creamy and light, about 4 minutes. Beat in the eggs one at a time, making sure each one is fully incorporated before adding the next. You're looking for a pale, very creamy batter. Beat in the flour, vanilla, and salt just until incorporated.

7. Pour half this cheesecake batter into the prepared springform pan, spreading it into an even layer without breaking or disturbing the phyllo sheets. Sprinkle the *dukka* spice mixture evenly over this layer. Then gently pour and scrape the remainder of the batter into the pan, taking care not to dislodge the *dukka* across the middle. Fold all the phyllo sheets over the top of the batter.

8. Bake until the phyllo has browned and the cake itself is set, if still waggly, when jiggled, about 1 hour 15 minutes. Cool in the springform pan on a wire rack to room temperature, about 1 hour. Store in the fridge, covered, until you're ready to unlatch the sides and serve the cake, cutting it into wedges.

GOAT CHEESE TAMALES

MAKES TWENTY-FOUR.

Dessert tamales are a Southwestern treat: often made with cheese and chopped fruit, topped with caramel. They're a bit of a pain to prepare, but you can do so in advance, storing them in the fridge for a day or two before steaming them just before you're ready to serve them. By the way, you might want to have more husks than the recipe calls for, perhaps half again as many, because they can tear and shred after being soaked in water for a while.

LESS TO DO

Omit making the *cajeta* and use warmed purchased caramel sauce instead.

24 corn husks for tamales

Boiling water

2 cups (455 g) **instant masa harina (marked** *for tamales* **on the package)**

½ cup (115 g) **shredded unsweetened dried coconut**

1 teaspoon **baking powder**

½ teaspoon **salt**

2 cups (480 ml) **regular or low-fat goat milk (or cow milk, if you must)**

⅔ cup (165 ml) **untoasted walnut oil**

2 cups (455 g) **chopped fresh pineapple**

1 pound (455 g) **fresh chèvre or soft goat cheese**

¼ cup (60 ml) **honey**

Butchers' twine

Cajeta **(page 148), warmed**

1. Place the husks in a large baking dish or roasting pan. Cover them with boiling water. Set a plate or a saucepan lid on top to weight them down in the hot water. Soak for 20 minutes.

2. Meanwhile, mix the masa harina, coconut, baking powder, and salt in a large bowl. Warm the milk and oil in a large saucepan over medium heat, just until the mixture is bathwater temperature. Pour this warm liquid into the masa mixture and stir to form a soft dough.

3. Mix the pineapple, fresh chèvre or soft goat cheese, and honey into the soft dough.

4. Now you're ready to start filling the tamales. Take a softened husk out of the hot water. Set it on your work surface, rough side down, and open it out. (Be gentle: it can tear.) Spread about 3 tablespoons of the masa filling into the husk, mounding it in the center but spreading it up and down the husk. Fold the husk's long sides over the filling, then fold the bottom (the part nearest you) and the top (the other end) over the filling as well, making a little rectangular packet, with the masa dough sealed inside. Tie this packet in two places (preferably once the long way and once the short way) with butchers' twine. Set aside and make more. The recipe can be made to this point in advance; store the tamales, covered, in a big bowl in the refrigerator for up to a couple days. Or they can be frozen at this point in a sealed container for up to 4 months. (No need to thaw them before the next step.)

5. Set up a large vegetable steamer with an inch or two (2.5 or 5 cm) of bubbling water underneath the steaming platform. Add all the tamales, stacking them to fit (or as many as you want to eat at one time). Cover, reduce the heat so the water simmers slowly, and steam for 1 hour. You'll need to check on the water occasionally to make sure it hasn't boiled away. Add more when necessary. Once steamed, serve the sweet tamales hot, letting everyone undo their packets—and pouring the warm *cajeta* as a sauce over the creamy filling. Don't be a Gerald Ford. He's said to have lost Texas in the presidential election because he tried to eat the husk. That's the part you toss into a bowl in the middle of the table.

Pouligny-Saint-Pierre (*poo-leen-YEE-seng-pee-YAIR*). This is one of the many Gallic pyramidal goat cheeses: a bumpy, beige-to-white rind covered with blue mold. The taste is the very definition of French chèvre: salty, sour, sweet, and umami, all bound with a silky moistness and texture.

Tessiner Geisskäse (*tuh-SEE-ner-GUYS-kay-zuh*). This Swiss goat cheese is not for everyone: stinky, very goaty, and quite pungent, but also hard, sometimes quite dry, made according to very old traditions (the curds must be cooked over wood fires). The rind is washed with brine to give it a rough, knobby appearance, sometimes seeping brown right down into the white cheese below.

Valençay (*vah-luhn-SAY*). This ripe, creamy goat cheese comes in the form of a brown, white-molded pyramid with its top lopped off—by some accounts, lopped off by Napoleon himself after liking the cheese but not wanting to be reminded of his troubles down in Egypt when he was off trying to pretend he was Alexander the Great. It's smooth, creamy, and moist, with a little whack from the sour and umami edges, a little goaty smack at the end—and probably best balanced with some quince paste or dried apricots.

GOAT CHEESE BLINTZES

SIXTEEN BLINTZES. FOUR, SIX, EIGHT SERVINGS?

Are blintzes for breakfast or dessert? Bruce and I have fought this one for years. He claims they're for whenever there's coffee. I, a Southern boy from prairie Protestants, find that eating them after 10:00 A.M. is a sign of rank indolence. Somehow, I think he's right—but I'm not willing to admit it.

For the crepes:

2 large eggs, at room temperature

1 cup (240 ml) regular or low-fat goat milk (or cow milk, if you must)

1 cup (125 g) all-purpose flour

¼ teaspoon salt

Goat butter (or unsalted cow butter, if you must), for greasing the skillet

For the filling:

8 ounces (225 g) fresh chèvre or soft goat cheese

1 large egg yolk

2 tablespoons sugar

½ teaspoon vanilla extract

4 tablespoons (55 g) goat butter (or unsalted cow butter, if you must)

1. Whir the two eggs and the milk in a blender (preferably) or a food processor fitted with the chopping blade until creamy. Add the flour and salt; blend or process until smooth.

2. Lightly grease an 8-inch (20-cm) nonstick skillet with a little butter on some wadded up paper towel. Set the skillet over medium heat, let it warm up a bit, then pour in 2 tablespoons of the flour batter. Swirl and shake the skillet so that the batter evenly covers its bottom. Cook until set, about 30 seconds. Flip the crepe, then cook for another 30 seconds or so, just until firm. Transfer the crepe from the skillet to a plate or cutting board; cover with a clean kitchen towel. Butter the skillet again, add 2 more tablespoons of batter, and keep going, repeating ad nauseam, until you have 16 crepes.

3. For the filling, stir the fresh chèvre or soft goat cheese, egg yolk, sugar, and vanilla in a big bowl until creamy. Set one of the crepes on your work surface, mound 2 teaspoons of this cheese mixture in the middle of the crepe, flatten the filling a little, fold the two sides of the crepe to your left and right over the filling, fold up the bottom, the part nearest you. Now roll the crepe away from you so that it folds up into a little packet. Set aside under a clean kitchen towel and continue filling all the crepes.

4. Heat a large skillet over medium heat. Add 2 tablespoons of the butter and about half the blintzes. Fry them on both sides until crisp and brown, about 4 minutes in all, turning once. Transfer these to a serving platter, add the remaining 2 tablespoons butter to the skillet, and fry the rest of them.

 GO ALL OUT! GO ALL OUT!

Before you roll them up, you can put a tablespoon or so of jam inside each blintz with the goat cheese filling: cherry, apricot, raspberry, or blueberry. Or how about some orange marmalade? For garnish, sift confectioners' sugar over the crepes, once they're fried.

IN WHICH A WORLD-CLASS POET SURPRISES ME WITH A GOAT TALE

WHEN YOU'RE INVITED OUT to dinner with a prestigious poet, the protégé of a Nobel laureate, a guy whose poetry you yourself have assigned in college courses, you have high expectations. At least, I do.

I'm not surrounded by academics anymore. Which is not a bad thing. I tend to get references to things like *The Simpsons* that I used to miss. But I also read in silence, as it were. Bruce and I talk about books, but we don't stake out and defend territories. So with the promise of a conversation with a poet of such renown, I was about to set the clock back to my bookish heyday.

I'd even studied up. OK, I wasn't really up on the latest post-post-post-structuralist theory or new-new-new-historicism, but I could probably fake it on context, once he said something. I'd heard Paul de Man was a Nazi. Maybe I could bring that up.

But when I finally got to have my important conversation, I got stumped. Not by literary theory. But by more prurient stuff.

Here's how I got to that moment. Last April, Bruce and I went to the Richmond, Virginia, Junior League Book and Author Dinner. If you ever think the book is dead, go there. A thousand people pay top dollar, enduring marginally acceptable banquet food, all to hear six authors discourse.

Like a dutiful writer—or more like a kid in a candy store—I'd read everyone's book before we arrived. They were all well-published types, and, to boot, one of them was married to said world-class poet, who had not come with her for the weekend. World-class poets don't tend to lurk around Richmond anymore.

As we were parting, Bruce told her we should all four have dinner some night. I was stunned. She herself was a great literary writer. But her husband? Well, you don't just invite those types to dinner. You stand around, admiring from afar. Years of academia had left me slack-jawed at the mere thought. Imagine Lucy with William Holden.

We met months later at a down-and-dirty joint in Manhattan's Chinatown, a restaurant that specialized in dishes from Shanghai: braised pork belly, lion's head meatballs.

Poetry didn't come up. Literature, either. Nor theory. I mentioned we were currently writing the first-ever all-goat book. We passed on to talk

about houses and cars. Did I mention this guy was anthologized? How can you talk about changing your oil with a guy who's in the Norton and Oxford greatest-hits books?

After the meal, we all decided to pack over to the Lung Moon Bakery for dessert.

On the walk, I made sure to pair myself up with the poet. I sort of pushed Bruce ahead. Ah, I thought, here it comes at last. I'm ready. I haven't done this in years. I remember sitting around in graduate school, tossing out literary allusions.

But before I could start, he leaned toward me and said, "Selkirk was surrounded by goats."

Oh, so it *is* going to be like graduate school. Because I had no idea what he was talking about.

"Selkirk?" I asked, stalling for time.

"Defoe," he answered.

Oh, right, the guy Defoe used as his model for Robinson Crusoe. In 1704, the real Alexander Selkirk was shipwrecked on what are now the Juan Fernández Islands off the coast of Chile. At least so it goes in some accounts. Others say he was put off there by his shipmates because he was such a miserable bastard.

"Oh, yes, that line between history and fiction." I laughed. I was almost there. Almost ready to drop a Derrida quote on him.

"He apparently got by for those four years with goats for companions," he said.

"Yes, they're very friendly. Dairy goats especially. On the farms we visited, they ran up . . ."

"Pleasure aids," he said.

Fancy French literary theory couldn't save me now.

Trying rather desperately to come up with something smart about the narrativization of sex, and goats, and the age of Western exploration, I waited just long enough for my world-class poet to get distracted by the Chinese pastries.

It all came to naught. And my only recompense? The vagaries of this career, a chuckle at the bottom of it all. Because life is comedy, not tragedy. Because writing books about food is way better than literary theory. And because I got to walk down a New York street with one of the greatest poets in the world and talk about some guy screwing goats. What could possibly be next?

ACKNOWLEDGMENTS

After eighteen books, it's hard to know where to begin.

This one had two editors. Luisa Weiss—how can you keep them in Manhattan when they've seen the bright lights of Berlin?—jumped at the mere notion of this title sometime during the photo shoot for our ham tome. But the project was actually shepherded by Natalie Kaire, a kind, patient voice in these turbulent times. We can't thank her enough for being the champion of this project.

While we're thinking of Stewart, Tabori & Chang, we must also thank our publisher, Leslie Stoker, for continuing to believe in our voice and vision; Katherine Camargo, the managing editor, for keeping the project moving along (despite our missed deadlines); Kerry Liebling for help with the marketing of what's a (to say the least) niche book; and Claire Bamundo for once again overseeing its publicity, so important for us in these days of way bigger noise machines.

There's just no way for us to say enough good things about Susan Ginsburg, our literary agent, who continues to keep our career on track after all these years. And thanks, too, to Bethany Strout, for patience and kindness—although she's now gone off on to higher publishing pastures.

While the words on a page may be an author's vision of a book, there's no way to talk about this book without the incredible design sensibilities of Alissa Faden, the drop-dead gorgeous photographs of Marcus Nilsson, and the spot-on prop stylings of Angharad Bailey.

Then there are the real heros: the food producers. Many thanks to Julie and Mike Bowen at North Hollow Farm for being willing to drop-ship goat meat so quickly. A huge thank-you to Jennifer Lynn Bice at Redwood Hill Farm and Mary Keehn at Cypress Grove Chevre for sending so much cheese both for recipe development and the book's photo shoot. Also thanks to Paul Trubey at Beltane Farms, Bill Niman at Niman Ranch, Laura Howard at Laloo's Goat's Milk Ice Cream Company, Sharon Bice at Redwood Hill Farm, Chuck Hellmer at Haystack Mountain Goat Dairy, Laini Fondiller at Lazy Lady Cheese, and Donna Pacheco at both the Pacheco Family Dairy and the Achadinha Cheese Company for their time and willingness to laze away a day talking to us about their fabulous art and craft. Thanks, too, to Kris Ellenberg at supergoat.org for organizing so much of the behind-the-scenes stuff that made this book go so easily.

Finally, we can't thank Jeffery Elliot enough for the beautiful Staub pots that got used in the photographs (and now grace the shelves of our kitchen). Also much thanks to AllClad and OXO for once again providing the tools that make recipe development so much fun.

INDEX

PAGE REFERENCES IN ITALIC REFER TO ILLUSTRATIONS

Accompaniments:
celery root raita, 135
corn pudding, 140, *141*
corn tortillas, 85
flour tortillas, 89
garlic and parsnip flans, 139
goat cheese mashed potatoes, 185
jicama salad with blood orange vinaigrette, 103
sweet and sour prunes preserved in red wine, 108
Achadinha Cheese Company, 147, 201
Affinage, 229
Age of goats, at slaughter, 14
Agglutinin, 120
Aleppo pepper, 189
Almond(s):
goat cheese cheesecake, 235–36
goat cheese rugelach, 226–27
tarragon pesto, 202, *203*
Alpine goats, 133
American goat cheeses:
Capricious, 201, 206
Caprino di Vino, 211
Harvest Cheese, 217
Humboldt Fog, 219
O'Banon, 236
Osage Orange, 236
Ancho chiles, 59
Angora goats, 133
Appetizers. *See* First courses
Apples, Normandy-inspired goat shanks with butter, cream and, 45–46
Apricots, dried, in *sali boti*, 72–74, *73*
Artichoke(s):
braised meatballs with fennel and, *98*, 99
fresh baby, preparing, 99
goat, and potato stew, 54
Arugula, 181

Back rib(s), goat:
chops, 17
pulled shoulder, 29
slices, in Masaman curry, 78–79
Banana–wheat germ muffins, 124–26, *125*
Basil, in almond-tarragon pesto, 202, *203*
Bean(s):
black, and goat cheese enchiladas, 210–11
black-eyed pea, goat cheese, and Swiss chard empanadas, 186–87
fava, in tagine with preserved lemon, 60, *61*
white, Italian-inspired goat shanks with lemon and, 48
see also Chickpeas
Beef, 13
Beltane Farm, 123, 175, 197–98, 229
Bice, Sharon, 209
Black bean and goat cheese enchiladas, 210–11
Blackberries, pan-roasted chops with sage and, 18, *19*
Black-eyed pea, goat cheese, and Swiss chard empanadas, 186–87
Blintzes, goat cheese, *242*, 243
Blondies, chocolate chip goat cheese, 232
Blood orange vinaigrette, jicama salad with, 103
Blueberry *tzatziki* soup, chilled, 138
Blue cheese, 198
Harbourne Blue, 217
Boer goats, 133
Bondes:
Bonde de Gâtine, 206
Chabichou du Poitou, 211
Bread(s):
croutons, 57

crumbs, fresh, 96
wheat germ–banana muffins, 124–26, *125*
yeast doughs that don't rise, 131
yoghurt brot, 130–31
Breakfast fare:
goat cheese blintzes, *242*, 243
goat cheese danishes, 127–29
wheat germ–banana muffins, 124–26, *125*
Breast of goat, 17, 54
braised, 26
goat *mole verde*, 88–89
visible fat on, 26
Brie, goat:
baked, 177
goat cheese quesadillas, 182, *183*
no-holds-barred mac and crab and goat cheese, 218–19
Briwat, *188*, 189
Brownies, goat cheese, 230–31
Browning meat, 26
Brunet, 206
Brunost, 191
Bulgur, in *kibbeh*, 114–17, *115*
Burgers, 92–93
Butter, goat, 120, 145
balancing recipe flavors and, 121
clarified, 81
corn pudding, 140, *141*
empanada dough, 186–87
goat cheese danishes, 127–29
substituting cow butter for, 180

Cabbage, goat shanks with port, vanilla and, 42–44, *43*
Cacciatore, goat, 24–25
Cajeta, 148, *149*
Cakes:
dukka cheesecake, 237–38, *239*
goat cheese cheesecake, 235–36
goat cheese sheet, with maple–goat cheese frosting, 233–34
Calcium, 120, 197

Canada:
Le Chèvre Noir from, 211
goat meat suppliers in, 15
Capricious, 201, 206
Caprino di Vino, 211
Capriole, 236
Caramel:
cajeta, 148, *149*
goat crème brûlée, 160–61
spiced flan, 158–59
Carrot-dill soup, creamy, *136*, 137
Casein, 170, 175, 191, 197
Cashews, in deconstructed *lassi*,
134
Cashmere goats, 133
Casseroles:
feta and greens pie, 207–8
goat cheese, crab, and tortilla,
212–13
mac and crab and goat cheese,
no-holds-barred, 218–19
meatball-and-rice, baked,
100–101
moussaka, 102–3
Cedar-planked goat cheese, 178,
179
Celery root raita, 135
Chabichou du Poitou, 211
Cheese, goat, 168–243
balls, chocolate-dipped, *224*, 225
beyond its prime, signs of, 178
and black bean enchiladas,
210–11
black-eyed pea, and Swiss chard
empanadas, 186–87
blintzes, *242*, 243
Brie, baked, 177
briwat, *188*, 189
brownies, 230–31
cedar-planked, 178, *179*
cheesecake, 235–36
chèvre truffles, 222–23
chocolate chip blondies, 232
corn pudding, 140, *141*
crab, and tortilla casserole,
212–13
croutons, radish and grape salad
with, 181
danishes, 127–29
dukka cheesecake, 237–38, *239*
feta, marinated, 176

feta and greens pie, 207–8
fondue, 192, *193*
fresh vs. aged, 201
gougères, 184
grated, spaghetti with oven-
roasted tomatoes, shiitake
mushrooms and, 199
history of, 168
lasagna with mushrooms,
spinach, and tarragon, 216–17
Lazy Lady Farm, 195
mac and crab and, no-holds-
barred, 218–19
making, with Paul Trubey at
Beltane Farm, 123, 175,
197–98, 229
mashed potatoes, 185
pizza with peaches, almond-
tarragon pesto and, 202, *203*
pizza with squash puree,
caramelized onion, pecans
and, 200–201
primary components of, 169–70,
191
and pumpkin ravioli with sage
butter, 214–15
quesadillas, 182, *183*
raw vs. pasteurized milk in, 175
ripened, two parts of, 176
rugelach, 226–27
saag paneer, 171–72, *173*
sandwiches, grilled, with
persimmons and honey
mustard, 194
savory shortbread rounds, 180
in Scandinavia, 191
sheet cake with maple–goat
cheese frosting, 233–34
-and-spinach dumplings, baked,
204, 205–6
storing, 208
tamales, 240–41
see also specific cheeses
Cheesecakes:
dukka, 237–38, *239*
goat cheese, 235–36
Cheese caves, 229
Cheesemongers, 176
Chestnut flour, 97
Chèvre, fresh, 168, 201
baked spinach-and-goat-cheese

dumplings, *204*, 205–6
briwat, *188*, 189
chocolate chip goat cheese
blondies, 232
chocolate-dipped goat cheese
balls, *224*, 225
corn pudding, 140, *141*
dukka cheesecake, 237–38, *239*
goat cheese, black-eyed pea,
and Swiss chard empanadas,
186–87
goat cheese, crab, and tortilla
casserole, 212–13
goat cheese and black bean
enchiladas, 210–11
goat cheese and pumpkin ravioli
with sage butter, 214–15
goat cheese blintzes, *242*, 243
goat cheese brownies, 230–31
goat cheese cheesecake, 235–36
goat cheese danishes, 127–29
goat cheese lasagna with
mushrooms, spinach, and
tarragon, 216–17
goat cheese mashed potatoes,
185
goat cheese rugelach, 226–27
goat cheese tamales, 240–41
goat crème brûlée, 160–61
goat gougères, 184
mac and crab and goat cheese,
no-holds-barred, 218–19
maple–goat cheese frosting,
233–34
pizza with goat cheese, peaches,
and almond-tarragon pesto,
202, *203*
pizza with goat cheese, squash
puree, caramelized onion, and
pecans, 200–201
pronunciation of, 176
radish and grape salad with goat
cheese croutons, 181
truffles, 222–23
*see also specific chèvres and
producers*
Chèvre Noir, Le, 211
Chevrotin des Aravis, 213
Chicken, 12
fried, 142–43
Chicken-fried goat with goat milk

gravy, 67–69, *68*

Chickpeas:
    Spanish-inspired leg of goat on
        bed of, with tomatoes and
        saffron, 38–40, *39*
    split, in *dalcha gosht*, 76–77

Chile powders, 49

Chiles:
    corn pudding, 140, *141*
    dried, 59
    pulled shoulder, 28–29
    safe handling of, 36

Chili, 58–59

Chimichurri, 111–13

Chipotle chiles, 59

Chocolate:
    chèvre truffles, 222–23
    chip goat cheese blondies, 232
    -dipped goat cheese balls, *224*,
        225
    goat cheese brownies, 230–31
    goat milk fudge, 150
    goat *mole negro*, 84–85
    panna cotta, 156, *157*
    pudding, 151
    tempering, 223

Chops, goat, 17
    see also Loin chops, goat; Rib
        chops, goat; Shoulder chops,
        goat

Cilantro, 78

Clarified goat butter, 81

Cocoa powder, Dutch-processed vs.
    natural, 151

Coconut, in goat cheese tamales,
    240–41

Collagen, 27

Corn:
    pudding, 140, *141*
    tortillas. *See* Tortilla(s), corn

Crab:
    goat cheese, and tortilla
        casserole, 212–13
    mac and goat cheese and, no-
        holds-barred, 218–19

Crème brûlée, goat, 160–61

Crepes, 243

Crottin de Chavignol, 213

Crottins, 199, 209

Croutons, 57
    goat cheese, 181

Cucumber:
    celery root raita, 135
    chilled blueberry *tzatziki* soup,
        138

Cultures, in cheese-making, 197,
    198

Curds, 170, 197, 198

Curries, 70–89
    dalcha gosht, 76–77
    dopiaza, 75
    goat vindaloo, 81
    Masaman, 78–79
    saag paneer, 171–72, *173*
    sali boti, 72–74, *73*

Custards:
    garlic and parsnip flans, 139
    goat crème brûlée, 160–61
    spiced flan, 158–59

Cypress Grove, 219

D

Dalcha gosht, 76–77

Danishes, goat cheese, 127–29

Daube de chèvre, 56–57

Deconstructed *lassi*, 134

Desserts:
    cajeta, 148, *149*
    chèvre truffles, 222–23
    chocolate chip goat cheese
        blondies, 232
    chocolate-dipped goat cheese
        balls, *224*, 225
    chocolate panna cotta, 156, *157*
    chocolate pudding, 151
    dukka cheesecake, 237–38, *239*
    fudge, goat milk, 150
    goat cheese blintzes, *242*, 243
    goat cheese brownies, 230–31
    goat cheese cheesecake, 235–36
    goat cheese rugelach, 226–27
    goat cheese sheet cake with
        maple–goat cheese frosting,
        233–34
    goat cheese tamales, 240–41
    goat crème brûlée, 160–61
    goat milk rice pudding, 162
    goat yogurt pie, 163–65, *164*
    honey goat milk gelato, 152–53
    raspberry frozen yogurt, 154
    spiced flan, 158–59

Dolmades, 109–10

Dopiaza, 75

Down-home stew, 94, *95*

Dressings:
    blood orange vinaigrette, 103
    creamy, 143

Drinks:
    deconstructed *lassi*, 134
    margarita, 178

Dukka cheesecake, 237–38, *239*

Dumplings:
    spinach-and-goat-cheese, baked,
        204, 205–6
    for stew, 94, *95*

Dutch ovens, 42

E

Eggplant, in moussaka, 102–3

Empanadas:
    goat cheese, black-eyed pea, and
        Swiss chard, 186–87
    meat, with *chimichurri*, 111–13

Enchiladas, goat cheese and black
    bean, 210–11

England, Harbourne Blue from, 217

F

Fargue, Léon-Paul, 169

Fat:
    balancing recipe flavors and, 121
    in goat milk, 120, 133, 169
    visible, in goat meat, 20, 26

Fava beans, in tagine with
    preserved lemon, 60, *61*

Fennel, braised meatballs with
    artichokes and, *98*, 99

Feta, goat:
    and greens pie, 207–8
    marinated, 176

First courses:
    baked goat Brie, 177
    briwat, *188*, 189
    cedar-planked goat cheese, 178,
        179
    deconstructed *lassi*, 134
    dolmades, 109–10
    goat cheese, black-eyed pea,
        and Swiss chard empanadas,
        186–87

goat cheese quesadillas, 182, *183*
goat gougères, 184
goat ragù with pappardelle, 55
marinated goat feta, 176
meat empanadas with
    chimichurri, 111–13
pâté de campagne, 106–8, *107*
radish and grape salad with goat
    cheese croutons, 181
savory shortbread rounds, 180
spaghetti with oven-roasted
    tomatoes, shiitake
    mushrooms, and grated goat
    cheese, 199
Fish sauce, 49
Flans:
    garlic and parsnip, 139
    spiced, 158–59
Flavor compounds, in goat milk,
    120–21, 169
    balancing recipes and, 121
    pasteurization and, 175
Flour tortillas. *See* Tortillas, flour
Folic acid, 120
Fondiller, Laini, 195
Fondue, goat cheese, 192, *193*
French cooking:
    daube de chèvre, 56–57
    goat gougères, 184
    Normandy-inspired goat shanks
        with butter, apples, and
        cream, 45–46
    pâté de campagne, 106–8, *107*
    seven-hour leg of goat, 30–31
French goat cheeses:
    Bonde de Gâtine, 206
    Chabichou du Poitou, 211
    Chevrotin des Aravis, 213
    Crottin de Chavignol, 213
    Le Lingot du Quercy, 201, 225
    Mothais sur Feuille, 227
    Persillé de Tignes, 236
    Pouligny-Saint-Pierre, 241
    Valençay, 241
French language, goat in, 30
French ovens, 42
Fried chicken, 142–43
Frosting, maple–goat cheese,
    233–34
Fudge, goat milk, 150

Game hens, tandoori, 144–45
Garlic:
    chimichurri, 111–13
    creamy salad dressing, 143
    and parsnip flans, 139
Garrotxa, 217
Gelato, honey goat milk, 152–53
German *yoghurt brot*, 130–31
Gjetost, 191
    goat cheese fondue, 192, *193*
    grilled goat cheese sandwiches
        with persimmons and honey
        mustard, 194
Goat lawn-mowing service, 155
Goat meat, 10–117
    authors' first experiences with,
        35, 40
    breeds of goat for, 133
    butchering practices and, 14, 17
    choosing, 14
    nutritional breakdown for, 13
    safe cooking temperature for, 18
    sources for, 14, 15
Goats:
    history of, 12–13
    raising, three options for, 133
    small- vs. large-scale production
        and, 12, 209
Gouda, goat, 201
    baked spinach-and-goat-cheese
        dumplings, *204*, 205–6
    goat cheese and black bean
        enchiladas, 210–11
    goat cheese fondue, 192, *193*
    grated, spaghetti with oven-
        roasted tomatoes, shiitake
        mushrooms and, 199
    mac and crab and goat cheese,
        no-holds-barred, 218–19
    pizza with goat cheese, peaches,
        and almond-tarragon pesto,
        202, *203*
    savory shortbread rounds, 180
Gougères, goat, 184
Grape and radish salad with goat
    cheese croutons, 181
Grape leaves, stuffed (*dolmades*),
    109–10
Gravy, goat milk, 67, *68*, 69

Greek flavors:
    braised meatballs with
        artichokes and fennel, *98*, 99
    chilled blueberry *tzatziki* soup,
        138
    dolmades, 109–10
    moussaka, 102–3
Greens and feta pie, 207–8
Grilled:
    cedar-planked goat cheese, 178,
        179
    goat cheese sandwiches with
        persimmons and honey
        mustard, 194
    goat skewers with vinegary herb
        sauce, 64–66, *65*
    herby chops, 20–21
    kofta, 97
    tandoori game hens, 144–45
Ground goat, 90–117
    baked meatball-and-rice
        casserole, 100–101
    braised meatballs with
        artichokes and fennel, *98*, 99
    burgers, 92–93
    dolmades, 109–10
    down-home stew, 94, *95*
    kibbeh, 114–17, *115*
    kofta, 97
    meat empanadas with
        chimichurri, 111–13
    meat loaf, 96
    moussaka, 102–3
    pâté de campagne, 106–8, *107*
Gruyère, goat, 201
    baked spinach-and-goat-cheese
        dumplings, *204*, 205–6
    goat cheese, crab, and tortilla
        casserole, 212–13
    goat cheese and black bean
        enchiladas, 210–11
    pizza with goat cheese, peaches,
        and almond-tarragon pesto,
        202, *203*
    savory shortbread rounds, 180
Guajillo chiles, 59

Harbourne Blue, 217
Harissa, 93

Harvest Cheese, 217
Hazan, Marcella, 55
Hazelnuts:
    creamy salad dressing, 143
    dukka cheesecake, 237–38, *239*
Heart, goat, 17
    in goat ragù, 55
Herb sauce, vinegary, 64
Hillman Farm, 217
Honey:
    goat milk gelato, 152–53
    mustard, 194
Humboldt Fog, 219
Hunter, Caitlin, 211

I

Ibores, 219
Indian flavors:
    celery root raita, 135
    deconstructed *lassi*, 134
    saag paneer, 171–72, *173*
    tandoori game hens, 144–45
    see also Curries
Italian flavors:
    chocolate panna cotta, 156, *157*
    goat shanks with white beans
        and lemon, 48
    honey goat milk gelato, 152–53
    see also Pasta; Pizza
Italy, Brunet from, 206

J

Jerk leg of goat, 36–37
Jicama salad with blood orange
    vinaigrette, 103
Juniper berries, 52

K

Kibbeh, 114–17, *115*
Kibbeh nayya, 117
Kiko goats, 133
Kofta, 97
Kubbeh matfuniya, 117

L

Lactic acid, 169, 175
Lactose, 169, 175

La Mancha goats, 133
Lamb, 13
Lasagna, goat cheese, with
    mushrooms, spinach, and
    tarragon, 216–17
Lassi, deconstructed, 134
Lazy Lady Farm, 195
Leg of goat, 17
    chicken-fried, with goat milk
        gravy, 67–69, *68*
    front vs. back, 17, 29
    goat skewers with vinegary herb
        sauce, 64–66, *65*
    jerk, 36–37
    schwarma, 32–34, *33*
    seven-hour, 30–31
    slicing meat from, 67
    Spanish-inspired, on bed of
        chickpeas, tomatoes, and
        saffron, 38–40, *39*
    tender vs. tough meat on, 64
Lemon:
    preserved, tagine with, 60, *61*
    tahini sauce, 34
Lingot du Quercy, Le, 201, 225
Liver, goat, in *pâté de campagne*,
    106–8, *107*
Locavore movement, 209
Loin chops, goat, 17
    grilled herby, 20–21
    with jerk rub, 37
    pan-roasted, with blackberries
        and sage, 18, *19*
    visible fat on, 20
Lunch fare:
    chilled blueberry *tzatziki* soup,
        138
    radish and grape salad with goat
        cheese croutons, 181

M

Mac and crab and goat cheese, no-
    holds-barred, 218–19
Majorero, 227
Makfoul, 62–63
Mangoes, in deconstructed *lassi*,
    134
Maple:
    goat cheese frosting, 233–34
    syrup, grades of, 222

Margarita, 178
Marinated goat feta, 176
Masa harina, in goat cheese
    tamales, 240–41
Masaman curry, 78–79
Meatball(s):
    braised, with artichokes and
        fennel, *98*, 99
    kibbeh, 114–17, *115*
    kofta, 97
    -and-rice casserole, baked,
        100–101
Meat empanadas with *chimichurri*,
    111–13
Meat loaf:
    goat, 96
    kibbeh, 114–17, *115*
Mexican flavors:
    chili, 58–59
    goat cheese and black bean
        enchiladas, 210–11
    goat cheese quesadillas, 182, *183*
    goat cheese tamales, 240–41
Middle Eastern flavors:
    briwat, *188*, 189
    goat skewers with vinegary herb
        sauce, 64–66, *65*
    harissa, 93
    kibbeh, 114–17, *115*
    kofta, 97
    schwarma, 32–34, *33*
    tahini sauce, 34
Milk, goat, 120–65
    balancing recipe flavors and, 121
    breeds of goat for, 133
    cajeta, 148, *149*
    chocolate panna cotta, 156, *157*
    chocolate pudding, 151
    corn pudding, 140, *141*
    creamy carrot-dill soup, *136*, 137
    crème brûlée, 160–61
    crepes, 243
    digestibility of, 120
    fat in, 120, 133, 169
    flavor profile of, 120–21, 169, 175
    fudge, 150
    garlic and parsnip flans, 139
    goat cheese danishes, 127–29
    gravy, 67, *68*, 69
    honey gelato, 152–53
    lactose in, 169

raw vs. pasteurized, 175
rice pudding, 162
saag paneer, 171–72, *173*
spiced flan, 158–59
substituting cow milk for, 180
wheat germ–banana muffins,
124–26, *125*
Milking goats, 123, 147
Mohair, 133
Mole(s), 82–89
negro, goat, 84–85
rojo, goat, 86, *87*
verde, goat, 88–89
Monte Enebro, 227
Moroccan flavors:
makfoul, 62–63
tagine with preserved lemon,
60, *61*
Mothais sur Feuille, 227
Moussaka, 102–3
Muffins, wheat germ–banana,
124–26, *125*
Mulato chiles, 59
Mushrooms:
goat cacciatore, 24–25
goat cheese lasagna with
spinach, tarragon and, 216–17
shiitake, spaghetti with oven-
roasted tomatoes, grated goat
cheese and, 199
Mustard:
-and-herb-rubbed rack of goat,
22, *23*
honey, 194
Myotonic goats, 133

Neck of goat, 54
Neck slices, 17
goat cacciatore, 24
goat *mole negro*, 84–85
Masaman curry, 78–79
sali boti, 72–74, *73*
New Mexico red chiles, 59
Niman, Bill, 57, 155
Normandy-inspired goat shanks
with butter, apples, and
cream, 45–46
Norway, goat cheese in, *191*
Nubian goats, 133

O'Banon, 236
Oberhasli goats, 133
Onion(s):
caramelized, pizza with goat
cheese, squash puree, pecans
and, 200–201
dopiaza, 75
makfoul, 62–63
Osage Orange, 236

Pachecos family, 147, 201
Panna cotta, chocolate, 156, *157*
Pappardelle, goat ragù with, 55
Paprika, smoked, 28
Parsley, in *chimichurri*, 111–13
Parsnip and garlic flans, 139
Pashmina goats, 133
Pasilla chiles, 59
Pasta:
goat cheese and pumpkin ravioli
with sage butter, 214–15
goat cheese lasagna with
mushrooms, spinach, and
tarragon, 216–17
goat ragù with pappardelle, 55
mac and crab and goat cheese,
no-holds-barred, 218–19
spaghetti with oven-roasted
tomatoes, shiitake
mushrooms, and grated goat
cheese, 199
Pasteurizing milk, 175
Pastries:
goat cheese danishes, 127–29
goat cheese rugelach, 226–27
see also Empanadas
Pâté de campagne, 106–8, *107*
Peaches, pizza with goat cheese,
almond-tarragon pesto and,
202, *203*
Pecans:
goat cheese sheet cake with
maple–goat cheese frosting,
233–34
pizza with goat cheese, squash
puree, caramelized onion and,
200–201

Pepitas (green pumpkin seeds), in
goat *mole verde*, 88–89
Pepper(corns):
Aleppo, 189
pink, 42
Peppers, roasted red, in creamy
salad dressing, 143
Persillé de Tignes, 236
Persimmons, grilled goat cheese
sandwiches with honey
mustard and, 194
Pesto, almond-tarragon, 202, *203*
Phyllo dough:
baked goat Brie, 177
dukka cheesecake, 237–38, *239*
feta and greens pie, 207–8
Pies:
feta and greens, 207–8
goat yogurt, 163–65, *164*
Pineapple, in goat cheese tamales,
240–41
Pink peppercorns, 42
Pistachios, in deconstructed *lassi*,
134
Pizza:
with goat cheese, peaches, and
almond-tarragon pesto, 202,
203
with goat cheese, squash puree,
caramelized onion, and
pecans, 200–201
Plantains, in goat *mole rojo*, 86, *87*
Pollan, Michael, 175
Pork, 13
jowl, in *pâté de campagne*,
106–8, *107*
Potassium, 120
Potato(es):
goat, and artichoke stew, 54
goat cheese mashed, 185
Pouligny-Saint-Pierre, 241
Prunes, sweet and sour, preserved
in red wine, 108
Puddings:
chocolate, 151
corn, 140, *141*
goat milk rice, 162
Puffs, goat cheese (goat gougères),
184
Pulled shoulder, 28–29
Pumpkin and goat cheese ravioli

with sage butter, 214–15
Pumpkin seeds:
  green (*pepitas*), in goat *mole verde*, 88–89
  yoghurt brot, 130–31

Q

Quesadillas, goat cheese, 182, *183*
Quince, goat stew with, 52–53

R

Rack of goat, mustard-and-herb-rubbed, 22, *23*
Radish and grape salad with goat cheese croutons, 181
Ragù:
  goat, with pappardelle, 55
  makfoul, 62–63
Raita, celery root, 135
Ras el hanout, 62
Raspberry frozen yogurt, 154
Ravioli, goat cheese and pumpkin, with sage butter, 214–15
Recipes, balancing flavors in, 121
Reduced-sodium products, 48
Redwood Hill Farm, 209
Rennet, 197–98
Rib chops, goat, 17
  grilled herby, 20–21
  with jerk rub, 37
  mustard-and-herb-rubbed rack, 22, *23*
  pan-roasted, with blackberries and sage, 18, *19*
  tandoori, 144
  visible fat on, 20
Rice:
  dolmades, 109–10
  meatball-and-, casserole, baked, 100–101
  pudding, goat milk, 162
Rouille, creamy salad dressing based on, 143
Rugelach, goat cheese, 226–27
Rye flour, in *yoghurt brot*, 130–31

S

Saag paneer, 171–72, *173*

Saanen goats, 133
Saffron, 38
Salads:
  celery root raita, 135
  jicama, with blood orange vinaigrette, 103
  radish and grape, with goat cheese croutons, 181
Sali boti, 72–74, *73*
Salt, 48, 229
Sandwiches:
  goat cheese quesadillas, 182, *183*
  grilled goat cheese, with persimmons and honey mustard, 194
Sauces:
  almond-tarragon pesto, 202, *203*
  cajeta, 148, *149*
  chimichurri, 111–13
  harissa, 93
  lemon tahini, 34
  vinegary herb, 64
Savanna goats, 133
Scandinavia, goat cheese in, *191*
Schad, Judy, 236
Schwarma, 32–34, *33*
Searing meat, 26
Selkirk, Alexander, 245
Semolina flour, 205
Sesame seeds:
  dukka cheesecake, 237–38, *239*
  yoghurt brot, 130–31
Seven-hour leg of goat, 30–31
Shanks, goat:
  with cabbage, port, and vanilla, 42–44, *43*
  Italian-inspired, with white beans and lemon, 48
  Normandy-inspired, with butter, apples, and cream, 45–46
  Vietnamese-inspired, ridiculously aromatic, 49
Shiitake mushrooms, spaghetti with oven-roasted tomatoes, grated goat cheese and, 199
Shortbread rounds, savory, 180
Shoulder(s), goat, 17, 54
  goat *mole verde*, 88–89
  pâté de campagne, 106–8, *107*
  pulled, 28–29
  roast, 27

roast, Spanish-inspired, on bed of chickpeas, tomatoes, and saffron, 40
Shoulder chops, goat, 17
  daube de chèvre, 56–57
  goat cacciatore, 24–25
  Masaman curry, 78–79
  Normandy-inspired, with butter, apples, and cream, 46
  pulled shoulder, 29
  sali boti, 72–74, *73*
Shrimp, 12, 13
  paste, 78
Side dishes. *See* Accompaniments
Skewers:
  goat, with vinegary herb sauce, 64–66, *65*
  kofta, 97
Soups:
  blueberry *tzatziki*, chilled, 138
  carrot-dill, creamy, *136*, 137
Southeast Asian flavors:
  kofta, 97
  Masaman curry, 78–79
  Vietnamese-inspired goat shanks, 49
Spaghetti with oven-roasted tomatoes, shiitake mushrooms, and grated goat cheese, 199
Spanish goat cheeses:
  Garrotxa, 217
  Ibores, 219
  Majorero, 227
  Monte Enebro, 227
Spanish-inspired leg of goat on bed of chickpeas, tomatoes, and saffron, 38–40, *39*
Spice blends:
  jerk rub, 36, 37
  ras el hanout, 62
Spiced flan, 158–59
Spinach:
  feta and greens pie, 207–8
  -and-goat-cheese dumplings, baked, *204*, 205–6
  goat cheese lasagna with mushrooms, tarragon and, 216–17
  saag paneer, 171–72, *173*
Spring roll wrappers, in *briwat*,

188, 189
Squash:
    pumpkin and goat cheese ravioli
      with sage butter, 214–15
    puree, pizza with goat cheese,
      caramelized onion, pecans
      and, 200–201
Starters. *See* First courses
Stews:
    chili, 58–59
    croutons for, 57
    cuts for, 17, 51, 54
    daube de chèvre, 56–57
    down-home, 94, *95*
    goat, potato, and artichoke, 54
    goat and quince, 52–53
    goat cacciatore, 24–25
    makfoul, 62–63
    tagine with preserved lemon,
      60, *61*
    see also Curries; Mole
Stock, goat, 74
Sumac, 97
Sunflower seeds, in *yoghurt brot*,
    130–31
Sweet and sour prunes preserved
    in red wine, 108
Swiss chard:
    feta and greens pie, 207–8
    goat cheese, and black-eyed pea
      empanadas, 186–87
Switzerland, Tessiner Geisskässe
    from, 241
Syrian *briwat*, *188*, 189

Tagine with preserved lemon, 60,
    61
Tahini sauce, lemon, 34
Tamales, goat cheese, 240–41
Tamarind paste and puree, 78
Tandoori game hens, 144–45
Tarragon:
    almond pesto, 202, *203*
    goat cheese lasagna with
      mushrooms, spinach and,
      216–17
Temperature, internal:
    collagen melt and, 27
    safety concerns and, 18

Tempering chocolate, 223
Tenderloins, goat, 17
    grilled herby, 21
Tennessee fainters, 133
Tessiner Geisskässe, 241
Tomatoes:
    makfoul, 62–63
    oven-roasted, spaghetti with
      shiitake mushrooms, grated
      goat cheese and, 199
Tongue, goat, 17
Tortilla(s), corn, 85
    goat cheese, and crab casserole,
      212–13
Tortillas, flour, 89
    goat cheese and black bean
      enchiladas, 210–11
    goat cheese quesadillas, 182, *183*
Tournevent, Fromagerie, 211
Trubey, Paul, 123, 175, 197–98, 209,
    229
Truffles, chèvre, 222–23
Twine, butchers', 28
Tzatziki soup, chilled blueberry,
    138

Umami, 121
United Kingdom, goat meat
    suppliers in, 15
USDA, 13, 18

Valençay, 241
Vietnamese-inspired goat shanks,
    ridiculously aromatic, 49
Vinaigrette, blood orange, 103
Vindaloo, goat, 81
Vinegary herb sauce, 64
Vitamin A, 120, 169
Vitamin B-12, 120
Vitamin D, 169
Vitamin E, 169
Vitamin K, 169

Water, in cheese-making process,
    170, 229

Wheat germ–banana muffins,
    124–26, *125*
Whey, 170, 191, 197, 198
Whipped cream, goat, 169
White beans, Italian-inspired goat
    shanks with lemon and, 48
Wool, goat, 133

Yeast doughs that don't rise,
    reasons for, 131
Yoghurt brot, 130–31
Yogurt, goat:
    balancing recipe flavors and, 121
    celery root raita, 135
    chilled blueberry *tzatziki* soup,
      138
    chocolate panna cotta, 156, *157*
    deconstructed *lassi*, 134
    fat in, 169
    fried chicken, 142–43
    goat cheese, crab, and tortilla
      casserole, 212–13
    pie, 163–65, *164*
    raspberry frozen, 154
    saag paneer, 171–72, *173*
    straining, 154
    tandoori game hens, 144–45
    yoghurt brot, 130–31

Published in 2011 by Stewart, Tabori & Chang
An imprint of ABRAMS

Text copyright © 2011 Bruce Weinstein and Mark Scarbrough
Photographs copyright © 2011 Marcus Nilsson

Library of Congress Cataloging-in-Publication Data

Weinstein, Bruce, 1960-
Goat : meat, milk, cheese / Bruce Weinstein and Mark Scarbrough ; Photographs by Marcus Nilsson.
p. cm.
Includes bibliographical references and index.
ISBN 978-1-58479-905-4 (alk. paper)
1. Cooking (Goat meat) 2. Goat milk. 3. Goat cheese. I. Scarbrough, Mark. II. Title.
TX749.5.G63W45 2011
641.6 639--dc22
2010032537
Editor: Natalie Kaire
Designer: Alissa Faden
Production Manager: Tina Cameron

The text of this book was primarily composed in Brothers, Lomba, and Frutiger.

Printed and bound in U.S.A.
10 9 8 7 6 5 4 3 2 1

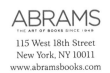

ABRAMS
THE ART OF BOOKS SINCE 1949

115 West 18th Street
New York, NY 10011
www.abramsbooks.com